The Overcrowded Barracoon

V. S. NAIPAUL

Vintage Books
A Division of Random House
New York

First Vintage Books Edition, May 1984
Copyright © 1958, 1962, 1963, 1964, 1965, 1966, 1967,
1968, 1969, 1970, 1971, 1972 by V.S. Naipaul
All rights reserved under International and Pan-
American Copyright Conventions. Published in the
United States by Random House, Inc., New York.
Originally published in Great Britain by André Deutsch,
Limited in 1972. Published in the United States by
Alfred A. Knopf, Inc. in 1973.

These pieces first appeared in *The Times Literary
Supplement, Encounter, The New Statesman, Daily
Telegraph Magazine, Sunday Times Magazine, The Listener,
The Reporter, The New York Review of Books,* and the
Illustrated Weekly of India.

Library of Congress Cataloging in Publication Data
Naipaul, V. S. (Vidiadhar Surajprasad), 1932–
The overcrowded barracoon.
I. Title.
PR9272.9.N320'9   1984   824'.914   83-40303
ISBN 0-394-72207-8 (pbk.)

Manufactured in the United States of America

Contents

I

An Unlikely Colonial

London

The Times Literary Supplement, 15 August 1958

FOR ME THE problem of mass communication is still only an academic problem. I have written three books in five years and made £300 out of them. The Americans do not want me because I am too British. The public here do not want me because I am too foreign. But I have been lucky in other ways. After only five years I am just able to make a living by writing. Many people here still feel that writing is an amateur activity and deserves gratuities rather than payment; but this is better than the attitude in, say, Trinidad, where it is felt that writing is its own reward. But for how long can I continue to live in London and continue writing?

I live in England and depend on an English audience. Yet I write about Trinidad, and more particularly the Indian community there. Few novels have been written about Trinidad and I cannot deny that this gives me some advantages. There is the additional advantage that Trinidad society is so far unformed; ambitions are not uniform; the class structure is so fluid as to be almost non-existent; there is a vague urge to respectability, but this can express itself in startling ways.

Superficially, because of the multitude of races, Trinidad may seem complex, but to anyone who knows it, it is a simple colonial philistine society. Education is desirable because it may lead to security, but any unnecessary acquaintance with books is frowned upon. The writer or the painter, unless he wins recognition overseas, preferably in England, is mercilessly ridiculed. This is only slowly changing. Respectability and class still mean very little. Money means a good deal more, and the only non-financial achievements which are recognized are those connected with sport and music. For these reasons Trinidadians are more recognizably "characters" than people in England. Only a man's eccentricities

can get him attention. It might also be that in a society without traditions, without patterns, every man finds it easier "to be himself".
Whatever the reason, this determination of people to be themselves, to cherish their eccentricities, to reveal themselves at once,
makes them easy material for the writer.

I have often heard people in this country deploring the disappearance of "characters". A well-known humorist once drove
me twenty miles on a Sunday morning to meet a man in a country
pub. He was recognizably, absurdly, a character, a cross between
Mr Pickwick and a Giles old man. He was holding court when we
arrived. To appreciate his remarks one had to know much of what
he had said in the past; he had his punch lines, which were coaxed
out of him and received with roars of laughter. The humorist
listened with awe, appreciation and a deepening depression. He
was positively gloomy when we left. "Great character," he said.
"Very few of them left nowadays." A few words about the
welfare state and the degeneracy of the country followed.

In *The Acceptance World* Anthony Powell gets to the heart of the
problem:

> I began to brood on the complexity of writing a novel about
> English life, a subject difficult enough to handle with
> authenticity even of a crudely naturalistic sort, even more
> to convey the inner truth of the things observed. Those South
> Americans sitting opposite, coming from a continent I had
> never visited, regarding which I possessed only the most
> superficial scraps of information, seemed in some respects
> easier to conceive in terms of a novel than most of the
> English people sitting round the room. Intricacies of social
> life make English habits unyielding to simplification, while
> understatement and irony – in which all classes of this
> island converse – upset the normal emphasis of reported
> speech. How, I asked myself, could a writer attempt to
> describe in a novel such a young man as Mark Members, for
> example, possessing so much in common with myself, yet so

different? . . . Viewed from some distance off, Members and
I might reasonably be considered almost identical units of
the same organism, scarcely to be differentiated even by the
sociological expert.

Might it not be because of this that English writers are depending
more and more on "gimmicks" – sex, snobbery, religion, anger?
It is a formidable problem and one which I do not have to face.
My material is abundant, new and easily grasped. I need no
gimmicks. But I have certain handicaps. The social comedies I
write can be fully appreciated only by someone who knows the
region I write about. Without that knowledge it is easy for my
books to be dismissed as farces and my characters as eccentrics.
There can also be misunderstanding: the critic of the *Observer*
thinks I get my dialect from Ronald Firbank. And there can be
simple exasperation: the critic of the *Yorkshire Post* says she is just
fed up with Trinidad and Trinidad dialect. This, from Yorkshire!
It isn't easy for the exotic writer to get his work accepted as being
more than something exotic, something to be judged on its merits.
The very originality of the material makes the work suspect. And
the exotic humorous writer is in a particularly delicate position.
Consider this comment on my first novel in a weekly paper, now
justly defunct: "His whole purpose is to show how funny
Trinidad Indians are." The *Daily Telegraph* says I look down a
long Oxford nose at the land of my birth. The *Evening Standard*,
however, thinks that I write of my native land with warm
affection. None of these comments would have been made about
a comic French or American novel. They are not literary judgments at all. Imagine a critic in Trinidad writing of *Vile Bodies*:
"Mr Evelyn Waugh's whole purpose is to show how funny
English people are. He looks down his nose at the land of his
birth. We hope that in future he writes of his native land with
warm affection."
    But – the English writer does not write for Trinidad. And I
write for England. And for me the regional barrier is much more
difficult than it is, say, for someone from Yorkshire. People are

used to reading about Yorkshire, used to the dialect. I am much more used to it than the critic of the *Yorkshire Post* is used to the Trinidad dialect.

And it isn't only that the dialect is new. People have been used to reading about non-Europeans through European eyes. India, with the vision of Kipling or Forster of J. R. Ackerley or John Masters, is best-selling territory. But what happens when R. K. Narayan writes about it? He has invention, warmth, humour, truth, a miraculous lightness of touch. Yet he remains comparatively unknown to the library reader. The alien, customary vision is missing.

There is, too, the prejudice of the European against the non-European. Forty years ago Sinclair Lewis was protesting against the indifference of English readers to American books. "I do think," Hugh Walpole wrote in 1922, "that it has been the fault of some of the newer American writers that, clever though they are, they have presented American life to us in so ugly a fashion – ugly in speech, in background, in thought." The ugliness remains, but today publishers fly over regularly to the United States to buy books. Is there, then, a political reason for interest in books from other countries? Does it depend on the size and power of the country one writes about? If this is so, Narayan may yet have a best-selling future. And I never will if I continue to write about Trinidad.

It is an odd, suspicious situation: an Indian writer writing in English for an English audience about non-English characters who talk their own sort of English. The Americans at least had their own audience. I cannot help feeling that it might have been more profitable for me to appear in translation. It would have been necessary then for the critic of the *Yorkshire Post* to do her job rather than express her exasperation; and there would have been no talk about the degree of affection with which I regarded my native land.

Most reviewers have judged me fairly. Some have been generous. I comment on those who have made political rather than literary judgments because I feel they represent the attitude of the reading public.

Yet there are writers in my position who have overcome public indifference. I have studied them closely and find that, apart, of course, from plain merit, there are three devices I can employ.

Sex, first of all. Sex, even in St Kitts, leaps through every barrier. But I cannot write Sex. I haven't the skill, or the wide experience which is necessary if one's work is to have variety. And then I would be embarrassed even at the moment of writing. My friends would laugh. My mother would be shocked, and with reason. Here are the publishers' notes about two successful books by Caribbean writers: one is described as a "boy's lust for women in the South American jungle"; the chief attraction of the other is its "quick-to-strip heroines".

Another device is to introduce an English or American character and write the story around him. This is the device used by British film-makers who put American characters in the most English setting. It is good business, but bad art.

Then there is Race. I wonder that no one has yet done a study on the reasons for the perennial popularity of books about racial discrimination. I believe they give a certain sadistic pleasure, a vicarious sense of power. The Sunday newspapers that serialize stories of oppression and humiliation by the oppressed and the humiliated are not going to try to lose their readers by attempting to uplift them: they respect them too well. To be successful, these chronicles of oppression must have clear oppressors and clear oppressed. This is not easy for an Indian. The most he can manage is something like Mulk Raj Anand's *Untouchable*. And for an Indian from an easy-going multi-racial society it is almost impossible. Oppressors and oppressed change so quickly. Even if I had any inclination to write that sort of book, eight years in England have shown me that the race issue is too complicated to be dealt with at best-seller, black-and-white level. It was unfortunate, for instance, that the *Manchester Guardian* should have carried a warm article by a Sinhalese about race discrimination in America at a time when his countrymen were killing Tamils in Ceylon.

These are the three ways open to me. I have to reject them all.

The only way out is to cease being a regional writer. People who wish me well have urged me to do so before it is too late. They say I have lived long enough in England to write about England. I would like nothing better. But there are difficulties.

The English writer benefits by travel but the foreign writer who comes to England benefits less. A few years ago I read that Simenon had come to England on a holiday and was dividing his time between Glasgow and Birmingham and Leeds. It sounded like a working holiday, but I don't believe anything came out of it.

It is a matter of climate. In a warm country life is conducted out of doors. Windows are open, doors are open. People sit in open verandas and cafés. You know your neighbour's business and he knows yours. It is easy for the visitor to get to know the country. He is continually catching people in off-duty positions. In England everything goes on behind closed doors. The man from the warm country automatically leaves the door open behind him. The man from the cold country closes it: it has become a point of etiquette. The moment the warm weather comes here the BBC urges people to turn down their radios: the open window is an event. The men of Muswell Hill, shopping on a Saturday morning, wear their summer clothes self-consciously, like a new uniform. And when pub doors are wedged open and people lounge in front gardens in shirt-sleeves what a disorderly, Southern, un-English aspect comes over this country!

And I feel I know so little about England. I have met many people but I know them only in official attitudes – the drink, the interview, the meal. I have a few friends. But this gives me only a superficial knowledge of the country, and in order to write fiction it is necessary to know so much: we are not all brothers under the skin. It might have been possible for me, at the end of my first year here, to write about England. First impressions, reinforced by what one reads in the newspapers, are often enough to give authenticity "of a crudely naturalistic sort". But now I feel I can never hope to know as much about people here as I do about Trinidad Indians, people I can place almost as soon as I see them.

The privacy of the big city depresses me. There are no communal pleasures in London. Between the activity and the response there is always the barrier of self-consciousness. You go to a restaurant or a night-club, you eat, you watch, you pay, you come out and look for a bus, feeling you have wasted your money. The theatre is a disappointment. There seems to be no complete communication between the actor and the audience, nothing to weld the audience together. You watch, you come out in the interval to smoke or have a drink, you watch again, and it is all over. You might have been at home, before the television set. However gay the musical or farce, however good the acting, you come out alone into the cold streets, private, sitting in a bus full of grim people who have left their pleasure behind them in the theatre. I like Spanish dancing but I do not care to see it in London. Something is missing; the communal element is not there; all you have is a remote spectacle. It isn't that the dances have been vulgarized – whole-hearted vulgarity is at least vigorous. They have been sterilized, by the audience. I have sat for half an evening in a cinema in the Kilburn High Road, watching Spanish dancing, wondering whether this was really the thing I liked in Spain. Then some Spaniards in the audience, who could bear it no longer, began shouting at the dancers – encouragement, raillery, a little abuse. By looks and action the dancers responded; the rest of the audience responded; for just that moment they had ceased to be individuals who had paid the price of their seat to witness a spectacle which was socially and culturally approved but with which they were not involved.

This may be a futile complaint. How can things be otherwise when London is so big and audiences so sophisticated? But that doesn't lessen my disappointment with the theatre in London. I get more pleasure from going to a cinema in Trinidad. As for the little theatres, the dedicated and dead hand of uplift and culture rests on their efforts. It is hard to imagine Pepys writing of a play today: "It was so mean a thing as, when they came to say it would be acted again tomorrow, both he that said it, Beeson, and the pit fell a-laughing."

My disappointment with the theatre symbolizes the barrenness of my life in London. The profession I follow may be partly responsible for this. Perhaps the fault is wholly mine. But after eight years here I find I have, without effort, achieved the Buddhist ideal of non-attachment. I am never disturbed by national or international issues. I do not sign petitions. I do not vote. I do not march. And I never cease to feel that this lack of interest is all wrong. I want to be involved, to be touched even by some of the prevailing anger.

And yet I like London. For all the reasons I have given it is the best place to write in. The problem for me is that it is not a place I can write about. Not as yet. Unless I am able to refresh myself by travel – to Trinidad, to India – I fear that living here will eventually lead to my own sterility; and I may have to look for another job.

Cricket

Encounter, September 1963

"Who is the greatest cricketer in the world?" The question came up in a General Knowledge test one day in 1940, when I was in the fourth standard at the Tranquillity Boys' School in Port of Spain. I saw it as a trap question. Though I had never seen him play, and he was reported to live in England, no cricketer was better known to me than Learie Constantine. Regularly in the *Trinidad Guardian* I saw the same picture of him: sweatered, smiling, running back to the pavilion bat in hand. To me the bat was golden: Constantine, in a previous General Knowledge test, had proved to be "the man with the golden bat" as, earlier, he had been "the man with the golden ball". But now – the greatest cricketer? I wrote "Bradman". This was wrong; the pencilled cross on my paper was large and angry. "Constantine" was the answer to this one too.

The teacher was a Negro, brown-skinned, but this is a later assessment and may be wrong: to me then, and for some time afterwards, race and colour were not among the attributes of teachers. It is possible now to see his propaganda for Constantine as a type of racialism or nationalism. But this would be only part of the truth. Racial pride pure and simple in the victories of Joe Louis, yes. But the teacher's devotion to Constantine was more complex. And it is with the unravelling of this West Indian complexity that C. L. R. James, politician, pamphleteer, historian, former cricket correspondent for the *Manchester Guardian*, is concerned. He has done his job superbly.

Beyond a Boundary, like Nirad Chaudhuri's *Autobiography of an Unknown Indian*, is part of the cultural boomeranging from the former colonies, delayed and still imperfectly understood. With one or two exceptions, a journalistic reaction to his material

– cricket – has obscured the originality of Mr James's purpose and method.

Since 1950 the newspapers have perhaps made us too familiar with calypsos at Lord's. For West Indians, as one cricket writer says, the game is a carnival. But what a game to choose for a carnival! It is leisurely, intricate, difficult to appreciate, its drama often concealed or curtailed; and the players stop for tea. Soccer, swift, short and brutal, would have been more suitable; or baseball, or bullfighting. But cricket has been chosen; and the conclusion must be that we are dealing with more than the picturesque. Consider just what cricket means to the West Indian: in Trinidad, with a population of 800,000, 30,000 can go to a test match on one day. Consider the mixed population. Here is Mr James describing the cricket field of his school in the 1910s:

> We were a motley crew. The children of some white officials and white business men, middle-class blacks and mulattoes, Chinese boys, some of whose parents still spoke broken English, Indian boys, some of whose parents could speak no English at all, and some poor black boys who had won exhibitions or whose parents had starved and toiled on plots of agricultural land and were spending their hard-earned money on giving the eldest boy an education. Yet rapidly we learned to obey the umpire's decision. . . . We learned to play with the team.

Racial generalizations – about certain people being good at ball games – won't help. There has been no West African cricketer; the only Chinese cricketers of standing have come from Trinidad; and, though the fact is seldom noticed, white West Indians have produced more first-class players per thousand of their population than any other community anywhere. Consider now the history of the islands: slavery until 1834, indentured labour until 1917. And then consider the cricket code: gentlemanliness, fair play, teamwork. The very words are tired and, in the West Indian situation, ridiculous, irrelevant. But they filled a need. In islands that had known only brutality and proclaimed greed, cricket and its code provided an area of rest, a release for much that was denied by the society: skill, courage, style: the graces, the very things that in a changed world are making the game archaic. And the code that came with the game, the code recognized by everyone, whatever his race or class, was the British public-school code:

> I learned and obeyed and taught a code, the English public-school code. Britain and her colonies and the colonial peoples. What do the British people know of what they have done there? Precious little. The colonial peoples, particularly West Indians, scarcely know themselves as yet.

Twenty years ago the colonial who wrote those words might have been judged to be angling for an OBE or MBE. But Mr James, who is over sixty, has a background of Marxism (he was a prominent follower of Trotsky) and African nationalism. He was the first of the emigrant West Indian writers; and his first book, published in 1933, was *The Case for West Indian Self-Government*. Self-government has more or less come to the West Indies; Sir Learie Constantine is now the Trinidad High Commissioner in London. The West Indies, captained for the first time by a black man, did great things in Australia in 1960–1. A quarter of a million people came out into the streets of Melbourne to say goodbye to the cricketers: West Indian cricket's finest moment, which Mr James sees as something more. "Clearing their way with bat and ball, West Indians at that moment had made a public entry into the comity of nations." It is a success story, then, that Mr James has to tell, but an odd one, since it is also the story of the triumph of the code. To Mr James Frank Worrell is more than the first black West Indian captain: "Thomas Arnold, Thomas Hughes and the Old Master himself would have recognized Frank Worrell as their boy."

This is the last sentence of Mr James's book, and this is his astounding thesis. To dismiss it would be to deny the curious position of the West Indies and West Indians in the Commonwealth, to fail to see that these territories are a unique imperial creation, where people of many lands, thrown together, "came to maturity within a system that was the result of centuries of development in another land, was transplanted as a hot-house flower is transplanted and bore some strange fruit". Stollmeyer, Gomez, Pierre, Christiani, Tang Choon, Ramadhin: the names of West Indian cricketers are sufficient evidence. To be a nationalist, Mr James says elsewhere, you must have a nation. The African in Africa had a nation; so had the Asian in Asia. The West Indian, whatever his community, had only this "system"; and my fourth standard teacher could only grope towards some definition of his position in the world by his devotion to Constantine.

It is part of the originality and rightness of Mr James's book that he should have combined the story of his development within the system with his view of West Indian political growth, and combined that with sketches of West Indian cricketers he knew and watched develop. In the islands the cricketers were familiar to many; they were as much men as cricketers. So they emerge in Mr James's pages, but even so they remain touched with heroic qualities, for their success, as with Constantine or Headley, was the only type of triumph the society as a whole knew. And their failure, as with Wilton St Hill who, achieving nothing in England in 1928, remained all his life a clerk in a department store, bitter tragedy.

How did Mr James become part of this "system"? He was born in a small Trinidad country town at the turn of the century. His father was a teacher. Yet slavery had been abolished only seventy years before, and "Cousin Nancy, who lived a few yards away, told many stories of her early days as a house-slave". Already, then, the slave society had been transformed, its assumptions destroyed; and this rapid transformation must be regarded as part of the West Indian good fortune. The family was not rich, but for the young James, as for every boy in the island, there was a narrow way out. Every year the government offered four exhibitions to one of the two secondary schools. There a boy could get a Senior Cambridge Certificate, which would ensure a modest job in the civil service. He could do more: he could win one of the three annual scholarships. With this he could get a profession in England, come back to Trinidad, make money and achieve honour. The form of promising boys was studied as carefully as that of racehorses; the course, from exhibition to scholarship, aroused island-wide interest and excitement.

James won his exhibition. He came from a house with books. Preparing for his exhibition, he became a "British intellectual long before I was ten, already an alien in my own environment". But he was ready for the public-school code of the Queen's Royal College, staffed for two generations by Oxford and Cambridge men. "Our masters, our curriculum, our code of morals, *everything* began from the basis that Britain was the source of all light and learning, and our business was to admire, wonder, imitate, learn." It was not hard. The colony might be ruled autocratically by Englishmen, but there was as yet no National Question and, within the school, no race question. "If the masters were so successful in instilling and maintaining their British principles as the ideal and norm it was because within the school, and particularly on the playing field, they practised them themselves. . . . They were correct in the letter and in the spirit." They were also not competing with any other system. Today, he says, these teachers with their "bristling Britishness" would be anachronisms. But was it possible to reject them then? Was it possible for Mr James, forty years later, at a public meeting in Manchester, to accept Mr Aneurin Bevan's sneers at public-school morality? As it was, however, the playing fields of Queen's Royal College undid Mr James. Cricket possessed him; he did not win the scholarship. But he had educated himself "into a member of the British middle class". In 1932, with the encouragement and help of Learie Constantine, he came to England. And he has been a wanderer ever since.

To me, who thirty years later followed in his path almost step by step – but I only watched cricket, and I won the scholarship – Mr James's career is of particular interest. Our backgrounds were

dissimilar. His was Negro, Puritan, fearful of lower-class con-
tamination; mine was Hindu, restricted, enclosed. But we have
ended speaking the same language; and though England is not
perhaps the country we thought it was, we have both charmed
ourselves away from Trinidad. "For the inner self," as Mr James
writes, "the die was cast."

In our absence the static society we knew has altered. Secondary
education is free. Not three, but more like thirty, scholarships are
given each year. With the new nationalism and confidence, the
public-school code has become as anachronistic as the masters who
taught it. What new code will be developed in a society so
clearly British-made? Cricket is no longer a substitute for
nationalism. Has it then served its purpose, and will it die in the
West Indies as it has died (in spite of Dexter, in spite of the Lord's
test) in England? Trinidad, we must remind ourselves, has produced no major player since Ramadhin, discovered in 1950. It
would be interesting to have Mr James's views. In the meantime
let us rejoice over what he has given us. *Beyond a Boundary* is one
of the finest and most finished books to come out of the West
Indies, important to England, important to the West Indies. It
has a further value: it gives a base and solidity to West Indian
literary endeavour.

Jasmine

The Times Literary Supplement, 4 June 1964

ONE DAY ABOUT ten years ago, when I was editing a weekly
literary programme for the BBC's Caribbean Service, a man from
Trinidad came to see me in one of the freelances' rooms in the old
Langham Hotel. He sat on the edge of the table, slapped down
some sheets of typescript and said, "My name is Smith. I write
about sex. I am also a nationalist." The sex was tepid, Maugham
and coconut-water; but the nationalism was aggressive. Women
swayed like coconut trees; their skins were the colour of the
sapodilla, the inside of their mouths the colour of a cut star-apple;
their teeth were as white as coconut kernels; and when they made
love they groaned like bamboos in high wind.

The writer was protesting against what the English language
had imposed on us. The language was ours, to use as we pleased.
The literature that came with it was therefore of peculiar
authority; but this literature was like an alien mythology. There
was, for instance, Wordsworth's notorious poem about the
daffodil. A pretty little flower, no doubt; but we had never seen
it. Could the poem have any meaning for us? The superficial
prompting of this argument, which would have confined all
literatures to the countries of their origin, was political; but it
was really an expression of dissatisfaction at the emptiness of our
own formless, unmade society. To us, without a mythology, all
literatures were foreign. Trinidad was small, remote and unimportant, and we knew we could not hope to read in books of
the life we saw about us. Books came from afar; they could offer
only fantasy.

To open a book was to make an instant adjustment. Like the
medieval sculptor of the North interpreting the Old Testament
stories in terms of the life he knew, I needed to be able to adapt.

All Dickens's descriptions of London I rejected; and though I might retain Mr Micawber and the others in the clothes the illustrator gave them, I gave them the faces and voices of people I knew and set them in buildings and streets I knew. The process of adaptation was automatic and continuous. Dickens's rain and drizzle I turned into tropical downpours; the snow and fog I accepted as conventions of books. Anything – like an illustration – which embarrassed me by proving how weird my own rec-rèation was, anything which sought to remove the characters from the make-up world in which I set them, I rejected.

I went to books for fantasy; at the same time I required reality. The gypsies of *The Mill on the Floss* were a fabrication and a disappointment, discrediting so much that was real: to me gypsies were mythical creatures who belonged to the pure fantasy of Hans Christian Andersen and *The Heroes*. Disappointing, too, was the episode of the old soldier's sword, because I thought that swords belonged to ancient times; and the Tom Tulliver I had created walked down the street where I lived. The early parts of *The Mill on the Floss*, then; chapters of *Oliver Twist, Nicholas Nickleby, David Copperfield*; some of the novels of H. G. Wells; a short story by Conrad called "The Lagoon": all these which in the beginning I read or had read to me I set in Trinidad, accepting, rejecting, adapting, and peopling in my own way. I never read to find out about foreign countries. Everything in books was foreign; everything had to be subjected to adaptation; and everything in, say, an English novel which worked and was of value to me at once ceased to be specifically English. Mr Murdstone worked; Mr Pickwick and his club didn't. *Jane Eyre* and *Wuthering Heights* worked; *Pride and Prejudice* didn't. Maupassant worked; Balzac didn't.

I went to books for a special sort of participation. The only social division I accepted was that between rich and poor, and any society more elaborately ordered seemed insubstantial and alien. In literature such a society was more than alien; it was excluding, it made nonsense of my fantasies and more and more, as I grew older and thought of writing myself, it made me despairingly conscious of the poverty and haphazardness of my own society. I might adapt Dickens to Trinidad; but it seemed impossible that the life I knew in Trinidad could ever be turned into a book. If landscapes do not start to be real until they have been interpreted by an artist, so, until they have been written about, societies appear to be without shape and *embarrassing*. It was embarrassing to be reminded by a Dickens illustration of the absurdity of my adaptations; it was equally embarrassing to attempt to write of what I saw. Very little of what I read was of help. It would have been possible to assume the sensibility of a particular writer. But no writer, however individual his vision, could be separated from his society. The vision was alien; it diminished my own and did not give me the courage to do a simple thing like mentioning the name of a Port of Spain street.

Fiction or any work of the imagination, whatever its quality, hallows its subject. To attempt, with a full consciousness of established authoritative mythologies, to give a quality of myth to what was agreed to be petty and ridiculous – Frederick Street in Port of Spain, Marine Square, the districts of Laventille and Barataria – to attempt to use these names required courage. It was, in a way, the rejection of the familiar, meaningless word – the rejection of the unknown daffodil to put it no higher – and was as self-conscious as the attempt to have sapodilla-skinned women groaning like bamboos in high wind.

With all English literature accessible, then, my position was like that of the maharaja in *Hindoo Holiday*, who, when told by the Christian lady that God was here, there and everywhere, replied, "But what use is that to *me*?" Something of more pertinent virtue was needed, and this was provided by some local short stories. These stories, perhaps a dozen in all, never published outside Trinidad, converted what I saw into "writing". It was through them that I began to appreciate the distorting, distilling power of the writer's art. Where I had seen a drab haphazardness they found order; where I would have attempted to romanticize, to render my subject equal with what I had read, they accepted.

They provided a starting-point for further observation; they did not trigger off fantasy. Every writer is, in the long run, on his own; but it helps, in the most practical way, to have a tradition. The English language was mine; the tradition was not.

Literature, then, was mainly fantasy. Perhaps it was for this reason that, although I had at an early age decided to be a writer and at the age of eighteen had left Trinidad with that ambition, I did not start writing seriously until I was nearly twenty-three. My material had not been sufficiently hallowed by a tradition; I was not fully convinced of its importance; and some embarrassment remained. My taste for literature had developed into a love of language, the word in isolation. At school my subjects were French and Spanish; and the pleasures of the language were at least as great as those of the literature. Maupassant and Molière were rich; but it was more agreeable to spend an hour with the big Harrap French-English dictionary, learning more of the language through examples, than with Corneille or Racine. And it was because I thought I had had enough of these languages (both now grown rusty) that when I came to England to go to university I decided to read English.

This was a mistake. The English course had little to do with literature. It was a "discipline" seemingly aimed at juvenile antiquarians. It by-passed the novel and the prose "asides" in which so much of the richness of the literature lay. By a common and curious consent it concentrated on poetry; and since it stopped at the eighteenth century it degenerated, after an intensive study of Shakespeare, into a lightning survey of minor and often severely local talents. I had looked forward to wandering among large tracts of writing; I was presented with "texts". The metaphysicals were a perfect subject for study, a perfect part of a discipline; but, really, they had no value for me. Dryden, for all the sweet facility of his prose, was shallow and dishonest; did his "criticism" deserve such reverential attention? *Gulliver's Travels* was excellent; but could *The Tale of a Tub* and *The Battle of the Books* be endured?

The fact was, I had no taste for scholarship, for tracing the growth of schools and trends. I sought continuously to relate literature to life. My training at school didn't help. We had few libraries, few histories of literature to turn to; and when we wrote essays on *Tartuffe* we wrote out of a direct response to the play. Now I discovered that the study of literature had been made scientific, that each writer had to be approached through the booby-traps of scholarship. There were the bound volumes of the Publications of the Modern Language Association of America, affectionately referred to by old and knowing young as PMLA. The pages that told of Chaucer's knowledge of astronomy or astrology (the question came up every year) were black and bloated and furred with handling, and even some of the pencilled annotations (*No, Norah!*) had grown faint. I developed a physical distaste for these bound volumes and the libraries that housed them.

Delight cannot be taught and measured; scholarship can; and my reaction was irrational. But it seemed to me scholarship of such a potted order. A literature was not being explored; it had been codified and reduced to a few pages of "text", some volumes of "background" and more of "criticism"; and to this mixture a mathematical intelligence might have been applied. There were discoveries, of course: Shakespeare, Marlowe, Restoration comedy. But my distaste for the study of literature led to a sense of being more removed than ever from the literature itself.

The language remained mine, and it was to the study of its development that I turned with pleasure. Here was enough to satisfy my love of language; here was unexpected adventure. It might not have been easy to see Chaucer as a great imaginative writer or to find in the *Prologue* more than a limited piece of observation which had been exceeded a thousand times; but Chaucer as a handler of a new, developing language was exciting. And my pleasure in Shakespeare was doubled. In Trinidad English writing had been for me a starting-point for fantasy. Now, after some time in England, it was possible to isolate the word, to separate the literature from the language.

Language can be so deceptive. It has taken me much time to realize how bad I am at interpreting the conventions and modes of

English speech. This speech has never been better dissected than in the early stories of Angus Wilson. This is the judgment of today; my first responses to these stories were as blundering and imperfect as the responses of Professor Pforzheim to the stern courtesies of his English colleagues in *Anglo-Saxon Attitudes*. But while knowledge of England has made English writing more truly accessible, it has made participation more difficult; it has made impossible the exercise of fantasy, the reader's complementary response. I am inspecting an alien society, which I yet know, and I am looking for particular social comment. And to re-read now the books which lent themselves to fantastic interpretation in Trinidad is to see, almost with dismay, how English they are. The illustrations to Dickens cannot now be dismissed. And so, with knowledge, the books have ceased to be mine.

It is the English literary vice, this looking for social comment; and it is difficult to resist. The preoccupation of the novelists reflects a society ruled by convention and manners in the fullest sense, an ordered society of the self-aware who read not so much for adventure as to compare, to find what they know or think they know. A writer is to be judged by what he reports on; the working-class writer is a working-class writer and no more. So writing develops into the private language of a particular society. There are new reports, new discoveries: they are rapidly absorbed. And with each discovery the society's image of itself becomes more fixed and the society looks further inward. It has too many points of reference; it has been written about too often; it has read too much. Angus Wilson's characters, for instance, are great readers; they are steeped in Dickens and Jane Austen. Soon there will be characters steeped in Angus Wilson; the process is endless. Sensibility will overlay sensibility: the grossness of experience will be refined away by self-awareness. Writing will become Arthur Miller's definition of a newspaper: a nation talking to itself. And even those who have the key will be able only to witness, not to participate.

All literatures are regional; perhaps it is only the placelessness of a Shakespeare or the blunt communication of "gross" experience as in Dickens that makes them appear less so. Or perhaps it is a lack of knowledge in the reader. Even in this period of "internationalism" in letters we have seen literatures turning more and more inward, developing languages that are more and more private. Perhaps in the end literature will write itself out, and all its pleasures will be those of the word.

A little over three years ago I was in British Guiana. I was taken late one afternoon to meet an elderly lady of a distinguished Christian Indian family. Our political attitudes were too opposed to make any discussion of the current crisis profitable. We talked of the objects in her veranda and of the old days. Suddenly the tropical daylight was gone, and from the garden came the scent of a flower. I knew the flower from my childhood; yet I had never found out its name. I asked now.

"We call it jasmine."

Jasmine! So I had known it all those years! To me it had been a word in a book, a word to play with, something removed from the dull vegetation I knew.

The old lady cut a sprig for me. I stuck it in the top buttonhole of my open shirt. I smelled it as I walked back to the hotel. Jasmine, jasmine. But the word and the flower had been separate in my mind for too long. They did not come together.

East Indian

The Reporter, 17 June 1965

IT WAS ABOUT thirteen or fourteen years ago. In those days Air France used to run an Epicurean Service between London and Paris. The advertisements taunted me. Poverty makes for recklessness, and one idle day in the long summer vacation I booked. The following morning I went with nervous expectation to the Kensington air terminal. There was another Indian in the lounge. He was about fifty and very small, neat with homburg and gold-rimmed spectacles, and looking packaged in a three-piece suit. He was pure buttoned-up joy: he too was an Epicurean traveller.

"You are coming from – ?"

I had met enough Indians from India to know that this was less a serious inquiry than a greeting, in a distant land, from one Indian to another.

"Trinidad," I said. "In the West Indies. And you?"

He ignored my question. "But you look Indian."

"I am."

"Red Indian?" He suppressed a nervous little giggle.

"East Indian. From the West Indies."

He looked offended and wandered off to the bookstall. From this distance he eyed me assessingly. In the end curiosity overcame misgiving. He sat next to me on the bus to the airport. He sat next to me in the plane.

"Your first trip to Paris?" he asked.

"Yes."

"My fourth. I am a newspaperman. America, the United States of America, have you been there?"

"I once spent twelve hours in New York."

"I have been to the United States of America three times. I also know the Dominion of Canada. I don't like this aeroplane. I don't like the way it is wibrating. What sort do you think it is? I'll ask the steward."

He pressed the buzzer. The steward didn't come.

"At first I thought it was a Dakota. Now I feel it is a Wiking."

The steward bustled past, dropping white disembarkation cards into laps. The Indian seized the steward's soiled white jacket.

"Steward, is this aircraft a Wiking?"

"No, sir. Not a Viking. It's a Languedoc, a French plane, sir."

"Languedoc. Of course. That is one thing journalism teaches you. Always get to the bottom of everything."

We filled in our disembarkation cards. The Indian studied my passport.

"Trinidad, Trinidad," he said, as though searching for a face or a name.

Before he could find anything the Epicurean meal began. The harassed steward pulled out trays from the back of seats, slapped down monogrammed glasses and liquor miniatures. It was a short flight, which perhaps he had already made more than once that day, and he behaved like a man with problems at the other end.

"Indian," the Indian said reprovingly, "and you are drinking?"

"I am drinking."

"At home," he said, sipping his aperitif, "I *never* drink."

The steward was back, with a clutch of half-bottles of champagne.

"Champagne!" the Indian cried, as though about to clap his tiny hands. "Champagne!"

Corks were popping all over the aircraft. The trays of food came. I grabbed the steward's dirty jacket.

"I am sorry," I said. "I should have told them. But I don't eat meat."

Holding two trays in one hand, he said, "I am sorry, sir. There is nothing else. The meals are not prepared on the plane."

"But you must have an egg or some fish or something."

"We have some cheese."

"But this is an Epicurean Service. You can't just give me a piece of cheese."

"I am sorry, sir."

I drank champagne with my bread and cheese.

"So you are not eating?"

"I am not eating."

"I enwy you." The Indian was champing through meats of various colours, sipping champagne and crying out for more. "I enwy you your wegetarianism. At home I am *strict* wegetarian. No one has even boiled an egg in my house."

The steward took away the remains of my bread and cheese, and gave me coffee, brandy, and a choice of liqueurs.

The Indian experimented swiftly. He sipped, he gulped. The flight was drawing to a close; we were already fastening our seat belts. His eyes were red and watery behind his spectacles. He stuck his hat on at comic angles and made faces at me. He nudged me in the ribs and cuffed me on the shoulder and giggled. He chucked me under the chin and sang: "*Wege-wege-wegetarian! Hin-du wege-tar-ian!*"

He was in some distress when we landed. His hat was still at a comic angle, but his flushed little face had a bottled-up solemnity. He was in for a hard afternoon. Even so, he composed himself for a farewell speech.

"My dear sir, I am a journalist and I have travelled. I hope you will permit me to say how much I appreciate it that, although separated by many generations and many thousands of miles of sea and ocean from the Motherland, you still keep up the customs and traditions of our religion. I *do* appreciate it. Allow me to congratulate you."

I was hungry, and my head was heavy. "No, no, my dear sir. Allow me to congratulate you."

To be a colonial is to be a little ridiculous and unlikely, especially in the eyes of someone from the metropolitan country. All immigrants and their descendants are colonials of one sort or another, and between the colonial and what one might call the metropolitan there always exists a muted mutual distrust. In England the image of the American is fixed. In Spain, where imperial glory has been dead for so long, they still whisper to you, an impartial outsider, about the loudness of *americanos* – to them people from Argentina and Uruguay. In an Athens hotel you can distinguish the Greek Americans, *back for a holiday* (special words in the vocabulary of immigrants), from the natives. The visitors speak with loud, exaggerated American accents, occasionally slightly flawed; the stances of the women are daring and self-conscious. The natives, overdoing the quiet culture and feminine modesty, appear to cringe with offence.

Yet to be Latin American or Greek American is to be known, to be a type, and therefore in some way to be established. To be an Indian or East Indian from the West Indies is to be a perpetual surprise to people outside the region. When you think of the West Indies you think of Columbus and the Spanish galleons, slavery and the naval rivalries of the eighteenth century. You might, more probably, think of calypsos and the Trinidad carnival and expensive sun and sand. When you think of the East you think of the Taj Mahal at the end of a cypress-lined vista and you think of holy men. You don't go to Trinidad, then, expecting to find Hindu pundits scuttling about country roads on motor-cycles; to see pennants with ancient devices fluttering from temples; to see mosques cool and white and rhetorical against the usual Caribbean buildings of concrete and corrugated iron; to find India celebrated in the street names of one whole district of Port of Spain; to see the Hindu festival of lights or the Muslim mourning ceremony for Husein, the Prophet's descendant, killed at the Battle of Kerbela in Arabia thirteen hundred years ago.

To be an Indian from Trinidad is to be unlikely. It is, in addition to everything else, to be the embodiment of an old verbal ambiguity. For this word "Indian" has been abused as no other word in the language; almost every time it is used it has to be qualified. There was a time in Europe when everything Oriental or everything a little unusual was judged to come from Turkey or India. So Indian ink is really Chinese ink and India paper first came from China. When in 1492 Columbus landed on the island of Guanahani he thought he had got to Cathay. He ought therefore to have called the people Chinese. But East was East. He called them Indians, and Indians they remained, walking Indian file through the Indian corn. And so, too, that American bird which to English-speaking people is the turkey is to the French *le dindon*, the bird of India.

So long as the real Indians remained on the other side of the world, there was little confusion. But when in 1845 these Indians began coming over to some of the islands Columbus had called the Indies, confusion became total. Slavery had been abolished in the British islands; the Negroes refused to work for a master, and many plantations were faced with ruin. Indentured labourers were brought in from China, Portugal, and India. The Indians fitted. More and more came. They were good agriculturalists and were encouraged to settle after their indentures had expired. Instead of a passage home they could take land. Many did. The indenture system lasted, with breaks, from 1845 until 1917, and in Trinidad alone the descendants of those immigrants who stayed number over a quarter of a million.

But what were these immigrants to be called? Their name had been appropriated three hundred and fifty years before. "Hindu" was a useful word, but it had religious connotations and would have offended the many Muslims among the immigrants. In the British territories the immigrants were called East Indians. In this way they were distinguished from the two other types of Indians in the islands: the American Indians and the West Indians. After a generation or two, the East Indians were regarded as settled inhabitants of the West Indies and were thought of as West Indian East Indians. Then a national feeling grew up. There was a cry for integration, and the West Indian East Indians became East Indian West Indians.

This didn't suit the Dutch. They had a colony called Surinam, or Dutch Guiana, on the north coast of South America. They also owned a good deal of the East Indies, and to them an East Indian was someone who came from the East Indies and was of Malay stock. (When you go to an Indian restaurant in Holland you don't go to an Indian restaurant; you go to an East Indian or Javanese restaurant.) In Surinam there were many genuine East Indians from the East Indies. So another name had to be found for the Indians from India who came to Surinam. The Dutch called them British Indians. Then, with the Indian nationalist agitation in India, the British Indians began to resent being called British Indians. The Dutch compromised by calling them Hindustanis.

East Indians, British Indians, Hindustanis. But the West Indies are part of the New World and these Indians of Trinidad are no longer of Asia. The temples and mosques exist and appear genuine. But the languages that came with them have decayed. The rituals have altered. Since open-air cremation is forbidden by the health authorities, Hindus are buried, not cremated. Their ashes are not taken down holy rivers into the ocean to become again part of the Absolute. There is no Ganges at hand, only a muddy stream called the Caroni. And the water that the Hindu priest sprinkles with a mango leaf around the sacrificial fire is not Ganges water but simple tap water. The holy city of Benares is far away, but the young Hindu at his initiation ceremony in Port of Spain will still take up his staff and beggar's bowl and say that he is off to Benares to study. His relatives will plead with him, and in the end he will lay down his staff, and there will be a ritual expression of relief.*

It is the play of a people who have been cut off. To be an Indian from Trinidad, then, is to be unlikely and exotic. It is also to be a little fraudulent. But so all immigrants become. In India itself there is the energetic community of Parsis. They fled from Persia to escape Muslim religious persecution. But over the years the very religion which they sought to preserve has become a matter of forms and especially of burial forms: in Bombay their dead are taken to the frighteningly named Towers of Silence and there exposed to vultures. They have adopted the language of the sheltering country and their own language has become a secret gibberish. Immigrants are people on their own. They cannot be

* Cremation is now permitted; ashes are scattered in the Caroni; and Ganges water is now imported.

judged by the standards of their older culture. Culture is like
language, ever developing. There is no right and wrong, no
purity from which there is decline. Usage sanctions everything.

And these Indians from Trinidad, despite their temples and
rituals, so startling to the visitors, belong to the New World.
They are immigrants; they have the drive and restlessness of
immigrants. To them India is a word. In moments of self-distrust
this word might suggest the Taj Mahal and an ancient civilization.
But more usually it suggests other words, fearfully visualized:
"famine", "teeming millions". And to many, India is no more
than the memory of a depressed rural existence that survived in
Trinidad until only the other day. Occasionally in the interior of
the island a village of thatched roofs and mud-and-bamboo walls
still recalls Bengal.

In Bengal lay the great port of Calcutta. There, from the vast
depressed hinterland of eastern India, the emigrants assembled for
the journey by sail, often lasting four months, to the West Indies.
The majority came from the provinces of Bihar and eastern Uttar
Pradesh; and even today – although heavy industry has come to
Bihar – these areas are known for their poverty and backwardness.
It is a dismal, dusty land, made sadder by ruins and place names
that speak of ancient glory. For here was the land of the Buddha;
here are the cities mentioned in the Hindu epics of three thousand
years ago – like Ayodhya, from which my father's family came,
today a ramshackle town of wholly contemporary squalor.

The land is flat, intolerably flat, with few trees to dramatize it.
The forests to which reference is often made in the epics have
disappeared. The winters are brief, and in the fierce summers the
fields are white with dust. You are never out of sight of low mud-
walled or brick-walled villages, and there are people everywhere.
An impression of tininess in vastness: tiny houses, tiny poor fields,
thin, stunted people, a land scratched into dust by an ever-growing
population. It is a land of famine and apathy, and yet a land of
rigid caste order. Everyone has his place. Effort is futile. His field
is small, his time unlimited, but the peasant still scatters his seed

broadcast. He lives from hand to mouth. The attitude is understandable. In this more than feudal society of India, everything once belonged to the king, and later to the landlord: it was unwise to be prosperous. A man is therefore defined and placed by his caste alone. To the peasant on this overpopulated plain, all of India, all the world, has been narrowed to a plot of ground and a few relationships.

Travel is still not easy in those parts, and from there a hundred years ago the West Indies must have seemed like the end of the world. Yet so many left, taking everything – beds, brass vessels, musical instruments, images, holy books, sandalwood sticks, astrological almanacs. It was less an uprooting than it appears. They were taking India with them. With their blinkered view of the world they were able to re-create eastern Uttar Pradesh or Bihar wherever they went. They had been able to ignore the vastness of India; so now they ignored the strangeness in which they had been set. To leave India's sacred soil, to cross the "black water", was considered an act of self-defilement. So completely did these migrants re-create India in Trinidad that they imposed a similar restriction on those who wished to leave Trinidad.

In a more energetic society they would have been lost. But Trinidad was stagnant in the nineteenth century. The Indians endured and prospered. The India they re-created was allowed to survive. It was an India in which a revolution had occurred. It was an India in isolation, unsupported; an India without caste or the overwhelming pressures towards caste. Effort had a meaning, and soon India could be seen to be no more than a habit, a self-imposed psychological restraint, wearing thinner with the years. At the first blast from the New World – the Second World War, the coming of Americans to the islands – India fell away, and a new people seemed all at once to have been created. The colonial, of whatever society, is a product of revolution; and the revolution takes place in the mind.

Certain things remain: the temples, the food, the rites, the names, though these become steadily more Anglicized and less recognizable to Indians; or it might be a distaste for meat, derived from a Hindu background and surviving even an Epicurean flight between London and Paris. Certainly it was odd, when I was in India two years ago, to find that often, listening to a language I thought I had forgotten, I was understanding. Just a word or two, but they seemed to recall a past life and fleetingly they gave that sensation of an experience that has been lived before. But fleetingly, since for the colonial there can be no true return.

In a Delhi club I met an Indian from Trinidad. I had last seen him fifteen years before. He was an adventurer. Now he was a little sad. He was an exile in the Motherland, and fifteen years had definitely taken him past youth; for him there were to be no more adventures. He was quiet and subdued. Then a worried, inquiring look came into his eyes.

"Tell me. I think we are way ahead of this bunch, don't you think?"

"But there's no question," I said.

He brightened; he looked relieved. He smiled; he laughed.

"I'm *so* glad you think so. It's what I *always* tell them. Come, have a drink."

We drank. We became loud, colonials together.

II

India

In the Middle of the Journey

The Illustrated Weekly of India, 28 October 1962

COMING FROM A small island – Trinidad is no bigger than Goa – I had always been fascinated by size. To see the wide river, the high mountain, to take the twenty-four-hour train journey: these were some of the delights the outside world offered. But now after six months in India my fascination with the big is tinged with disquiet. For here is a vastness beyond imagination, a sky so wide and deep that sunsets cannot be taken in at a glance but have to be studied section by section, a landscape made monotonous by its size and frightening by its very simplicity and its special quality of exhaustion: poor choked crops in small crooked fields, undersized people, undernourished animals, crumbling villages and towns which, even while they develop, have an air of decay. Dawn comes, night falls; railway stations, undistinguishable one from the other, their name-boards cunningly concealed, are arrived at and departed from, abrupt and puzzling interludes of populousness and noise; and still the journey goes on, until the vastness, ceasing to have a meaning, becomes insupportable, and from this endless repetition of exhaustion and decay one wishes to escape.

To state this is to state the obvious. But in India the obvious is overwhelming, and often during these past six months I have known moments of near-hysteria, when I have wished to forget India, when I have escaped to the first-class waiting room or sleeper not so much for privacy and comfort as for protection, to shut out the sight of the thin bodies prostrate on railway platforms, the starved dogs licking the food-leaves clean, and to shut out the whine of the playfully assaulted dog. Such a moment I knew in Bombay, on the day of my arrival, when I felt India only as an assault on the senses. Such a moment I knew five

months later, at Jammu, where the simple, frightening geography
of the country becomes plain – to the north the hills, rising in
range after ascending range; to the south, beyond the temple
spires, the plains whose vastness, already experienced, excited only
unease.

Yet between these recurring moments there have been so many
others, when fear and impatience have been replaced by enthusiasm and delight, when the town, explored beyond what one
sees from the train, reveals that the air of exhaustion is only
apparent, that in India, more than in any other country I have
visited, things are happening. To hear the sounds of hammer on
metal in a small Punjab town, to visit a chemical plant in
Hyderabad where much of the equipment is Indian-designed and
manufactured, is to realize that one is in the middle of an
industrial revolution, in which, perhaps because of faulty publicity,
one had never really seriously believed. To see the new housing
colonies in towns all over India is to realize that, separate from the
talk of India's ancient culture (which invariably has me reaching
for my *lathi*), the Indian aesthetic sense has revived and is now
capable of creating, out of materials which are international,
something which is essentially Indian. (India's ancient culture,
defiantly paraded, has made the Ashoka Hotel one of New
Delhi's most ridiculous buildings, outmatched in absurdity only
by the Pakistan High Commission, which defiantly asserts the
Faith.)

I have been to unpublicized villages, semi-developed and undeveloped. And where before I would have sensed only despair,
now I feel that the despair lies more with the observer than the
people. I have learned to see beyond the dirt and the recumbent
figures on string beds, and to look for the signs of improvement
and hope, however faint: the brick-topped road, covered though
it might be with filth; the rice planted in rows and not scattered
broadcast; the degree of ease with which the villager faces the
official or the visitor. For such small things I have learned to look:
over the months my eye has been adjusted.

Yet always the obvious is overwhelming. One is a traveller

and as soon as the dread of a particular district has been lessened by familiarity, it is time to move on again, through vast tracts which will never become familiar, which will sadden; and the urge to escape will return.

Yet in so many ways the size of the country is only a physical fact. For, perhaps because of the very size, Indians appear to feel the need to categorize minutely, delimit, to reduce to manageable proportions.

"Where do you come from?" It is the Indian question, and to people who think in terms of the village, the district, the province, the community, the caste, my answer that I am a Trinidadian is only puzzling.

"But you look Indian."

"Well, I am Indian. But we have been living for several generations in Trinidad."

"But you look Indian."

Three or four times a day the dialogue occurs, and now I often abandon explanation. "I am a Mexican, really."

"Ah." Great satisfaction. Pause. "What do you do?"

"I write."

"Journalism or books?"

"Books."

"Westerns, crime, romance? How many books do you write a year? How much do you make?"

So now I invent: "I am a teacher."

"What are your qualifications?"

"I am a BA."

"Only a BA? What do you teach?"

"Chemistry. And a little history."

"How interesting!" said the man on the Pathankot–Srinagar bus. "I am a teacher of chemistry too."

He was sitting across the aisle from me, and several hours remained of our journey.

In this vast land of India it is necessary to explain yourself, to define your function and status in the universe. It is very difficult.

If I thought in terms of race or community, this experience of

India would surely have dispelled it. An Indian, I have never before been in streets where everyone is Indian, where I blend unremarkably into the crowd. This has been curiously deflating, for all my life I have expected some recognition of my difference; and it is only in India that I have recognized how necessary this stimulus is to me, how conditioned I have been by the multi-racial society of Trinidad and then by my life as an outsider in England. To be a member of a minority community has always seemed to me attractive. To be one of four hundred and thirty-nine million Indians is terrifying.

A colonial, in the double sense of one who had grown up in a Crown colony and one who had been cut off from the metro-polis, be it either England or India, I came to India expecting to find metropolitan attitudes. I had imagined that in some ways the largeness of the land would be reflected in the attitudes of the people. I have found, as I have said, the psychology of the cell and the hive. And I have been surprised by similarities. In India, as in tiny Trinidad, I have found the feeling that the metropolis is elsewhere, in Europe or America. Where I had expected large-ness, rootedness and confidence, I have found all the colonial attitudes of self-distrust.

"I am craze phor phoreign," the wife of a too-successful con-tractor said. And this craze extended from foreign food to German sanitary fittings to a possible European wife for her son, who sought to establish his claim further by announcing at the lunch table, "Oh, by the way, did I tell you we spend three thousand rupees a month?"

"You are a tourist, you don't know," the chemistry teacher on the Srinagar bus said. "But this is a terrible country. Give me a chance and I leave it tomorrow."

For among a certain class of Indians, usually more prosperous than their fellows, there is a passionate urge to explain to the visitor that they must not be considered part of poor, dirty India, that their values and standards are higher, and they live per-petually outraged by the country which gives them their liveli-hood. For them the second-rate foreign product, either people or manufactures, is preferable to the Indian. They suggest that for them, as much as for the European "technician", India is only a country to be temporarily exploited. How strange to find, in free India, this attitude of the conqueror, this attitude of plundering – a frenzied attitude, as though the opportunity might at any moment be withdrawn – in those very people to whom the developing society has given so many opportunities.

This attitude of plundering is that of the immigrant colonial society. It has bred, as in Trinidad, the pathetic philistinism of the *renonçant* (an excellent French word that describes the native who renounces his own culture and strives towards the French). And in India this philistinism, a blending of the vulgarity of East and West – those sad dance floors, those sad "western" cabarets, those transistor radios tuned to Radio Ceylon, those Don Juans with leather jackets or check tweed jackets – is peculiarly frightening. A certain glamour attaches to this philistinism, as glamour attaches to those Indians who, after two or three years in a foreign country, proclaim that they are neither of the East nor of the West.

The observer, it must be confessed, seldom sees the difficulty. The contractor's wife, so anxious to demonstrate her Westernness, regularly consulted her astrologer and made daily trips to the temple to ensure the continuance of her good fortune. The schoolteacher, who complained with feeling about the indiscipline and crudity of Indians, proceeded, as soon as we got to the bus station at Srinagar, to change his clothes in public.

The Trinidadian, whatever his race, is a genuine colonial. The Indian, whatever his claim, is rooted in India. But while the Trinidadian, a colonial, strives towards the metropolitan, the Indian of whom I have been speaking, metropolitan by virtue of the uniqueness of his country, its achievements in the past and its manifold achievements in the last decade or so, is striving towards the colonial.

Where one had expected pride, then, one finds the spirit of plunder. Where one had expected the metropolitan one finds the colonial. Where one had expected largeness one finds narrowness.

Goa, scarcely liberated, is the subject of an unseemly inter-State squabble. Fifteen years after Independence the politician as national leader appears to have been replaced by the politician as village headman (a type I had thought peculiar to the colonial Indian community of Trinidad, for whom politics was a game where little more than PWD contracts was at stake). To the village headman India is only a multiplicity of villages. So that the vision of India as a great country appears to be something imposed from without and the vastness of the country turns out to be oddly fraudulent.

Yet there remains a concept of India – as what? Something more than the urban middle class, the politicians, the industrialists, the separate villages. Neither this nor that, we are so often told, is the "real" India. And how well one begins to understand why this word is used! Perhaps India is only a word, a mystical idea that embraces all those vast plains and rivers through which the train moves, all those anonymous figures asleep on railway platforms and the footpaths of Bombay, all those poor fields and stunted animals, all this exhausted plundered land. Perhaps it is this, this vastness which no one can ever get to know: India as an ache, for which one has a great tenderness, but from which at length one always wishes to separate oneself.

Jamshed into Jimmy

New Statesman, 25 January 1963

"You've come to Calcutta at the wrong time," the publisher said. "I very much fear that the dear old city is slipping into bourgeois respectability almost without a fight."

"Didn't they burn a tram the other day?" I asked.

"True. But that was the first tram for five years."

And really I had expected more from Calcutta, the "nightmare experience" of Mr Nehru, the "pestilential behe-moth" of a recent, near-hysterical American writer, a city which, designed for two million people, today accommodates more than six million on its pavements and in its *bastees*, in conditions which unmanned the World Bank Mission of 1960 and sent it away to write what the *Economic Weekly* of Bombay described as a "strikingly human document".

Like every newspaper-reader, I knew Calcutta as the city of tram-burners and students who regularly "clashed" with the police. A brief news item in *The Times* in 1954 had hinted memorably at its labour troubles: some disgruntled workers had tossed their manager into the furnace. And during my time in India I had been following the doings of its Congress-controlled Corporation, which, from the progressive nationalist citadel of the twenties, has decayed into what students of Indian affairs consider the most openly corrupt of India's multitudinous corrupt public bodies: half the Corporation's five hundred and fifty vehicles disabled, many of them stripped of saleable parts, repair mechanics hampered, accounts four years in arrears, every obstacle put in the way of "interference" by State Government, New Delhi and a despairing Ford Foundation.

At every level I found that Calcutta enjoyed a fabulous reputation. The Bengali was insufferably arrogant ("The *pan*-seller doesn't so much as look at you if you don't talk to him in Bengali"); the Bengali was lazy; the pavements were dyed red with betel-juice and the main park was littered with used sanitary towels ("very untidy people", had been the comment of the South Indian novelist). And even in Bombay, the seat of gastro-enteritis, they spoke of Calcutta's inadequate (thirteen out of twenty-two Corporation tubewells not working) and tainted water supply with terror.

I had therefore expected much. And Howrah station was promising. The railway officials were more than usually non-committal and lethargic; the cigarette-seller didn't look at me; and in the station restaurant a smiling waiter drew my attention to a partly depilated rat that was wandering languidly about the tiled floor. But nothing had prepared me for the red-brick city on the other bank of the river which, if one could ignore the crowds, the stalls, the rickshaw-pullers and the squatting pissers, suggested, not a tropical or Eastern city, but central Birmingham. Nothing had prepared me for the Maidan, tree-dotted, now in the early evening blurred with mist and suggesting Hyde Park, with Chowringhee as a brighter Oxford Street. And nothing had prepared me for the sight of General Cariappa in the Maidan, dark-suited, English-erect, addressing a small relaxed crowd on the Chinese invasion in Sandhurst-accented Hindustani, while the trams, battleship-grey, with wedge-shaped snouts, nosed through the traffic at a steady eight miles an hour, the celebrated Calcutta tram, ponderous and vulnerable, *bulging* at entrances and exits with white-clad office workers, the neon lights beyond the Maidan gay in the mist: the invitations to espresso bars, cabarets, air travel. Here, unexpectedly and for the first time in India, one was in the midst of the big city, the recognizable metropolis, with street names – Elgin, Allenby, Park, Lindsay – that seemed oddly at variance with the brisk crowds, incongruity that deepened as the mist thickened to smog and as, travelling out to the suburbs, one saw the factory chimneys smoking among the palm trees.

And where in that bright heart, forgetting the pissers, were the piles of filth and refuse I had been told about, and the sanitary towels? In fact, as the publisher said, I had come to Calcutta at the wrong time. The city had recently been subjected to a brief and frenzied clean-up by the "volunteers" of the new Chief Minister of Bengal; it had been hoped that this would fill the Corporation's professionals with "enthusiasm". An "Operation Bull" had sought to clear the main streets of bulls which the devout Hindu releases into central Calcutta to service the holy cow. The idea was that the cows would follow the bulls. As it turned out, the cows had stayed; the bulls were returning. And no inhabitant of Calcutta doubted that with the withdrawal of the volunteers, and with so many things in India suspended because of the Emergency – suspension and prohibition being the administration's current substitute for action – the filth too would return. But for the moment some of the unfamiliar gloss remained.

All the four main cities in India were developed by the British, but none has so British a stamp as Calcutta. Lutyens's New Delhi is a disaster, a mock-imperial joke, neither British nor Indian, a city built for parades rather than people, and today given a correctly grotesque scale by the noisy little scooter-rickshaws that scurry about its long avenues and endless roundabouts. Madras, though possessing in Fort St George one of the finest complexes of eighteenth-century British architecture outside Britain, is elsewhere lazily colonial. Bombay owes much to its Parsi community, enterprising, civic-minded, culturally ambiguous; the hysterical American already quoted speaks of Bombay's "bandbox architecture", and indeed this city, the best-run in India, is cosmopolitan to the point of characterlessness. Calcutta alone appears to have been created in the image of England, the British here falling, unusually, into the imperialist practice of the French and the Portuguese. And what has resulted in Calcutta is a grandeur more rooted than that of New Delhi: "the city of palaces", they called Calcutta, the palaces Indian or British, built in a style which might best be described as Calcutta Corinthian: Calcutta, for long the capital of British India, the second city of the British Empire.

In India the confrontation of East and West was nowhere more violent than in Calcutta, and two buildings, both now regarded as monuments, speak of this violence: the Mullick Palace and the Victoria Memorial. Decaying now, with servants cooking in the marble galleries, the Mullick Palace still looks like a film set. It is dominated by tall Corinthian columns; Italian fountains play in the grounds; its excessively chandeliered marble rooms are crowded out with the clutter of a hundred nineteenth-century European antique shops, this dusty plaster cast of a Greek nymph hiding that faded, unmemorable painting of red-coated soldiers repulsing some native attack. In the courtyard four marble figures represent the major continents; and on the lower floor the monumental statue of a youthful Queen Victoria makes a big room small. None of the dusty treasures of the Mullick Palace is Indian, save perhaps for a portrait of the collector: the original Bengali babu, anxious to prove to the supercilious European his appreciation of European culture. And on the Maidan stands the Victoria Memorial, Curzon's answer to the Taj Mahal, as studiedly derivative as the Mullick Palace, here recalling the Taj, there recalling the Salute. "Passing through the Queen's vestibule into the Queen's Hall under the dome," says Murray's *Handbook*, which characteristically gives twice as much space to this Raj Taj as to the Kailasa Temple at Ellora,

> one sees the dignified statue of Queen Victoria at the age when she ascended the throne (the work of Sir Thomas Brock RA); this gives the keynote to the whole edifice.

Yet out of this confrontation there emerged something new in India, an explosive mixture of East and West, a unique culture which, however despised by the non-Calcutta Bengali as jumped-up and camp-following, gave Indian nationalism many of its prophets and heroes. The Bengali will tell you that British officials were urged to treat the South Indian as a slave, the Punjabi as a friend, and the Bengali as an enemy. But when the Bengali tells you this he is speaking as of lost glories, for today, with Independence and the partition of Bengal (in Calcutta the words are

synonymous), the heart has gone out of Calcutta. It is a city
without a hinterland, a dying city. Even the Hooghly is silting
up, and everyone agrees that Calcutta has ceased to grow economically, however much it might spread physically. Though there are
endearing vestiges of the Mullick Palace mentality in, say, the
literary criticism of Professor Sadhan Kumar Ghosh (compassion-
ately dealt with in the *New Statesman* by Malcolm Muggeridge),
Calcutta is exhausted, its people withdrawn. It has Satyajit Ray,
the film director; it has in Sunil Janah a photographer of world
stature; Bengali typography, nervously elegant, is perhaps the
best in India. But the glory lies in the past, in Tagore, in Bankim
Chandra Chatterji, in the terrorists, in Subhas Chandra Bose.
(1962 was a good year for the Bose legend: one libel action
brought by a member of the family against an Englishwoman,
and another reported reappearance, this time as a sadhu in the
Himalayas.)

Calcutta remains what it always has been through growth,
creative disorder, quiescence. It is still, despite the strong challenge
of Bombay, India's principal commercial city, and the element of
Calcutta culture which might be said to be dominant is that
represented by the business buildings of Dalhousie Square and
the squat business houses of Imperial Tobacco and Metal Box on
Chowringhee. There in air-conditioned offices may be found the
young Indian business executives, the box-wallahs, the new
Indian élite. A generation ago such positions would not have been
acceptable to any Indian of birth; and he almost certainly would
not have been accepted. But the Indian genius for compromise is
no less than that of the British. The box-wallah culture of
Calcutta is of a peculiar richness, and if it has not yet been explored
by Indian writers this is because they have been too busy plagi-
arizing, or writing harrowing stories about young girls drifting
into prostitution to pay the family's medical bills and stories about
young girls, poor or pretty, who inexplicably die. This culture,
though of Calcutta, is not necessarily Bengali. Commerce is controlled by the British and increasingly since Independence by the
Marwaris – it is almost with pride that the Bengali tells you there

is no Bengali businessman worth the name. The Marwaris are Indian but are spoken of throughout India as a community even more alien than the British: the feeling against them in Calcutta is something you can cut with a knife. No one of standing wishes to be directly employed by the Marwaris. The conditions are not as good as those offered by the British who are reputable; in the public mind Marwari businessmen are associated with black-marketing and speculation. No one who works for the Marwaris can therefore properly be considered a box-wallah – your true box-wallah works only for the best British firms. ("Tell me," they were asked at Imperial Tobacco, "was that very large painting of the Queen put up especially for the Queen's visit?" "No," was the box-wallah reply. "It is *always* there.")

No one in Calcutta is sure of the origin of the word box-wallah. It has been suggested that it comes from the street pedlar's box; but in Calcutta the word has too grand and restricted a significance, and it seems to me more likely to have been derived from the Anglo-Indian office-box of which Kipling speaks so feelingly in *Something of Myself*. Perhaps the office-box, like the solar topee (still worn with mournful defiance by those ICS officers who despair of further promotion), was a symbol of authority; and though the symbols have changed, the authority has been transferred and persists.

The Calcutta box-wallah comes of a good family, ICS, Army or big business; he might even have princely connections. He has been educated at an Indian or English public school and at one of the two English universities, whose accent, through all the encircling hazards of Indian intonation, he rigidly maintains. When he joins his firm his first name is changed. The Indian name of Anand, for example, might become Andy; Dhandeva will become Danny, Firdaus Freddy, Jamshed Jimmy. Where the Indian name cannot be adapted, the box-wallah will most usually be known as Bunty. It is a condition of Bunty's employment that he play golf; and on every golf course he can be seen with an equally unhappy Andy, both enduring the London-prescribed mixture of business and pleasure.

Bunty will of course marry well, and he knows it will be counted in his favour if he contracts a mixed marriage; if, say, as a Punjabi Hindu he marries a Bengali Muslim or a Bombay Parsi. Bunty and his wife will live in one of the company's luxury flats; they will be called Daddy and Mummy by their two English-speaking children. Their furnishings will show a happy blend of East and West (Indian ceramics are just coming in). So too will their food (Indian lunch followed by Western-style dinner), their books, their records (difficult classical Indian, European chamber music) and their pictures (North Indian miniatures, Ganymed reproductions of Van Gogh).

Freed of one set of caste rules, Bunty and his wife will adopt another. If his office has soft furnishings he will know how to keep his distance from Andy, whose furnishings are hard; and to introduce Andy, who shares an air-conditioned office with Freddy, into the home of Bunty, who has an office to himself, is to commit a blunder. His new caste imposes new rituals on Bunty. Every Friday he will have lunch at Firpo's on Chowringhee, and the afternoon-long jollity will mark the end of the week's work. In the days of the British this Friday lunch at Firpo's celebrated the departure of the mail-boat for England. Such letters as Bunty sends to England go now by air, but Bunty is conscious of tradition.

It is impossible to write of Bunty without making him appear ridiculous. But Bunty is the first slanderer of his group; and enough has been said to show how admirable, in the Indian context, he is. Where physical effort is regarded as a degradation and thick layers of fat are still to many the marks of prosperity, Bunty plays golf and swims. Where elections are won on communal campaigns, Bunty marries out of his community. Bunty is intelligent and well-read; like most educated Indians, he talks well; though he has abandoned the social obligations of the Indian joint family, he is generous and hospitable; he supports the arts. Not least of his virtues is that he keeps a spotless lavatory. East and West blend easily in him. For him, who has grown up in an independent India, Westernization is not the issue it was to his grandfather and even his father. He carries no chip on his shoulder; he does not feel the need to talk to the visitor about India's ancient culture.

Occasionally, very occasionally, the calm is disturbed. "These damned English!" Bunty exclaims. "When are they going to learn that 1947 really happened?" The words are like an echo from the Mullick Palace. But it is a passing mood. Soon Bunty will be out on the golf course with Andy. And golf is a game they both now love.

Indian Autobiographies

New Statesman, 29 January 1965

THE DERELICTION OF India overwhelms the visitor; and it seems reasonable to imagine that the Indian who leaves his country, and all its assumptions, for the first time is likely to be unsettled. But in Indian autobiographies* there is no hint of unsettlement: people are their designations and functions, and places little more than their names. "We reached Southampton, as far as I can remember, on a Saturday." This is Gandhi writing in 1925 of his arrival in England as a student in 1889. That it was a Saturday was more important to him than that he had exchanged Bombay for Southampton. He had landed in a white flannel suit and couldn't get at his luggage until Monday. So Southampton is no more than an experience of embarrassment and is never described; as later London, never described, is converted into a series of small spiritual experiences, the vows of vegetarianism and chastity being more important than the city of the 1890s. A place is its name.

> London was just too big for me and the two days I spent there so overwhelming that I was glad to leave for Manchester. My brother had arranged some digs in advance so that I settled in straight away.

We are forty years beyond Gandhi, but the tone in *Punjabi Century*, the memoirs of a high business executive, remains the same. India is one place, England another. There can be no contrast, no shock in reverse. It is only near the end of *My Public*

---

* *The Story of My Experiments with Truth*, by M. K. Gandhi, translated by Mahadev Desai, 1966.
Punjabi Century, by Prakash Lal Tandon, 1963.
My Public Life, by Mirza Ismail, 1954.
A Passage to England, by Nirad Chaudhuri, 1959.
The Autobiography of an Unknown Indian, by Nirad Chaudhuri, 1951.

Life that Sir Mirza Ismail, after listing the recommendations he made to President Sukarno for the improvement of the Indonesian administration – he recommended four new colleges, five new stadiums and "publication of the President's speeches in book form" – it is only after this that he observes:

> The standard of living is higher in Indonesia than in India. People are better clad and better fed, although cloth is much dearer. One hardly sees the miserable specimens of humanity that one comes across in the big cities in India, as well as in rural areas.

The effect is startling, for until that moment the talk had mostly been of parks and gardens and factories, and of benevolent and appreciative rulers. We have to wait until Nirad Chaudhuri's *Passage to England*, published in 1959, for something more explicit.

> I failed to see in England one great distinction which is basic in my country. When I was there I was always asking myself, "Where are the people?" I did so because I was missing the populace, the commonalty, the masses. . . .

The attitude might be interpreted as aristocratic; in no country is aristocracy as easy as in India. But we are in reality dealing with something more limiting and less comprehensible: the Indian habit of exclusion, denial, non-seeing. It is part of what Nirad Chaudhuri calls the "ignoble privacy" of Indian social organization; it defines by negatives. It is a lack of wonder, the medieval attribute of a people who are still surrounded by wonders; and in autobiographies this lack of wonder is frequently converted into a hectic self-love.

For its first half Gandhi's autobiography reads like a fairy-tale. He is dealing with the acknowledged marvels of his early life; and his dry, compressed method, reducing people to their functions and simplified characteristics, reducing places to names and action to a few lines of narrative, turns everything to legend. When the action becomes more complex and political, the method fails; and the book declines more obviously into what it always was: an obsession with vows, food experiments, recurring illness, an obsession with the self. "Thoughts of self," Chaudhuri writes in *The Autobiography of an Unknown Indian*,

> are encouraged by a religious view of life, because it emphasizes our lone coming into the world and our lone exit from it and induces us to judge values in their relation to the individual voyager, the individual voyage, and the ultimate individual destiny.

In *Punjabi Century* Prakash Tandon seems to set out to tell the story of the transformation of the Punjab from 1857 to 1947. He barely attempts the theme. He minutely describes festivals, marriage customs, his father's engineering duties, the various family houses; and the book is transformed into a tribute to his province, his caste, his family and himself: it contains an embarrassing account of his courtship in Sweden, to which is added an injured and recognizably Indian account of his difficulties in getting a job. "Friends not only in my own country but scattered on three continents have suggested I should write my memoirs," Sir Mirza Ismail says.

> It is not easy, however, to write about oneself, and partly for this reason, and partly in order to make the memoirs more interesting, I have quoted from letters received.

Not a few of these letters are tributes to the writer. "You're a wonder!" writes Lord Willingdon. "I would like to name a road after you," writes the Maharaja of Jaipur.

An old-fashioned Muslim vizier, a modern Hindu businessman, the Mahatma: assorted personalities, but recognizably of the same culture. "Writing an autobiography is a practice peculiar to the West," a "God-fearing" friend said to Gandhi on the Mahatma's day of silence. "I know of nobody in the East having written one except amongst those who have come under western influence." And it is in this bastard form – in which a religious view of life, laudable in one culture, is converted steadily into self-love, disagreeable in another culture – that we can begin to see the misunderstandings and futility of the Indo-English encounter.

The civilizations were, and remain, opposed; and the use of English heightens the confusion. When Gandhi came to England for the Round Table Conference in 1931 he stayed for a night at a Quaker guest-house in the Ribble Valley. The garden was in bloom. In the evening Gandhi, in sandals, dhoti and shawl, walked among the flowers. He scarcely looked at them. The story is told by Tandon, who got it from the warden.

I consoled him that it was quite characteristic of Gandhiji that though he passionately advocated a return to nature he completely lacked interest in its beauty.

But was it strictly a "return to nature" that Gandhi advocated? Wasn't it something more complex? Was Gandhi's aim to re-awaken wonder, or was it rather an unconscious striving after a symbolism acceptable to the Indian masses, a political exploitation, however unconscious, of the "ignoble privacy" of Indian attitudes? The Gandhian concept is not easily translated. A "return to nature" and "patriotism": in India the concepts are linked; and the Indian concept of patriotism is unique. Tandon tells how, in 1919, the Independence movement made its first impression on his district.

These visitors spoke about the freedom of India, and this intrigued us; but when they talked in familiar analogies and idiom about the Kal Yug, we saw what they meant. Had it not been prophesied that there were seven eras in India's life and history: there had been a Sat Yug, the era of truth, justice and prosperity; and then there was to be a Kal Yug, an era of falsehood, of demoralization, of slavery and poverty. . . . These homely analogies, illustrated by legend and history, registered easily, but not so easily the conclusion to which they were linked, that it was all the fault of the Angrezi Sarkar.

We are in fact dealing with the type of society which Camus described in the opening chapter of *The Rebel*: a society which has not learned to see and is incapable of assessing itself, which asks no questions because ritual and myth have provided all the answers, a society which has not learned "rebellion". An unfortunate word perhaps, with its juvenile, romantic 1950s associations; but it is the concept which divides, not the East from the West, but India from almost every other country. It explains why so much writing about India is unsatisfactory and one-sided, and it throws into relief the stupendous achievement of Nirad Chaudhuri's *Autobiography of an Unknown Indian* which, containing within itself both India and the West, has had the misfortune of being taken for granted by both sides.

Chaudhuri's *Autobiography* may be the one great book to have come out of the Indo-English encounter. No better account of the penetration of the Indian mind by the West – and, by extension, of the penetration of one culture by another – will be or can now be written. It was an encounter which ended in mutual recoil and futility. For Chaudhuri this futility is an almost personal tragedy. Yet we can now see that this futility was inevitable. To the static, minutely ordered Indian society, with its pressures ever towards the self, England came less as a political shock than as the source of a New Learning. Chaudhuri quotes from *Rajani*, a Bengali novel by Bankim Chandra Chatterji:

> He did not disclose his business, nor could I ask him outright. So we discussed social reform and politics. . . . The discussion of ancient literature led in its turn to ancient historiography, out of which there emerged some incomparable exposition of the classical historians, Tacitus, Plutarch, Thucydides, and others. From the philosophy of history of these writers Amarnath came down to Comte and his *lois des trois états*, which he endorsed. Comte brought in his interpreter Mill and then Huxley; Huxley brought in Owen and Darwin; and Darwin Buchner and Schopenhauer. Amarnath poured the most entrancing scholarship into my ears, and I became too engrossed to remember our business.

The astonishing thing about this novel is its date, which is 1877. Kipling's *Plain Tales* were to appear in book form just eleven years later, to reveal the absurdity of this New Learning, nourished

by books alone. Between the New Learning and its representatives
in Simla there was a gap. Dead civilizations alone ought properly
to provide a New Learning. This civilization survived; it had
grown suburban and philistine, was soon to become proletarian;
and it was fitting that from 1860 to 1910, which Chaudhuri fixes
as the period of the Indian Renaissance, the educated Bengali
should have been an object of especial ridicule to the English, to
whom the unintellectual simplicities of the blue-eyed Pathan were
more comprehensible. Chaudhuri, lamenting the death of the
Indian Renaissance, and the corrupting, "elemental" Westernization that took its place, pays little attention to this aspect of the
encounter.

The élite Indo-English culture of Bengal was as removed from
the Anglo-Indian culture of Simla as it was removed from the
culture of the Indian masses. It was a growth of fantasy; the
political liberalism it bred could not last. It was to give way to the
religious revivalism of a mass movement, to all the combative
hocus-pocus of revived "Vedic" traditions such as the launching
of ships with coconut-milk instead of champagne, and finally to
that cultural confusion which some sentences of Tandon's illustrate
so well:

> Gandhi rechristened India Bharat Mata, a name that evoked
> nostalgic memories, and associated with Gao Mata, the
> mother cow. . . . He . . . spoke about the peace of the British
> as the peace of slavery. Gradually a new picture began to
> build in our minds, of India coming out of the Kal Yug into
> a new era of freedom and plenty, Ram Rajya.

Language has at last broken down. Gao Mata, Ram Rajya: for
these there are no English equivalents. We can see "national pride"
now as an applied phrase, with a special Indian meaning. In the
definition of Ram Rajya the true stress falls on "plenty", while
"freedom" is an intrusive English *word*. Here is the futility of the
Indo-English encounter, the intellectual confusion of the "new"
India. This is the great, tragic theme of Chaudhuri's book.

The Last of the Aryans

Encounter, January 1966

YOU DON'T HAVE to wait long for the characteristic Nirad
Chaudhuri note in *The Continent of Circe*. It occurs, unmistakably,
almost before the book begins; yet it has the effect of a climax.
There is a frontispiece with two views from the author's veranda
in Delhi: one looking up to clouds, one looking down to refugee
tents. The title page has a Latin device: *De rerum indicarum natura:
Exempla gentium et seditionum.* The motto – "Know Thyself" –
follows, in five Indo-European languages. Seven detailed contents
pages come next. And then we come to text: six pages, a chapter
almost, headed "In Gratitude". Chaudhuri begins by thanking
Khushwant Singh, "the well-known Sikh writer, good companion, and man-about-town, for the loan of his portable typewriter". This seems straightforward enough; but it soon becomes
clear that we have to do with an incident.

It is like this. Chaudhuri is tapping away on Khushwant's
machine. He is nearing the end of one of the sections of his book
and his gratitude to Khushwant, as he says, is at its highest. A
"public print" comes his way. It is "the official publication of the
American Women's Club of Delhi". It contains "An Interview
with Khushwant Singh":

INTERVIEWER: Who is the best Indian writer today?
KHUSHWANT SINGH: In non-fiction? Without a doubt Nirad
Chaudhuri. . . . A bitter man, a poor man. He doesn't even
own a typewriter. He borrows mine a week at a time.

Chaudhuri is "struck all of a heap":

My poverty is, of course, well known in New Delhi and
much further afield, and therefore I was not prepared to see

it bruited about by so august a body as the American Women's Club of Delhi.

Khushwant explains. His statement has been given the wrong emphasis. He thought he was only entertaining a lady to tea; he had no idea what her real intention was. He offers Chaudhuri a brand-new portable typewriter as a gift:

> I tried to show that I bore no grudge by again borrowing the machine after the publication of the article and by most gratefully accepting the present of the new typewriter.

And a footnote adds:

> Having read Pascal early in life I have always tried to profit by his wisdom: "*Si tous les hommes savaient ce qu'ils disaient les uns des autres, il n'y aurait pas quatre amis dans le monde.*"

So much about the typewriters on which the book was written; the Americans, though, continue to receive attention for a whole page.

It is impossible to take an interest in Nirad Chaudhuri's work without becoming involved with his situation and "personality". This has been his extra-literary creation since the publication in 1951 of his *Autobiography of an Unknown Indian*. The book made him known. But in India it also made him disliked. Cruelly, it did not lessen his poverty; this mighty work, which in a fairer world would have made its author's fortune and seen him through old age, is now out of print. So, persecuted where not neglected, as he with some reason feels, he sits in Delhi, massively disapproving, more touchy than before, more out of touch with his fellows, never ceasing to attract either the slights of the high or the disagreeable attentions of the low.

His fellow passengers on the Delhi buses wish to know the time. Without inquiry they lift his wrist, consult his wrist-watch, and then without acknowledgement let his wrist drop. Sometimes he walks; and, in a land of "massive staticity", where when men walk it is as if "rooted trees were waving in the wind", he walks "in the European manner, that is to say, quickly and with a sense of the goal towards which I am going". Elderly people shout after him, "Left! Right! Left! Right!" Boys call out, "Johnnie Walker!" Sometimes they come right up to him and jeer in Hindi: "*Aré Jahny*." It is not even the Johnnie Walker of the whisky label they refer to, but "a caricature of him by an Indian film star":

> Friends ask me why I do not go for these impertinent young fellows. I reply that I retain my common sense at least to the point of forcing myself to bear all this philosophically. But being also a naturally irascible man, I sometimes breathe a wish that I possessed a flame-thrower and was free to use it. In my conduct and behaviour, however, I never betray this lack of charity.

Indoors it is hardly less dangerous. The London Philharmonic Orchestra comes to Delhi. Chaudhuri talks music to Sir Malcolm Sargent; an English lady whispers to Mrs Chaudhuri, "What a bold man he is!" He goes to the concert the next day; the British Council has provided tickets. He finds that he is separated from his wife by the aisle. An upper-class Indian lady claims that he is sitting on her chair. She is wrong; she objects then to his proximity; she calls the upper-class usherettes to her aid. He yields; he takes his chair across the aisle to join his wife.

The extra-literary Chaudhuri "personality" is more than a creation of art; the suffering, however self-induced, is too real. Nearly seventy, he is a solitary, in hurtful conflict at every level with his environment.

FAILURE: it is Chaudhuri's obsession. There is the personal failure: twenty years of poverty and humiliation dismissed in a single, moving sentence in the *Autobiography*. There is the failure as a scholar, recorded in the *Autobiography* and echoed in the present book.

I shall mention the names of four men whom I regard as truly learned. They are Mommsen, Wilamowitz-Moellendorf, Harnack, and Eduard Meyer. When young and immature I cherished the ambition of being the fifth in that series. So I could not have been very modest. But a standard is a standard.

There is the failure, or rather the futility, of the nineteenth-century Anglo-Bengali culture, Chaudhuri's own, set against the larger futility of British rule. These were the interwoven themes of the monumental *Autobiography*. Now Chaudhuri addresses himself to a more encompassing failure: the failure of his country, his race, and the land itself, *Aryavarta*, the land of the Aryans.

He has called *The Continent of Circe* an "Essay on the Peoples of India". But his subject is really the Hindus; and his starting-point is the incomprehension, rapidly giving way to rage, which the Hindus have immemorially aroused in non-Hindus. Even E. M. Forster, Chaudhuri says, is more drawn to Muslims; and for all his pro-Indian sentiment, "there are few delineations of the Indian character more insultingly condescending" than those in *A Passage to India*. Forster's plea for Indo-British friendship reminds Chaudhuri of the poem:

> *Turn, turn thy hasty foot aside,*
> *Nor crush that helpless worm!*
> *The frame thy wayward looks deride*
> *Required a God to form.*

"This massive, spontaneous, and uniform criticism by live minds . . . cannot be cancelled by afterthoughts which have their source in the *Untergang des Abendlandes*." And Chaudhuri wishes to cancel nothing. He seeks only to explain. But the act of explaining frequently drives *him* to rage. Where the *Autobiography* was analytic, detached and underplayed, the Essay is strident and tendentious. Chaudhuri's sense of failure and vulnerability, that personality, comes in the way; and it is as a display of personality that *The Continent of Circe* is best to be relished. It is at its most delicious when it is most passionate; and it is most passionate when, one suspects, it is most personal: in the account, for instance, of the "sob-chamber" of Hindu family life, where the only competition is in gloom and people can legitimately consider themselves provoked if they are told they are looking well. So, in Chaudhuri's essay as much as in the work of any uncomprehending foreigner, "Hindu" ends by being almost a word of abuse.

Hindus pacifist? Rubbish, says Chaudhuri. Hindus are militarist, have always been; it is only their inefficiency that makes them less of a menace to the world. To prove this he gives selective historical examples and interprets the frontier conflict with China in a way that will not be faulted in Peking. Again: "The industrial revolution in India at its most disinterested is an expression of anti-European and anti-Western nationalism." This is possible; but it cannot be squared with what immediately follows: "a far stronger force, in actual fact the positive force, is the Hindu's insatiable greed for money". This, at first, seems too meaningless a statement even for simple denial. But he is making an important point; he is speaking of what some people in India call the "pigmy mentality" of the Indian capitalist:

> The American industrialist is the old European Conquistador in a new incarnation. . . . But the Hindu money-maker can never be anything but his *paisa*-counting sordid self. . . . His spirit is best symbolised by the adulteration of food, medicine, and whatever else can be adulterated.

So that the Indian industrial revolution, so far from being an expression of anti-Western nationalism, turns out to be a very petty, private thing indeed. Its cynicism might appear to some to be an extension of caste attitudes. And it might be expected that Chaudhuri would be critical of caste. Not at all. He asks us to keep off the caste question if we don't want to pound India to dust. Caste is the only thing that holds Indian society together. It is "a natural compensation for man's convergent zoological evolution and divergent psychological evolution". Caste did not suppress mobility; that came only with the *Pax Britannica*. And the Chaudhuri flourish is added:

3

If the system suppressed anything it was only ambition un-related to ability, and watching the mischief from this kind of ambition in India today I would say that we could do with a little more of the caste system in order to put worthless adventurers in their place.

It might seem then that Chaudhuri, in an attempt to make a whole of Hindu attitudes, has succumbed to any number of Hindu con-tradictions. But I also feel that Chaudhuri, living in Delhi, endur-ing slights and persecution, has at last succumbed to what we might call the enemy. He sees India as too big; he has lost his gift of detachment, his world view. He seeks to expose where exposure is not really necessary. He has been taken in by the glitter of "the diplomatic" at Delhi, the flurry of visitors, the cultural displays of competing governments. He exaggerates the importance of India and the interest taken in India. People in England, he says, "are still longing after [India] with the docility of cattle", and the words make sad reading in London in 1965.

But this is the theme of his polemic: that tropical India is the continent of Circe, drugging and destroying those whom it attracts, and that the Aryans, now Hindus, were the first to be lured from a temperate land, "denatured" and destroyed. Their philosophy is the philosophy of the devitalized. It is rooted in secular distress, the anguish of flesh on the Gangetic Plain, where everything quickly decomposes and leads to *tamas*, a comprehen-sive squalor:

> The tragedy of all the systems of Hindu philosophy is that they confront men with only one choice: remain corrupt-ible and corrupt flesh, or become incorruptible and incorrupt stone.

Be neurotically fussy about cleanliness; or – the greater spirituality – show your indifference to the extent of being able to eat excre-ment. Hindus are not philosophers; nor do they reverence philo-sophy. "What we respect are the sadhus, possessors of occult power."

In Chaudhuri's argument it follows without contradiction that a people obsessed with religion, really a "philosophy of sorrow", are obsessed with sex. It is the great anodyne. "Defeat was on the fleshly plane. . . . Rehabilitation must also be in the flesh." The sex act in Hindu sculpture is not symbolic of any sort of spiritual union, as is sometimes said: it is no more than what it appears to be. With a loss of vitality this celebration of the senses declines into the "sex-obsessed chastity of the Hindu, which is perhaps the most despicable ethical notion ever created in the moral evolution of any people":

> Their admiration of the supposed superior sexual knowledge and dexterity of the Hindus is putting ideas in the heads of a particularly depraved set of Occidentals, who are coming to India and working havoc with what sexual sanity . . . we still have.

Well said; but it is on the subject of sex that Chaudhuri becomes most fanciful. Tracing the decline of vitality, he makes too much, one feels, of the emphasis in Sanskrit erotic writings on the pleasures of the *purushayita* or reversed position. Wasn't it in such a position, if one reads right, that Lucius and Fotis first came together in *The Golden Ass*?

Chaudhuri writes of India as though India has never been written about before. He pays little attention to received ideas; he mentions no authorities:

> I am old, and I cannot spend the few years that are left to me tilting at theories which I have taken a lifetime to outgrow. . . . I must therefore be resigned to being called a fool by those who believe in ghosts. . . . Historical conferences in India always reminds me of séances.

He places the Aryan settlement of the Gangetic Plain in the seventh century BC. This will be offensive to those Indians who think of India as the Aryan heartland and, playing with millennia, like to think of Rome as a recent, and peripheral, disturbance. He

allows no civilization worth the name to the indigenous Austra-
loids, whom he calls the Darks. Rigid barriers were set up against
them, and Chaudhuri – going back on some of his old views –
claims that no significant intermingling of the races took place.
The Darks, in their free or servile state, remain to this day geneti-
cally stable; and to this day, it might be added, the burning of a
giant effigy of a Dark is the climax of an annual Hindu pageant-
play. Hindu *apartheid* quickly gave the Darks the psychology of
a subject race. Chaudhuri retells a story from the *Ramayana*, the
Hindu epic. It is reported one day to Rama, the Aryan hero, that
the son of a brahmin has died suddenly. There can be only one
explanation: an act of impiety. Rama goes out to have a look and,
sure enough, finds that a young Dark has been performing Aryan
religious rites. The Dark is at once decapitated and the brahmin's
son comes back to life. In later versions of the story the Dark dies
happily: death at the hands of an Aryan is a sure way to heaven.
Not even slavery created so complete a subjection.

So that, as Chaudhuri tells it, the continent of Circe has played
a cruel joke on the Hindus. The first white people to come into
contact with a black race, and the first and most persistent practi-
tioners of *apartheid*, they have themselves, over the centuries,
under a punishing sun, grown dark. The snow-capped Himalayas
have become objects of pilgrimage; and some Hindus, in their
hysteria, look beyond that to the North Pole, of which modern
map-makers have made them aware. There, someone will tell you
in all the blaze of Madras, there at the North Pole lies the true
home of the Hindus:

> The theme of paradise lost and regained is one of the major
> stories of Hindu mythology, and it must date from the Iranian
> sojourn of the Indian Aryans. In the stories the gods recover
> their heaven. . . . But in history paradise is lost for ever; and
> the curse begins to work: in sorrow shalt thou eat of it all
> the days of thy life.

This is the true Chaudhuri mood; and, for all Chaudhuri's fanciful
flights and parenthetic rages, it must be respected: the Hindu sense

of exile and loss is real. Yet the layman must ask certain questions. Chaudhuri places the Aryan settlement just two or three generations before the birth of the Buddha. Could the philosophy of sorrow and the devitalization of the Aryan have occurred so soon? Could the Aryan, even the settler in the South, have undertaken the colonization of South-east Asia a thousand years later? The reader of Chaudhuri's book, working from Chaudhuri's clues, might easily come to a different conclusion from Chaudhuri. He might feel that the Hindus, so far from being denatured Aryans, have continued, in their curious and self-willed isolation, to be close to their elemental Aryan origins. For the Aryan in India, Chaudhuri says, both sensibility and effort became parts of piety; and this surely makes many Hindu attitudes less mysterious. The attitudes remain; the gloss varies with historical circumstance. Chaudhuri writes with some sharpness of Hindus who now use European rationalism to excuse their "irrational urges and taboos". Yet we have seen how he himself uses a borrowed language to defend caste, a primitive institution. Hindus can be found today to defend Gandhi's assassination on the grounds that the assassin was a brahmin. This is outrageous; but it becomes intelligible and logical if we see it as an extension of the old Aryan approval of Rama's slaying of the impious, and complaisant, Dark in the *Ramayana* story.

And there is the erotic sculpture. It cannot be ignored. It cannot be talked away. It is too widespread, too casual. It is of a piece with the open sensuality of the *Rig Veda*, the earliest Hindu sacred book. This has been called the first recorded speech of Aryan man. Chaudhuri translates a sample:

> *He achieves not – he whose penis hangs limp between*
> *his thighs;*
> *Achieves he alone whose hairy thing swells up when*
> *he lies.*

It is Indrani, the Queen Goddess, who speaks; and she is a match for her consort who, for his lechery, was punished by the appearance all over his body of a thousand *pudenda muliebria*. This is a camp-fire, peasant lewdness. And when all is said and done this is what *aryan* means: he is one who tills the soil.

Chaudhuri's plea that Hindus should turn their backs on Asia and recover their Aryan or European personality is, if narrowly interpreted, meaningless. Part of the trouble is that Chaudhuri makes "Aryan" and "European" interchangeable. But "European" surely needs to be more closely defined, and dated. It is a developing concept; "Aryan" is fixed. And Chaudhuri's plea becomes very thin indeed when we find that for *homo europaeus* in his present predominant and proliferating variety Chaudhuri has no high regard:

> The most vapid and insignificant class of human beings which so far has been evolved in history [is] the modern urban lower middle class of the West.

The absurd thing is that in India Aryan racial pride still has point; in Europe it has little. Of this pride Chaudhuri's book might be seen as the latest expression. He is not European; with his poetic feeling for rivers and cattle, his insistence on caste, he remains Aryan.

> Make a European society with India's religion. Become an occidental of occidentals in your spirit of equality, freedom, work, and energy, and at the same time a Hindu to the very backbone in religious culture, and instincts.

This is not Chaudhuri. It is Vivekananda, the Vedantist, writing at the turn of the century. A Bengali, like Chaudhuri, a reformer, a product of the Anglo-Bengali culture; and the message, with all its imprecisions and contradictions, is like Chaudhuri's. The Anglo-Bengali culture survives. To its passionate introspection *The Continent of Circe* is a late addition, quirky, at times wild, but rich and always stimulating.

Theatrical Natives

New Statesman, 2 December 1966

THE KIPLING REVIVAL is curious. It seems to be mainly academic – and therefore self-perpetuating – and its interest seems to be less in the work than in the man. Kipling is more complex than his legend. It is easy for the critic to be made possessive by this discovery and to go through the work just looking for clues. It can be shown, for instance, from a story like "The Bridge-Builders", that Kipling was not insensitive to the subtleties of Hindu iconography. The fact is interesting, but it doesn't make the story any less obscure or unsatisfactory. The fact is also awkward: it doesn't fit with other facts. And so it happens that attempts to set the legend right often end in simple tabulation, of matter and motif. This is the method of Mr Stewart's *Rudyard Kipling*, which does little more than celebrate a reading of the Kipling canon.

The legend survives. "The Kipling that Nobody Read" – the title of Mr Edmund Wilson's essay – is still the Kipling nobody reads. Kipling revaluations are self-defeating, since they lead back more surely to the only Kipling of value, which is the Kipling of the legend. It is the legend of the brief serene decade of British India, when the Mutiny finally became a memory and nationalism was still to come: a moment of order and romance, vanishing even as it was apprehended, later to embarrass, sadden, anger and be explained away, until it became historical. The legend can be accepted now. Mr Cornell accepts it: it is one of the merits of his book. *Kipling in India* is the most balanced analysis I have read of Kipling's literary achievement. Mr Cornell says that his subject is Kipling's apprenticeship, which contained the legendary achievement: the fixing, for all time, of that moment of British India.

It was the unlikely achievement of a very young man who took his unimportant journalistic work seriously; who abandoned the graver literary ambitions of his school-days to become a kind of club-writer; who aimed at ordinariness, and feared above all to offend. The club was at first the Punjab Club, of which Kipling became a member at seventeen. Soon it was all British India. This artificial, complete and homogeneous world did not require explanations. "Dedication," Mr Cornell says, "walked hand in hand with triviality." The triviality was the triviality of "good-fellowship, not savage mockery"; there were limits to self-satire. Kipling followed the rules and didn't sink. Like the Lama in *Kim*, he acquired merit.

Mr Cornell is right to stress the club, for it is from his function as a club-writer that Kipling's virtues came, and especially that allusive, elliptical prose, easy but packed, which, almost one hundred years later, still seems so new. Mr Cornell's account of the development of this prose is fascinating. This is Kipling at seventeen, describing a Hindu pageant in Lahore:

To the great delight of the people, Ramachandra and his brothers, attired in the traditional costume and head-dress, were mounted aloft and held the mighty bow, the breaking of which shook the world to its centre. But it must be admitted that Sita, uncomfortably astride a broad-backed wicker-work bull, supported by an uneasy Rama, buried in tinsel and attended by bearers ... was a spectacle more comic than imposing.

This, as Mr Cornell says, is cheap, obvious and anonymous. It is without Kipling's later "visual clarity". It is also the work of an outsider: the Anglo-Indian was closer to the country. But two years later the tone changes. Here is another fair scene:

Presently the bolder spirits among them would put out a horny finger, and carefully touch one of the bullocks. Then as the animal was evidently constructed of nothing more terrible than clay ... the whole hand would be drawn gently over its form; and, after an appreciative pat, the adventurous one would begin a lengthy dissertation to the bystanders at large.

The outsider has drawn closer. And sixteen months later the prose is like this:

> Suddhoo sleeps on the roof generally, except when he sleeps in the street. He used to go to Peshawar in the cold weather to visit his son who sells curiosities near the Edwardes' Gate, and then he slept under a real mud roof. Suddhoo is a great friend of mine, because his cousin had a son who secured, thanks to my recommendation, the post of head-messenger to a big firm in the Station. Suddhoo says that God will make me a Lieutenant-Governor one of these days. I daresay his prophecy will come true.

This is the accomplished club-writer. He has mastered his subject and he knows his audience. He deals in an irony so private it might be missed by an outsider. To the Anglo-Indian, as Mr Cornell points out, simple phrases like "a great friend of mine" and "a real mud roof" would have precise meanings. On the difference between the first and last quotations, he writes:

> In the earlier piece, Indian life appeared as no more than a passing show to be judged and dismissed on its aesthetic merits by a superior – and very young – English spectator. In the 1886 story, however, Kipling has penetrated to the heart of the Anglo-Indian's historical dilemma with amazing swiftness and economy.

The judgment is typical of Mr Cornell's balance and perception. He has not been tempted to make use of "The House of Suddhoo" to amend the legend; he makes a *literary* judgment, and it is correct.

Kipling's prose was later to go beyond this. It was to become a superb instrument of narration, concise, full of flavour and speed, and wonderfully pictorial. But the club-writer always needed the club, the common points of reference; he needed the legend, which perhaps his own stories had helped to create. Kipling can best be savoured in a group of related stories: to this extent the tabulators are justified. A story by Chekhov is complete in itself;

a story by Kipling isn't. It is either too slight or too longwindedly anecdotal. A legitimate delay in an Indian story would lose its point elsewhere.

> There were the usual blue-and-white striped jail-made rugs on the uneven floor; the usual glass-studded Amritsar *phulkaris* draped to nails driven into the flaking whitewash of the walls; the usual half-dozen chairs that did not match, picked up at sales of dead men's effects. . . . The little windows, fifteen feet up, were darkened with wasp-nests, and lizards hunted flies between the beams of the wood-ceiled roof.

"William the Conqueror", from which the passage is taken (it is quoted by Mr Stewart), is not a good story. It is pure comic-strip and – it is a love story set against a background of famine and corpses – it is horrifying to some. But details like these make it a true and acceptable part of Kipling's Indian work. In another setting comparable details would tell less. They wouldn't be as intimate; the "usual" would have less meaning; and "dead men's effects" would not speak of that dedication which was part of the Anglo-Indian's myth. Kipling's Anglo-Indians are always slightly embarrassing when they are on leave in England; there is a similar embarrassment, of ordinariness, it might be said, even in an Indian story like "The Gadsbys", from which India is almost totally subtracted.

Just as in that passage detail adds to detail, and we would be without none of them, so each of Kipling's Indian stories adds to the others and is supported by them. Kipling's stories are not like Chekhov's; they are like Turgenev's hunting sketches or Angus Wilson's stories of the late forties. They make one big book; they have to be taken together. They catch – or create – a complete society at a particular moment. It is in its search for the independent, good Kipling story that Kipling criticism becomes aggressive and tabulatory. Even Mr Cornell succumbs. He notices the frequency of disguises, hoaxes and frauds in the stories; and he makes much of this. He should have ignored it. The fact would have been important if Kipling were more interested in people than in the types with whom he filled his club, never allowing himself satire, mockery or anger beyond what the club permitted. As it is, such tabulation shows up the limitations of the too homogeneous club as a source for material, and it shows up the limitations of the club-writer, whose closest literary friend, later in England, was to be Rider Haggard.

The irony, like the legend, remains. The "long-coated theatrical natives discussing metaphysics in English and Bengali" – threats to order and romance, and therefore to be ceaselessly satirized – were to lead to a writer like Nirad Chaudhuri and a film-maker like Ray. The club has disappeared. By becoming its spokesman and jester, by brilliantly creating its legend, Kipling made the disappearance of the club certain.

A Second Visit

Daily Telegraph Magazine, 11–18 August 1967

I
TRAGEDY: THE MISSING SENSE

THE RAJA RECLINES below a broken chandelier in a dark narrow room right at the back of the palace. The room is in the third courtyard, the only part of the palace that still works. The raja's armchair belongs to an extensive "sofa-set" – English suburban, 1930 – distributed down the length of the room; the magenta upholstery is grimy. A rag-carpet completely covers the floor. It has been cut out from a more enormous piece, and is folded under where it doesn't fit. It is in a violent pattern of yellow and green that camouflages the million flies that buzz in and out of the rags. A photograph of the raja's father hangs forward from the wall; flat against the wall are a photograph of a family group, a hunting print in a rustic frame, and, at the top, in the yellowing colours of an unsuccessful reproduction process, a row of misty European landscapes.

Against this the raja sits, young, plump, cool in loose white cotton, and listens without expression to his last courtier, who sits at his feet on the rag-carpet and, holding a creased typewritten memorandum of many pages, outlines once again the complications of the inter-family litigation about the property that remains. The courtier is gaunt, his bony face finer than his master's; his clothes are dingier. He is a BA – the achievement is still fresh in his mind. He entered the service of the raja's family nearly fifty years ago, and now – his own son is dead – he has nowhere else to go.

Lunch is ordered for the visitors. The raja's younger brother, lean, elegant in movement – he is an attractive badminton player

- offers to show the sights. The palace is in the nondescript Lucknow style, and not old. Most of what we see was built in the 1920s, at a cost of half a million pounds. The family's revenue then was £60,000. An oval-shaped garden in the forecourt, over-grown. Tall carved wooden doors from a provincial exhibition of 1911 (the Raj then in its glory, with at least two society magazines in Calcutta, the capital). The clock-tower courtyard, with crude roundels down the archway: an English couple be-tween the Hindu and the Muslim: he in broad-lapelled jacket and sun-helmet, she in the loose lines of the 1920s. Beyond, the apartments, miniature palaces, of the former raja's wives: the source of the present litigation.

The raja's younger brother says there are six hundred rooms in all. The statement is disturbing. It is surely an exaggeration. Exaggeration does not belong to tragedy; it destroys the mood. And once, just twenty-five, thirty years ago, five hundred servants looked after the twenty-five members of the family. Round figures again, no doubt. But the palace had its own generating plant, stables for horses and elephants, its own zoo, its own reservoir. All this is shown from the clock-tower, the English machinery broken, the plaster broken. But the view from the clock-tower also shows no other building of consequence. It shows only the grass roofs of the bazaar settlement just outside the palace gates, and the flat scorched fields.

The eagerness of the raja's brother denies sadness. And there can be no sadness. Because there was no true grandeur. There was only excess and exaggeration, dying at the stroke of the legisla-tor's pen that abolished large estates. The palace rose out of this dust; it expressed this dust, nothing more; it is returning to dust again; and the cycle had been unfruitful (the sofa-set, the land-scape prints). Peasant, briefly prodigal, is turning to peasant again, as the kitchens of the third courtyard show. There is no vacuum; litigation totally engages the calm mind. There is no tragedy. There is, as perhaps there always has been, drabness. In this plain landscape wealth itself had been just another simplicity, an event, like decay.

This is the hoax of India. We take the country too personally. We
go with a sense of tragedy and urgency, with the habit of contemplating man as man, with ideas of action; and we find ourselves
unsupported.

There was a famine in Bihar. It had taken some time to prepare;
and in this time the wits of Delhi had called it the "shamine". Now
it was real: thirty million people were starving, bodies wrecked
beyond redemption. But famine was never the subject of conversation; there was more about it in foreign newspapers than in
Indian newspapers, which continued to be occupied with the post-
election manœuvring and speeches of politicians. The Films
Division made a film about the famine; in Bombay and Delhi it
was discussed as a film, a documentary breakthrough. The famine
was like something in a foreign country, like the war in Vietnam.
It was something you went to; it tested the originality of artists.

The civil servant in Calcutta said: "Famine? Can that be news
to us?" The editor in Delhi said: "Famine? Can I turn that into
news every day?"

It was the pattern of Indian conversation. After the frenzy, the
reasoned catalogue of disasters and threats – China, Pakistan,
corruption, no leaders, devaluation, no money, no food – after
this the frenzy burnt itself out, and the statement was made that
it didn't really matter, that it wasn't news. The young poet I met
in Delhi had made the statement in a long English poem on which
he had been working for months. The poem was a dialogue
between historical India and spiritual India; its subject was "the
metaphysical timelessness" of India. The absurd words had a
meaning. The poet was saying, with the civil servant and the
editor, that there was no disaster, no news, that India was infinitely
old and would go on. There was no goal and therefore no failure.
There were only events. There was no tragedy.

It was what, in his own stylish way, the Maharishi Mahesh Yogi
was telling the inaugural meeting of his Spiritual Regeneration
Movement. The red-and-black cotton banner hung out on the
Delhi Ring Road, next to the Indian Institute of Public Administration; and inside, in the shuttered gloom, the Maharishi, small,

black-locked, bearded, in a cream silk gown, flowers and garlands about him, sat cross-legged before the microphone, backed on the platform by his American, Canadian and other white disciples on chairs, the men in dark suits, the women and girls in silk saris: India, it might be said, getting a dose of her own medicine from the West.

The Maharishi reproved his reverential middle-class Indian audience for running after "isms" and failing to keep in tune with the infinite which lay below flux. No wonder the country was in a mess. The reproof was rubbed in by the glamorous figures on the platform who went one by one to the microphone, now raised, and gave witness to the powers of Indian meditation, the key to the infinite. A youngish, grey-haired Canadian was described by the Maharishi as a man who had given up drilling for oil to drill for truth. He gave his witness; and then, apparently on behalf of the world, thanked India. So that at the end it was all right. Everybody had just been talking; there was no problem; everything was as before.

The infinite, metaphysical timelessness: it always came to this. From whatever point they started – the Maharishi had even mentioned Bihar and glancingly attacked the folly of giving land to ignorant peasants, as though that would solve the food problem – there always came a moment when Indians, administrator, journalist, poet, holy man, slipped away like eels into muddy abstraction. They abandoned intellect, observation, reason; and became "mysterious".

It is in that very area that separates India from comprehension that the Indian deficiency lies. To see mysteriousness is to excuse the intellectual failure or to ignore it. It is to fall into the Indian trap, to assume that the poverty of the Indian land must also extend to the Indian mind. It is to deal in *Bengal Lancer* romance or *Passage to India* quaintness. It is, really, to express a simple wonder.

Because it is the simplicity of India which disappoints and in the end fatigues. There is a hoax in that quaintness. The barbaric religious rites of Hinduism are barbaric; they belong to the ancient world. The holy cow is absurd; it is, as Nirad Chaudhuri suggests in *The Continent of Circe*, an ignorant corruption of an ancient Aryan reverence. The caste-marks and the turbans belong to a people who, incapable of contemplating man as man, know no other way of defining themselves. India lies all on the surface. Once certain basic lessons are learnt, it is possible to make everything up, to chart conversations, to gauge the limit of comprehension. It was even possible for me to anticipate much of what was said at the inaugural meeting of the Spiritual Regeneration Movement. Where there is no play of the intellect there is no surprise.

The beatniks of America, Australia and other countries have now recognized India as their territory. Their instinct is true. Five years ago Ginsberg left America to make an initial exploration. He found the local Indians friendly; they were flattered by the attention of someone with a name so bright and modern; it was another tribute to the East from the West. Now the beatniks are everywhere, withdrawn, not gay, and sometimes in moving little domestic groups: papa beatnik, mama beatnik, baby beatnik, the man protected by his beard and jeans, the thin young woman more exposed, the dirt showing on her sandalled feet and on the tanned but pale skin of her bony, finely-wrinkled face. They are guests in temples (the Sikhs feed everybody); they thumb lifts on the highways and travel third on the railways; sometimes they compete with the beggars in cities; they attach themselves to the camps of holy men, like the one I heard about in Hyderabad, whose big trick was to pull a prick (I never found out whose) out of his mouth. In India they have rediscovered the wayfaring life of the middle ages.

There is a difference, of course. The maimed to the maimed, the West returning mysteriousness and negation to the East, while the humiliating deals are made in New Delhi and Washington for arms and food: it is like a cruel revenge joke played by the rich, many-featured West on the poor East that possesses only mystery. But India does not see the joke. In March the glossy *Indian Hotelkeeper and Traveller* introduced a "Seers of India" series:

India's seers and sages have something to offer to the world outside. To some of the materially affluent but psychologically sick and spiritually rudderless foreigners from far-flung corners of the world, India's saints and sadhus provide irresistible magnets of attraction. India, steeped in spirituality, has a singularly unique facet to project to the world outside which at once commands attention and admiration.

The absurdity of India can be total. It appears to ridicule analysis. It takes the onlooker beyond anger and despair to neutrality.

We were far from the drought and famine area. But even here no rain had fallen for some time, and on the leafless trees in the administrator's compound the sharp spring sun had brought out the bougainvillaea like drops of blood. Twenty miles away hailstones destroyed a village's crops. The villagers, relishing the drama, the excuse for a journey, came in a body to report. We went to have a look. On the way we made surprise stops.

We stopped first at a primary school, a small three-room brick shelter beside a banyan tree. Two brahmins in spotless white cotton, each washed and oiled, each with his top-lock of caste, each "drawing" 90 rupees a month, were in charge. Twenty-five children sat on the broken brick floor with their writing boards, reed pens and little pots of liquid clay. The brahmins said there were two hundred and fifty children at the school.

"But there are only twenty-five here."

"We have an attendance of a *hundred* and twenty-five."

"But there are only twenty-five here."

"What can you do, sahib?"

Beyond the road some of the children not at school rolled in the dusty fields. Even with twenty-five children the two rooms of the school were full. In the third room, protected from sun and theft, were the teachers' bicycles, as oiled and cared for as their masters.

At the next school, a few miles down the road, the teacher was asleep in the shade of a tree, a small man stretched out on his tiny teacher's table, his feet balanced on the back of the chair, so that he looked like a hypnotist's subject. His pupils sat in broken rows on strips of matting that had been soaked and pressed into the earth and was of its colour. The teacher was so soundly asleep that though our jeep stopped about eight feet away from his table he did not immediately awaken. When he did – the children beginning to chant their lessons in the Indian fashion as soon as they saw us – he said he was not well. His eyes were indeed red, with illness or sleep. But redness disappeared as he came to life. He said the school had three hundred and sixty pupils; we saw only sixty.

"What is the function of a schoolteacher?"

"To teach."

"But why?"

"To create better citizens."

His pupils were in rags, unwashed except by snot, their hair, red from sun and malnutrition, made stiff and blond with dust.

Two or three and stop. The Hindi slogan on the walls of the family planning centre looked businesslike, but the centre itself was empty except for charts and more slogans and a desk and chair and calendar, and it was some time before the officer came out, a good-looking young man in white with a neat line moustache and a wristwatch of Indian manufacture. He said he spent twelve days a month on family planning. He led discussions and "motivated" people to undergo vasectomy.

"How many people did you motivate last month?"

"Three."

"Your target is one hundred."

"The people here, sahib, they laugh at me."

"How many discussions did you lead last month?"

"One."

"How many people were there?"

"Four."

"What were you doing when we came?"

"I was taking food and little rest."

"What did you do this morning?"

"Nothing."

"Show me your diary."

Loose forms for travelling expenses fell out of the diary. The diary itself hadn't been filled for two months. The young man had been holding down the job for two years; every month he drew 180 rupees.

"Try to motivate me," the administrator said. "Come on. Tell me why I should go in for family planning."

"To raise the standard of living."

"How would family planning raise the standard of living?"

It was an unfair question, because concrete, and because it hadn't been put to him before. He didn't answer. He had only the abstraction about the standard of living.

Birth control here; and, not far away, the artificial insemination centre. A peasant sat on the concrete culvert of an abandoned flower-bed, holding his white cow by a rope. In a stall at the other end of the garden was the black zebu bull. Contraception, insemination: whatever the aim, nature was taking her own way in this district. It was clear what was about to happen wasn't going to be artificial: the male villagers were gathering to watch. And the centre was well-equipped. It had a refrigerator; it had all the obscene paraphernalia of artificial insemination. But the bull, the officer said, had lost its taste for artificial stimuli; which was not surprising. The bull itself was running down. Certain potent rations had been fixed for it by the authorities, but the rations hadn't been collected. Seventy natural inseminations had taken place in the last year. But no one could tell the percentage of success, in spite of the ledgers in filing cabinets and the multi-coloured charts on the walls. It hadn't occurred to the follow-up officer that he had to follow up.

"What is the purpose of artificial insemination?"

"It allows one bull to cover many cows."

This explained everything. The larger purpose – the gradual improvement of cattle in the district – had escaped him. Where the mind did not deal in abstractions, it dealt, out of its bewilderment, in the literal and the immediate.

To abstraction itself, then: to the district degree college, the

humanities, and the Professor of Literature. He was a tiny man in
a white shirt and flagrant yellow trousers belted without tightness
over a gentle little paunch bespeaking total contentment. He
looked very frightened now: the visit wasn't fair. His mouth was
open over his projecting top teeth, which were short, fitted
squarely one against the other, and made a perfect ivory arc. He
said he taught the usual things. "We begin with Eshakespeare.
And – " Then he went shy.

"The Romantics?" the head prompted, turning it into a
supporting inquiry.

"Yes, yes, the Romantics. Eshelley."

"No moderns?" asked the administrator. "Ezra Pound, people
like that."

The Professor grunted. Shoulder against the head's table, he
leaned forward over his little paunch, his mouth collapsed, his eyes
terrified. But he kept up with modern writing. "Yes, yes. I have
been reading *so* much Esomerset Maugham."

"What do you think is the point of teaching literature in a
country like ours, Professor?"

"Self-culture." He had been asked that before. "Even if there
is dirt and filth, the cultured mind, as Aristotle says, gets this
purge. And this catharsis, as they call it, helps the self-culture.
Because it is the cultured mind that even from all this dirt and
filth gets the education the lower sort of mind cannot get."

"Lady Chatterley?" the head interrupted. He had, mysteriously,
understood.

The Professor cast him a swift look of gratitude and ended with
relief, "This is the value of literature."

Poor Professor, poor India. Yet not poor – that was only the
estimate of the onlooker. The Professor, and the other officers we
had met, considered themselves successful. In the midst of insecurity, they drew their rupees. The rupees were few but regular;
they set a man apart. All of India that was secure was organized
on this tender basis of mutual protection; no one would apply to
others the sanctions he feared might one day be applied to himself.

Survival – the regularity of the rupees – was all that mattered. Standards, of wealth, nourishment, comfort, were low; and so, inevitably, were those of achievement. It took little to make a man happy and free him of endeavour. Duty was irrelevant; the last thing to ask in any situation of security was *why*. A colleague of the Professor's had said that the problems of teachers in the district were two: "Estatus and emolument." (But he liked alliteration; he described his pupils as "rustics or ruffians".)

So the abstractions and good intentions of New Delhi – the dangerous administrative capital, all words and buildings, where chatterers flourished and misinterpreted the interest of the world, where analysts who had never considered the vacuum in which they operated reduced the problems India to the day-to-day schemings of politicians, and newspapers, which had never analysed their function, reported these schemings at length and thought they had done their duty to a country of five hundred million – so the abstractions of New Delhi remained abstractions, growing progressively feebler, all the way down. Insecurity merged with the Indian intellectual failure and became part of the Indian drabness.

And the physical drabness itself, answering the drabness of mind: that also held the Indian deficiency. Poverty alone did not explain it. Poverty did not explain the worn carpets of the five-star Ashoka Hotel in New Delhi, the grimy armchairs in the serviceless lounge, the long-handled broom abandoned there by the menial in khaki who had been cleaning the ventilation grills. Poverty did not explain the general badness of expensive, over-staffed hotels, the dirt of first-class railway carriages and the shanty-town horror of their meals. Poverty did not explain the absence of trees: even the Himalayan foothills near the resort of Naini Tal stripped to brown, heat-reflecting desert. Poverty did not explain the open stinking sewers of the new middle-class Lake Gardens suburb in Calcutta. This was at the level of security, the rupees regularly drawn. It did not speak only of an ascetic denial of the senses or of the sands blowing in from the encroaching desert. It spoke of a more general collapse of sensibility, of a people grown barbarous, indifferent and self-wounding, who, out of a shallow perception of the world, have no sense of tragedy.

It is what appals about India. The palace crumbles into the dust of the countryside. But prince has always been peasant; there is no loss. The palace might rise again; but, without a revolution in the mind, that would not be renewal.

II

MAGIC AND DEPENDENCE

A year or so ago an Indian holy man announced that he had ful-filled an old ambition and was at last able to walk on water. The holy man was claimed by a progressive Bombay weekly of wide circulation. A show was arranged. Tickets were not cheap; they went to among the highest in the land. On the day there were film teams. The water tank was examined by distinguished or sceptical members of the audience. They found no hidden devices. At the appointed time the holy man stepped on the water, and sank.

There was more than embarrassment. There was loss. Magic is an Indian need. It simplifies the world and makes it safe. It com-plements a shallow perception of the world, the Indian intellectual failure, which is less a failure of the individual intellect than the deficiency of a closed civilization, ruled by ritual and myth.

In Madras State the Congress had been overthrown in the elections. The red-and-black flags of the Dravidian party were out everywhere, and it was at first like being in a colony celebrating independence. But this was a victory that could be fully under-stood only in Hindu terms. It was the revenge of South on North, Dravidian on Aryan, non-brahmin on brahmin. Accounts had been squared with the Hindu epics themselves, sacred texts of Aryan victory: no need now to rewrite them from the Dravidian side, as had been threatened.

The students of a college held a meeting to "felicitate" – the Indian English word – a minister-designate. "The evening is cool and mild winds are tickling us," a student said in his speech of welcome. He was heckled; the evening was hot. But we had moved away from reality already: the student was inviting the minister-designate to drown the audience "in the honey of his oration". The minister-designate responded with pieces of advice. A cunning man never smiled; at the same time it was wrong for anyone to keep on laughing all the time. Some people could never forget the loss of a small coin; others could lose six argosies on the ocean and be perfectly calm. Reality was now destroyed, and we were deep in the world of old fairy-tale: the folk-wisdom, the honey, that was the satisfying substitute, even among politically active students, for observation, analysed experience and inquiry.

The national newspaper that reported this reception also reported a religious discourse:

MEDITATION ON GOD ONLY WAY TO REDEMPTION
Madras, March 9
Even an exceptionally intellectual and astute person is likely to falter and indulge in a forbidden act and perform a suicidal act under the influence of destiny. One has to suffer the consequences of his errors in previous life . . .

This, in South India, was still news. There had been an election, though, a process of the twentieth century. And here, on the main news page of another newspaper, were post-election headlines:

MASSES MUST BE EDUCATED TO MAKE DEMOCRACY A SUCCESS
– Prof Ranga
PAST MISTAKES RESPONSIBLE FOR CURRENT PROBLEMS
– Ajoy Mukherjee
CONGRESS REVERSES ATTRIBUTED TO LACK OF FORESIGHT

A nation ceaselessly exchanging banalities with itself: it was the impression Indians most frequently gave when they attempted analysis. At one moment they were expressing the old world, of myth and magic, alone; at another they were interpreting the new in terms of the old.

There is an 1899 essay, *Modern India*, in which Swami Vivekananda, the Vedantist, takes us closer to the Indian bewilderment and simplicity. Vivekananda came from Bengal, the quickest province of India. He was pained by the subjection of his country and his own racial humiliation. He was also pained by the caste divisions of Hinduism, the holy contempt of the high for the low, the "walking carrion" of Aryan abuse. Vivekananda himself was of the Kayastha caste, whose status is still in dispute. In religion Vivekananda later found compensation enough: he exported the Vedas to the West itself, and found admirers. *Modern India* can be seen as a link between Vivekananda's political distress and its religious resolution. It is an interpretation of Indian history in apocalyptic Hindu terms which barely conceal ideas borrowed from the West.

Every country, Vivekananda states axiomatically, is ruled in succession by the four castes of priests, warriors, merchants and *shudras*, the plebs. India's top castes have decayed. They have failed in their religious duties, and they have also cut themselves off from the source of all power, the *shudras*. India is therefore in a state of "*shudra*-hood", which perfectly accommodates the rule of the *vaishya* or merchant power of Britain. *Shudra* rule, though, is about to come to the West; and there is the possibility, in India as well as in the West, of a "rising of the *shudra* class, *with their* shudra-*hood*". The emphasis is Vivekananda's; and from his curious position he appears to welcome the prospect, while saying at the same time that *shudra*-hood can be rejected by India, just as "Europe, once the land of *shudras* enslaved by Rome, is now filled with *kshatriya* [warrior] valour".

So, out of mock-Western historical inquiry, out of borrowed ideas and personal pain, Vivekananda reduces the condition of his country to a subject for simple, though slightly distorted, Hindu religious contemplation. Failure was religious; redemption can come only through religion, through a rediscovery by each caste of its virtuous duty and – at the same time – through a discovery by India of the brotherhood of all Indians.

Modern India is part of the unread but steadily reprinted litera-

ture of Indian nationalism. It is not easy to read. It wanders, is
frequently confused, and is full of the technicalities of Hindu
metaphysics. It could never have been easily understood. But with
Indian sages like Vivekananda, utterance is enough; the message
is not important. A nation exchanging banalities with itself: it
cannot be otherwise, when regeneration is believed to come, not
through a receptiveness to thought, however imperfect, but
through magic, through reverential contact with the powerful,
holy or wise. The man himself is the magic.

There is a whole department of the Central Government at
work on The Complete Works of Mahatma Gandhi; they have
an entry, under that name, in the Delhi telephone directory. But
The Hindu newspaper of Madras reported in March that ninety
per cent of high-school students in one district knew nothing of
Gandhi except that he was a good man who had fought for independence. In a southern city I met a twenty-year-old Dravidian
student. He was a product of independence, privileged; and we
met at, of all twentieth-century things, an air show. The uncertain
native, of Jabalpur or Gerrard's Cross, seeks to establish his standing in the eyes of the visitor by a swift statement of his prejudices.
And all this student's social attitudes were anti-Gandhian. This
was news to him. He reverenced the name. It was the name alone,
the incantatory magic, that had survived.

Mind will not be allowed to play on the problems of India. It
is part of the Indian frustration.

But now Indians have a sense of wrongness. They have begun to
feel, like the Spaniards, that they are an inadequate people; and,
like the Spaniards, they feel they are inadequate only because they
are uniquely gifted. "Intelligent" is the word Indians use most
often to describe themselves, and the romantic view is gaining
ground that they might be intelligent to the point of insanity. In
India self-examination is abortive. It ends only in frenzy or in
generalities about the Indian "character".

The humanities are borrowed disciplines that always turn discussions about famine or bankruptcy into university tutorials.

There can be no effective writing. The ritual of Indian life
smothers the imagination, for which it is a substitute, and the
interpretation of India in the Indian novel, itself a borrowed form,
is at a low, unchanging level. "I don't wait for another *novel*,"
Graham Greene says of the Indian writer he admires; he waits for
an encounter with another stranger, "a door on to yet another
human existence". The Delhi novelist R. Prawer Jhabvala has
moved away from the purely Indian themes with which she
started; she feels unsupported by the material.

In such a situation the novel is almost part of autobiography,
and there have been many Indian autobiographies. These – always
with the exception of the work of Nirad Chaudhuri – magnify
the Indian deficiency. Gandhi drops not one descriptive word
about London in the 1880s, and even Mr Nehru cannot tell us
what it was like to be at Harrow before 1914. The world in these
books is reduced to a succession of stimuli, and the reacting
organism reports codified pleasure or pain; the expression of an
egoism so excluding that the world, so far from being something
to be explored, at times disappears, and the writers themselves
appear maimed and incomplete. All Indian autobiographies appear
to be written by the same incomplete person.

So the sense of wrongness remains unresolved. But it is possible
now for the visitor to raise the question and at times to tease out a
little more, especially from men under thirty-five. At a dinner
party in Delhi I met a young businessman who had studied in
America and had felt himself at a disadvantage. He said, "I felt
that intellectually" – the Indian pride! – "they were far below me.
But at the same time I could see they had something which I didn't
have. How shall I say it? I felt they had something which had been
excised out of me. A sort of motivational drive, you might call
it."

The jargon was blurring, but I felt that, for all his businessman's
adventurousness, he was like the peasants I had met some hundreds
of miles away. It was a late afternoon of dust and cane-trash, and
golden light through the mango trees. The peasants were boiling
down sugar-cane syrup into coarse brown sugar. The bullocks

turned the mill; a black cauldron simmered over a fire-pit. A
bare-backed, well-built young man scraped up sugar from the
shallow brick trough level with the ground and pressed it into
balls. His father chewed *pan* and watched. He said, just giving
information, that his son had to write an examination in the
morning. He would fail, of course; another son had written an
examination six months before and had failed. In his mind, and
perhaps in his son's mind, there was no link between failure and
this labour in the fields. The peasants were Kurmis, a caste who
claim Rajput ancestry. The British-compiled gazeteers of the last
century are full of praise for the Kurmis as diligent and adaptable
cultivators; they are praised in exactly the same way by Indian
officials today. But they have remained Kurmis, demanding only
to have their Rajput blood acknowledged.

What had been excised out of the Kurmis had been excised
out of the businessman: "motivational drive", that profound
apprehension of cause and effect, which is where magic ends and
the new world begins.

Causation: it was the theme of the Buddha 2,500 years ago in the
distressed land of Bihar. It was the theme one hundred and fifty
years ago of Raja Rammohun Roy, the first British-inspired Indian
reformer. It is the necessary theme today. It is depressing, this
cycle of similar reform and similar relapse. Reform doesn't alter;
it temporarily revives. Ritual and magic forever claim the world,
however new its structure.

The process of relapse can be charted in our own time in the
work of Vinoba Bhave, the Gandhian land-reformer of Bihar,
who fifteen years ago made the cover of *Time* magazine. "I have
come," *Time* reported him saying, "to loot you with love." His
programme was simple: he would ask landowners to give away
land to the landless. It was the spiritual way of India. "We are a
people wedded to faith in God and do not give ourselves to the
quibblings of reason. We believe in what our Rishis [sages] have
taught us. I have the feeling that the present-day famines and
other calamities are all due to our sins." It was not therefore his

business to think in any practical way of the food problem or of creating economic units of land. "Fire merely burns; it does not worry whether anyone puts a pot on it, fills it with water and puts rice into it to make a meal. It burns and that is the limit of its duty. It is for others to do theirs."

With this there went ideas about education. "Human lives are like trees, which cannot live if they are cut off from the soil. . . . Therefore, everyone must have the opportunity to tend the soil. . . ." Agricultural work will also keep the population down, because it takes the mind off sex. Care has to be taken in choosing a craft for a school, though. Fishing, for example, wouldn't do, because "I have to show (the children) how to deceive the fish"; poultry-keeping is better. Literature should not be neglected. "It is a fault in the Western system of education that it lays so little stress on learning great lines by heart." But the best education is the one Krishna, the mythological-religious figure, received. "Shri Krishna grazed cattle, milked them, cleaned the cowshed, worked hard, hewed firewood . . . ; later, as Arjuna's charioteer, he not only drove his horses but also cared for them."

It isn't only that so much of this is absurd, or that Bhave was taken seriously until recently. It is that Bhave's sweetness adds up to a subtle but vital distortion of the Mahatma's teaching. The stoic call to action and duty becomes, with Bhave, an exercise in self-perfection, an act of self-indulgence and holy arrogance. He will not see his responsibility through to the end; it is the duty of fire only to burn. He separates, in a way the Mahatma never did, the private religious act from its social purpose. He misapplies the doctrine of bread-labour by which the Mahatma hoped to ennoble all labour, including that of the untouchables. Bhave says that the untouchables do work which is "not worthy of human dignity"; they must become tillers and landowners. He leaves them, in effect, where he finds them. And he does nothing to solve the food problem which, in India, is related to the ignorant use of land.

Bhave goes back again and again to the scriptures: their redis-covery becomes an end in itself. So, in the name of reform, the

Mahatma and goodness, Bhave slips into reaction. The old world claims its own.

Indians are proud of their ancient, surviving civilization. They are, in fact, its victims.

Reform this time will be more brutal. China presses; Pakistan threatens; non-alignment collapses and America drives hard bargains. The new world cannot be denied. Incapable of lasting reform, or of a correct interpretation of the new world, India is, profoundly, dependent. She depends on others now both for questions and answers; foreign journalists are more important in India than in any other country. And India is fragmented; it is part of her dependence. This is not the fragmentation of region, religion or caste. It is the fragmentation of a country held together by no intellectual current, no developing inner life of its own. It is the fragmentation of a country without even an idea of a graded but linked society.

There is no true Indian aristocracy, no element that preserves the graces of a country and in moments of defeat expresses its pride. There have been parasitic landowners, tax-farmers; there have been rulers. They represented a brute authority; they were an imposed element on a remote peasantry; in moments of stress they have – with exceptions – proclaimed only their distance. They are the aptly named "native princes"; and though here and there their brute authority, of money or influence, has been reasserted, they have disappeared and nothing marks their passing. In Hyderabad you wouldn't have known that the Nizam had just died, that a dynasty older than Plassey had expired. Every Indian, prince or peasant, is a villager. All are separate and, in the decay of sensibility, equal.

There are contractors and civil servants in Delhi, where a "society lady" is usually a contractor's wife. There are business executives in Calcutta, which still has an isolated, ageing set with British titles. There are the manufacturers and advertising men and film people of Bombay, where "suave", "sophisticated" and "prestigious" are words of especial approval. But these are trade guilds; they do not make a society. There is an absence of that element, to which all contribute and by which all are linked, where common standards are established and a changing sensibility appears to define itself. Each guild is separate. Even the politicians, with the state withering away for lack of ideas, are sterilized in their New Delhi reserve. And each trade – except the entertainment trade – is borrowed.

Every discipline, skill and proclaimed ideal of the modern Indian state is a copy of something which is known to exist in its true form somewhere else. The student of cabinet government looks to Westminster as to the answers at the back of the book. The journals of protest look, even for their typography, to the *New Statesman*. So Indians, the holy men included, have continually to look outside India for approval. Fragmentation and dependence are complete. Local judgment is valueless. It is even as if, without the foreign chit, Indians can have no confirmation of their own reality.

But India, though not a country, is unique. To its problems imported ideas no longer answer. The result is frenzy. The journals of revolt are regularly started; they are very private ventures, needing almost no readership and having responsibility to no one; within weeks they are exhausted and futile, part of the very thing they are revolting against. Manners deteriorate. Each Indian wishes to be the only one of his sort recognized abroad: like Mr Nehru himself, who in the great days was described, most commonly, by visiting writers as the lonely Indian aristocrat – his own unexplained word – presiding over his deficient but devoted peasantry. Each Indian, looking into himself and discovering his own inadequacy, attributes inadequacy to every other Indian; and he is usually right. "Charlatan" is a favourite word of Indian abuse. The degree of this self-destructive malice startles and depresses the visitor. "The mutual hatred of men of their own class – a trait common to *shudras*": the words are Vivekananda's: they describe a dependent people.

This dependent frenzy nowadays finds its expression in flight. Flight to England, Canada, anywhere that lets Indians in: more than a flight to money: a flight to the familiar security of second-class citizenship, with all its opportunities for complaint, which implies protection, the other man's responsibility, the other man's ideas.

It was written, of course. It was the price of the independence movement.

The movement, as it developed under Gandhi, became a reforming religious movement, and it was in the Indian tradition that stretched back to the Buddha. Gandhi merged the religious emphasis on self-perfection in the political assertion of pride. It was a remarkable intuitive achievement. But it was also damaging. It was not concerned with ideas. It committed India to a holy philistinism, which still endures.

At the beginning of the nineteenth century Raja Rammohun Roy had said that forty years of contact with the British would revivify Indian civilization. He spoke before the period of imperialist and racialist excess; the technological gap was not as wide as it later became; the West, to the forward-looking Indian, was then less the source of new techniques than the source of a New Learning. But the gap widened and the mood changed. The independence movement turned away, as it had to, from people like Roy. It looked back to the Indian past. It made no attempt to evaluate that past; it proclaimed only glory. At the same time the imaginative probing of the West was abandoned. It has never been resumed. The fact escapes notice. The West, so much more imitable today than in 1800, might be pillaged for its institutions and technology; its approval is valuable. But the political-religious–philistine rejection still stands. The West is "materially affluent but psychologically sick"; the West is a sham. No Indian can say why. But he doesn't need to; that battle has been won; independence is proof enough.

A scholar in Delhi reminded me that Macaulay had said that all the learning of India was not worth one shelf of a European library. We had been talking of aboriginal Africa, and Macaulay was brought in to point out the shortsightedness of a certain type of obvious comment. Later it occurred to me, for the first time, that Macaulay had not been disproved by the Indian revolution. He had only been ignored. His statement can be reaffirmed more brutally today. The gap between India and the West is not only the increasing gap in wealth, technology and knowledge. It is, more alarmingly, the increasing gap in sensibility and wisdom. The West is alert, many-featured and ever-changing; its writers and philosophers respond to complexity by continually seeking to alter and extend sensibility; no art or attitude stands still. India possesses only its unexamined past and its pathetic spirituality. The Indian philosopher specializes in exegesis; the holy man wishes to rediscover only what has been discovered; in 1967 as in 1962 the literary folk squabble like schoolmen, not about writing, but about the proprieties of translation from all their very ancient languages. India is simple; the West grows wiser.

Her revolution did not equip India for a twentieth-century independence. When that came, it existed within an assumption of a continuing dependence: an accommodating world, of magic, where Indian words had the power Indians attributed to them. The bluff had to be called; the disaster had to come.

One by one India has had to shed ideas about herself and the world. Pain and bewilderment can no longer be resolved by the magical intervention of a Vivekananda, a Gandhi, a Nehru, a Vinoba Bhave. Fifteen years ago Bhave said, more or less, that his aim was the withering away of the state. He called it "the de-centralized technique of God"; and even the pious dismissed him as a dreamer. The state has now withered away. Not through holiness; it is just that the politicians, homespun villagers in New Delhi, no longer have an idea between them. Magic can no longer simplify the world and make it safe. India responds now only to events; and since there can be no play of the mind each disagree-able event – the Chinese attack, the Pakistan war, devaluation, famine and the humiliating deals for food with the United States – comes as a punishing lesson in the ways of the real world. It is as if successive invasions, by the reaction they provoked, that special Indian psychology of dependence, preserved an old world which should have been allowed to decay centuries ago; and that now, with independence, the old world has at last begun to disintegrate.

The crisis of India is not political: this is only the view from Delhi. Dictatorship or rule by the army will change nothing. Nor is the crisis only economic. These are only aspects of the larger crisis, which is that of a decaying civilization, where the only hope lies in further swift decay. The present frenzy cannot be interpreted simply as a decline from stability. That was the stability of a country ruled by magic, by slogans, gestures and potent names. It was the stability of a deficient civilization that thought it had made its peace with the world and had to do no more. The present mood of rejection has dangers. But it alone holds the possibility of life. The rejection is not religious, even when its aims are avowedly the protection of a religion. It does not attempt reform through self-perfection. The *mode* is new, and of the new world.

It may be that I exaggerate; that I forget the holy man putting his thumb in his mouth and pulling out a prick, to applause; that I forget the pious who, in a time of famine, pour hundreds of gallons of milk over a monumental idol while an Air Force helicopter drops flowers. But magic endures only when it appears to work. And it has been proved that man, even in India, can no longer walk on water.

4

The Election in Ajmer

Sunday Times Magazine, 15–22 August 1971

I

WHOM TO VOTE FOR? the English-language poster in New Delhi asked. And when, in mid-February, a fortnight before the first polling day, I went south to Ajmer in Rajasthan, it seemed that the half a million voters of this Indian parliamentary constituency, part urban, part rural, part desert, had a problem. The Congress had won freedom for India, and for more than twenty years, through four election victories, it had ruled. Now the Congress had split. The split had led to this mid-term election. But both sides continued to use the name. *Kangrace ko wote do*, the posters of both sides said: Vote Congress. And the same saffron, white and green flag flew from rival campaign jeeps: the jeep the favoured campaign vehicle, authoritative and urgent in the dusty streets of Ajmer, among the two-wheeled tonga carriages, the battered buses, bicycles by the hundred, handcarts and bullockcarts.

Both sides would have liked to use the old election-winning Congress symbol of the pair of yoked bullocks. But the courts had decided that the yoked bullocks shouldn't be used at all; and both sides had devised complicated and naturalistic symbols of their own. A cow licking a sucking calf: that was the Congress that was with Mrs Gandhi, the Prime Minister. A full-breasted woman at a spinning-wheel (the fullness of the breasts always noticeable, even in stencilled reproductions): that was the old or Organization Congress, that had gone into opposition. Both symbols, in India, were of equal weight. The spinning-wheel was Gandhian, the cow was sacred. Both symbols proclaimed a correct, Congress ancestry.

It was in some ways like a family quarrel, then. And, as it

happened, for this Ajmer seat the candidates of the two Congresses were related. There were five candidates in all. Three were independents and of no great consequence. "They are only contesting by way of their hobby," a man from the Election Department said. "They will put down their security of 500 rupees. They will get a few thousand votes and forfeit their deposit and sit quietly, that is all. It is only their hobby."

The main candidates were Mr Mukut Bharvaga and Mr Bishweshwar Bhargava. Mr Mukut was standing for the old Congress and all its opposition associates. He was the uncle of Mr Bishweshwar, who was defending his seat for the Indira Congress. And here – a local reflection of the national quarrel about legitimacy – was the first issue in Ajmer: who was morally in the wrong? The uncle, for fighting the nephew? Or the nephew, for fighting the uncle?

Mr Mukut, the uncle, was sixty-eight years old, a lawyer, and blind. He was famous in Rajasthan for his prodigious memory and his skill in matters of land revenue. His fees were said to be as high as 1,000 rupees a day, about £50; his earnings were put at two lakhs a year, about £10,000. But Mr Mukut was also known for his free services to peasants, who still came to Ajmer to look for "the lawyer without eyes". Mr Mukut was an old Congressman and freedom fighter and he had gone to jail in 1942. His political career since independence had been unspectacular, but steady and without blemish: he was perhaps best known for his campaign to have clarified butter easily distinguishable from its groundnut-based substitute. He had won the Ajmer seat for Congress in 1952, 1957 and 1962. In 1967, at the age of sixty-four, he had retired, handing over the Ajmer seat to his thirty-six-year-old nephew and protégé, Mr Bishweshwar. Now, with the Congress split, Mr Mukut wanted his seat back; and, to get it, he had allied himself with all his old political enemies. Was Mr Mukut right? Was Mr Bishweshwar wrong, for resisting?

The answer, overwhelmingly, was that Mr Bishweshwar was wrong. He should have withdrawn; he should not have fought his uncle, to whom he owed so much. It was what Mr Mukut's son, who was Mr Mukut's election agent, said; and it was what Mr Bishweshwar's agent said. Mr Mukut himself always spoke of the contest with a sense of injury. "The State Congress chose the meanest weapon," he said, "setting my own nephew to fight me. They know I'm a man of strong family feeling and they were hoping *I* would withdraw." The Maharana of Udaipur, who was supporting Mr Mukut, told an election meeting, "The Indira Congress is dividing the country, and not only ideologically. They are breaking up families." And the Rajput village headman, loyal to his Maharana, agreed. "A nephew who cannot love the members of his own family, how can he love the public?"

But wasn't the uncle also wrong to try to pull down his nephew? "I didn't want my father to fight this election," Mr Mukut's son said. "I said, 'Bapuji, you are old now, you are disabled.' But then I was overwhelmed by his answer. It brought tears to my eyes. He said, 'This is a time for sacrifice'."

Sacrifice: it wasn't a claim Mr Bishweshwar could make, and for much of the campaign he looked harassed and uncertain and sometimes hunted. Unlike his uncle, who always spoke freely, even elaborately, Mr Bishweshwar had little to say; and his manner discouraged conversation. He stared blankly through his glasses, like a man alerted not to say anything that might be used against him. Once he said, "I cannot understand how my uncle can go against all those principles I imbibed from him." It was the only comment on his uncle I heard him make, and it was spoken very quickly, like a prepared line.

Mr Bishweshwar wasn't a popular man. He suffered from all comparisons with his uncle. Mr Mukut was small and lean and brown, an ascetic politician of the old school, with a jail-record. Mr Bishweshwar was as tall and plump as a film star. He was a post-independence politician, an organization man. People in his own party said of him: "Politics is his profession." And: "If politics were taken away from him he would hardly be having two square meals a day." And: "His uncle massacred hundreds of party workers for him." But that wasn't held against the uncle; that was held against Mr Bishweshwar.

"I'm not working for Bishweshwar," his campaigners said. "I'm working for Indira." And this was what they said even on polling day, waiting in the brightly coloured party tents for voters. "The people aren't voting for Bishweshwar. They're voting for Indira."

Which, as everybody said, was what the election was about: Indira, Mrs Gandhi, that formidable lady in New Delhi, who had done a de Gaulle on the Congress and taken over, who had abolished the old consensus politics of the Congress. She had declared war on privilege; her appeal was to the poor, the untouchables, the minorities. She had nationalized the banks; she had "de-recognized" the princes; and, to deprive the princes of their privy purses, she intended to change the constitution.

Indiscipline, people like old Mr Mukut said, grieving for all those old members of the party who had fallen. *Indira Hatao*, the opposition posters said: Remove Indira. And on the other side: *Garibi Hatao*, Remove Poverty. The rich, the poor: the wonder was that, in India, this basic division had taken such a long time to be politically formulated. The socialists and communists hadn't done that: they offered theologies. And this was the first election in Ajmer in which the parties had issued manifestoes.

Rich and poor. But there was a regional complication. Rajasthan is a land of princes. Ajmer itself, though in the centre of Rajasthan, hadn't been a princely state and had no maharaja. But the Ajmer constituency was vast: two hundred miles, mainly of desert, rock and jagged brown hills, between Ajmer and Char Bazaar: more than six hours in a jeep. Two of its districts belonged to the former state of Udaipur; and the Maharana of Udaipur, who had supported Mr Bishweshwar at the last election, had declared for Mr Mukut in this. The princes of Rajasthan, "de-recognized" by the government, their privy purses threatened, were in their different ways up in arms against the government. And they could take their case to the people and get a hearing, because they were princes.

For other people in the opposition, supporters of Mr Mukut,

it wasn't so easy. Mr Kaul, an old Congressman of Mr Mukut's age, was now a member of the Indian Upper House. Mr Kaul ate only one meal a day and he said he had acquired the habit during his time in jail in 1932. But there was no jail-taint to him now; the post-independence years of power, honour and politicking had worn him smooth; and Mr Kaul thought that personal canvassing should be banned.

"We issue our manifestoes. Why should we go to the people personally? By canvassing the way is found for bribing them. Our people are poor; they don't understand what we are fighting for. Their ignorance is being exploited. The Indira Congress is spending crores of rupees, spoiling them, the peasants, the villagers, the uneducated and the labour classes. Giving them slogans. All slogans. It's our national character."

I asked him about the national character.

"Our people don't think in terms of country first."

"What do they think of?"

"*Nothing.*" He laughed. "Haven't you noticed? They're indifferent."

And on that first day in Ajmer the election seemed far away. The tongas carried advertisements for the Apollo Circus; walls everywhere were painted with family-planning slogans in Hindi. It was a Tuesday, the day of the weekly service at the Hanuman temple; and monkeys from the temple hopped from tree to tree on the nearby Circuit House hill. At the top of the hill there was a view of the clear lake beside which Ajmer is built, the water a surprise after the dust of the streets. On the black rocks at the lake-edge scores of washermen were beating the cotton clothes of the poor to death, swinging the twisted wet hanks with a steady circular motion and grunting competitively at every blow.

The sun rose higher. The brown mist lifted over the brown hills. The washermen spread out their lengths of cotton, white and coloured, and went away. Hawks hovered over the lake, at whose margin clouds of midges swirled and thinned like cigarette smoke in a wind, and then re-formed. From the flat-roofed white-and-ochre town below there came the sound of a loudspeaker: cinemas announcing their attractions. In the late afternoon there was music: a wedding procession.

The Ajmer calendar was full. On Saturday there was the eighty-ninth prize-giving of Mayo College, one of India's important English-style public schools, founded for the education of the sons of princes. Three days later came the Hindu festival of Shivratri and the opening of the Ajmer Flower Show. So, quickly, after the disorder of the main street – the mixed traffic, the cows, the rubble and dust, the exposed food-stalls – Ajmer revealed itself as excessively ordered. There was the railway town with its great locomotive workshops and its severely graded housing. There was the medieval, narrow-laned town around the famous Muslim shrine, an object of pilgrimage. There were the newer residential areas; there was the bazaar, an extension of the disorder of the main street; and there were the ordered acres of Mayo College, where only the servants' quarters spoke of India.

Beyond the brown hills were the smaller towns and the thousand villages that made up the constituency, each village as fragmented and ordered as Ajmer itself: every man in his caste, his community, his clan: divisions not strictly racial and not strictly social: more as if, in an English village, where everyone more or less looked alike, spoke the same language and had the same religion, every man yet remembered that he was Dane or Saxon or Jute and stuck to his kind. Cow-and-calf, spinning-wheel: poor and rich, left and right: how could these divisions apply?

In the evening I went to the Honeydew, one of the three recognizable cafés that Ajmer, with a population of 300,000, just about supports. It was air-conditioned and dim and the waiters were in white. A young man I fell in with told me that the Honeydew was for the young and "modern" of Ajmer. He spoke sardonically but he too wanted it known that he was modern. "My father was a semi-literate. He joined the Railways in 1920 and retired thirty-seven years later. Then he died. At the end of his life he was making 300 rupees a month. For my father it was his luck, his *karma.* What he had sown in a past life he was reaping in this. I am not like that. I am only making 400. But let people look at my suit and tie and see me spending in the Honeydew and think I'm rich."

A cup of Honeydew coffee cost about three pennies. You could ask the waiter for a cigarette; he would place an open packet on your table and you paid only for those you took. Luxuries were small in India and little gestures were fundamental acts of defiance. To wear a tie, when money was immemorially scarce, to have a coffee in the Honeydew: that was more than extravagance. That was to deny one's *karma*, to challenge the basis of one's father's faith.

And it was of defiance that Mr Desai, once Mrs Gandhi's Deputy Prime Minister, now in the opposition and supporting Mr Mukut, was speaking in Naya Bazaar that evening. In the bazaar lanes the narrow shops, raised on platforms, glittered with electric light, tempting custom. In the wide open area of Naya Bazaar itself, beyond the heads of the crowd, beyond the flags and bunting and posters strung across the street, and at the end of two little colonnades of fluorescent tubes, there was another platform, very clean and very bright, and there – with Mr Mukut and Mr Kaul and others no doubt sitting at his feet – Mr Desai, not looking his seventy-four years, was talking about "the Indira psychosis", nationalization and the danger to the constitution.

At first it seemed, to use the Indian word, "sophisticated". But an election address, in that street, before that crowd, without an analysis of the distress that was so visible, without a promise for the future! An election address, about economic and legal matters, cast in terms of personal injury! But when Mr Desai was talking of nationalization he was talking of more than an economic issue. He was talking of an act of defiance, a threat to order and *dharma*, an impious shaking of the world. In the place of that defiance he was offering himself: his Gandhi-cap, his white homespun, his simple brown waistcoat, his well-known asceticism, his Gandhian habit of spinning: all his personal merit built up through many years of service. Religion, *dharma*, the Hindu "right way", given a political expression: the crowd was in tune with what was being said. They listened respectfully; there was even some slight applause.

Garibi Hatao, Remove Poverty: it was possible to understand why no one before Mrs Gandhi had raised this simple political slogan. And it was also possible to understand why it was said in Ajmer that the issues of the election – Remove Poverty, Remove Indira – were too abstract and remote. There would have been more interest, people said, in elections for the State Assembly, when the politicians could play on the more immediate issues of caste and community and offer tangible rewards: a tarred road, a water-tank, electricity.

But that evening, less than twenty miles away, on the Jaipur road, the forty-six-year-old Maharaja of Kishangarh, politically active on the opposition side, a member of the State Assembly, was murdered.

Kishangarh was part of the neighbouring constituency. It is one of the lesser names of princely Rajasthan – the state, as it existed in 1947, was just over 650 square miles – but the Maharaja was linked by blood to the great houses. He was well known in Ajmer. He played badminton at the Ajmer Club and tennis on the Mayo College courts.

That evening he and the Maharani were going to a wedding. They were about to leave when the telephone rang. Kishangarh took the call himself. Then he told the Maharani he had to go out for a little and would be back in ten minutes. When he left the palace, driving himself in a little Indian-made Fiat, he had a revolver and many rounds of ammunition; he also had about 1,500 rupees. A few miles from the palace, on a straight stretch of the Jaipur-Ajmer road, the car stopped or was made to stop; and Kishangarh was shot in the right ear. His revolver was taken; his money wasn't touched.

This was the story that broke the next morning. And it was strange, at eleven, in the bright desert light, neem trees and cactus beside the road, thorn trees scattered about the dug-out brown land, to see the little "champagne-green" Fiat, not princely or

4 *

tragic, not a dent anywhere, not a window cracked, only a finger-wipe of blood on the driving door, at rest on the sandy verge with its front bumper against a tall clump of the *ker* shrub, by whose red flowers the strength of the monsoon can be foretold. The princely licence-plate, white on red, said: *Kishangarh No 11*. A line of stones marked the course of the car as it had come off the road. On the other side of the road were the jeeps of the district police and a crowd of dhoti-clad, turbanned peasants.

Some local politicians were also there, among them Mr Makrana, small and fat and grim, with dusty trousers, a worn green pullover and a very white muslin turban the size and shape of a scooter tyre. "I am a Marwari," he said, "and we Marwaris wear these turbans, white or khaki, at sad deaths, funerals." Mr Makrana was a member of the State Assembly and the whip of the party to which the Maharaja had belonged. "The Maharaja was having a very nice influence for us. Some big person is behind this killing." Once Mr Makrana had owned about 2,500 acres of land. "I lost my land when the *jagir* system went out." Under this system his tenants used to give him a third or a half of what they made. "With that percentage we used to manage our establishment. Now I am in the marble business. I couldn't survive if I had to depend on politics. I live from the marble. Politics is only my hobby." And, leaving me, he began again to walk up and down the road before the still peasants, his plump face set and petulant, his white turban on his head, very visibly mourning a member of his party.

The Ajmer District Magistrate, in a suit, and two senior police officers, in khaki, came in a black saloon which flew a blue police pennant. The peasants watched; Mr Makrana himself stopped to watch. A smiling green-bereted sub-inspector from the Jaipur Dog Squad arrived and reported. And then Mr Kaul, the member of the Indian Upper House, turned up. He scrambled briskly out of his car – tight white trousers stylishly creased, long brown coat – and hurried across the road to the officials, like a man used to being well received everywhere; and then gravely, as though looking at the corpse itself, he examined the Fiat.

Mr Kaul wasn't a man for white turbans and country mourning. His manner was of New Delhi; and very soon he was to issue a statement, in English: ". . . dastardly murder . . . general atmosphere of lawlessness and violence . . . leaders of the Ruling Party from the Prime Minister downwards . . . using such derogatory epithets against the so-called capitalist, industrialist and feudal order . . . inciting the feelings and sentiments of the masses, particularly of the Youth of the lower rungs of Society. . . ."

In Kishangarh the shops were shut, but the streets were full of people, stunted, thin-limbed peasants from the interior who, as soon as the news had broken that morning, had begun to make their way on foot or cycle to the palace. It was a ramshackle Indian country town, the new concrete buildings all balconies and balustrades at the top, slum at road-level, with rough additional lean-tos roofed with canvas or thatch. The asphalt road was like an irregular black path through dust and dung, unpaved sidewalks, heaps of rubble and old gravel. Then, unexpectedly, there was a lake, and in the centre of the lake an old stone building, possibly a summer pavilion; and at the end of the lakeside road the high walls of Kishangarh fort and the old town.

Inside, the procession had started to the cremation ground and the waiting pyre, prepared with sandalwood and other scents. The road and the city walls were packed, ablaze with the colours of peasant Rajasthan, red and orange and saffron. The open jeep with the body came out of the palace gate. The relations of the dead Maharaja were in white. White here the terrible colour of mourning.

In the middle of the afternoon the Fiat was still where it had been, against the *ker* bush. Some of the marker stones had been scattered. No one watched now. Some distance away two or three peasants sat in the shade of a thorn tree. The brown hills were pale in the glare. The private tragedy was over. Mr Mukut and Mr Kaul had already addressed a condolence meeting.

The Kishangarh affair had upset Mr Bishweshwar's schedule, and when I went to his house only his wife was there. The house was in an open area at the end of a dirt lane where Mr Mukut also had his law office. The ambiguous Congress flag hung limp in the little garden where flowers and shrubs grew out of bald earth.

I had been told that Mr Bishweshwar lived simply. The trellis-enclosed veranda where I sat first of all had a dark, tarnished, homely air, with rough-and-ready furniture and a strip of dirty matting. The small terrace upstairs was even less formal, with a plain concrete floor, and local five-rupee basket chairs brought out as required. A servant squatted on the floor in a small room near the steps and scoured dishes. A Hindu country interior: there was nothing, except perhaps the telephone, to suggest that this was one of the rising political households of Rajasthan and that Mrs Bishweshwar's father had been in his time a famous politician, so fierce in faction fights against Mr Kaul that Mr Nehru had had to intervene.

Mrs Bishweshwar was a pretty woman of thirty-three, pale and slightly pinched, with her head covered modestly with a dark-red sari. At first she spoke only in Hindi. She said she couldn't speak English well; but later she relented, and it turned out that she spoke English impeccably. She had been educated in a pastoral institution that her father had founded. There she had studied Indian classical music and had learned to spin. Later she took her BA in music and English and Hindi literature. She still spun. "I believe in Gandhiji's teachings." But she had let the literature go. "I don't like modern literature. I can't understand it. I don't like Hindi modern literature either. I like Shakespeare, Browning, Shelley."

She didn't like political life. "My husband is not a politician. He is a worker." It was the Gandhian word: a doer of good works. "I too am an ardent believer in improving the lot of the down-trodden. But I want to work silently. I don't want publicity for myself. But I would like a lot more for my husband. People should recognize his ability. If he is a sincere and hardworking man, people should know."

Mr Bishweshwar arrived, tall and plump, in trousers and a brown sports shirt. He looked harassed and winded and had clearly been rattled by the Kishangarh affair. He had also missed a meeting at a village called Saradhna; and it was for Saradhna that we immediately started, accompanied – perhaps for luck on this unlucky day, perhaps for reasons of piety – by a small, energetic sadhu clad from top to toe in saffron. The sadhu seemed about to chatter with cold; it was the effect of his saffron head-dress, which was cunningly tied from one piece of cotton and looked like a cross between a mitre and a jester's cap, with flaps over the ears.

The Rajasthan village huddles together, a solid built-up mass where space is suddenly scarce. Saradhna was like this. We stopped near the two tea-shacks, their fires glowing in the dark. There was no one to receive us and we walked around to the other side of the village. Then, at a great pace, Mr Bishweshwar began to walk through the village, kicking up dust, the rubber-sandalled sadhu running at his heels, ear-flaps sticking out. We raced past stripped trees, over piles of rubble, past broken courtyards, over runnels of filth. The narrow lane twisted and turned and opened abruptly into miniature squares. We passed a group of smokers sitting peaceably in the thick warm dust around a brass plate with their smoking things; and then we were out of the village and near the tea-shacks again.

Some men came to Mr Bishweshwar then and whispered. *Unanimous, unanimous*: the English word was quite clear in all the Hindi. Not far away a man squatted in the dust, cooking some mess in a tiny black pot over an enormous straw blaze.

Mr Bishweshwar said, "They held their own meeting. The whole village has decided to support me."

"*Unanimous*," a black-capped villager said, shaking his head from side to side.

It was hard to push the matter any further; and our business was therefore, quite unexpectedly, over.

As we were driving back to Ajmer it occurred to me that Mr Bishweshwar's trousers and shirt were unusual for a campaigning Congress politician. I said, "So you don't wear homespun?"

He thought I was criticizing. He plucked at the sleeve of his brown sports shirt and said, "This is homespun. Sometimes I wear trousers for the convenience. But I often wear the dhoti. I like the dhoti."

So he was only out of uniform. He wasn't, as I had thought, the new-style politician, matching Mrs Gandhi's new-style campaign. He was a Congressman, aspiring after the old style; he had, as he had said, imbibed his principles from his uncle. When the Congress had split, leaving Mrs Gandhi at the head of a minority government, the leaders of the local State Congress had hesitated about which side to join; and Mr Bishweshwar, as he admitted, had hesitated with them. When they had declared for Mrs Gandhi, he had gone along with them. The new-style politics was Mrs Gandhi's, and Mrs Gandhi's alone. In Rajasthan the Congress organization, the whole structure of Congress control, remained what it was. It was Mrs Gandhi who had appeared to turn this party, ruling since independence, into the party of protest.

But for Mr Bishweshwar it remained a gamble. In 1967 he had got 145,000 votes; his main opponent, from the party known as the Jan Sangh (The National Party) had got 108,000. But in 1967 Mr Bishweshwar had had the support of Mr Mukut and the Maharana of Udaipur. Now Udaipur and the Jan Sangh were supporting Mr Mukut. Udaipur could take away Rajput votes from Mr Bishweshwar; the Kishangarh affair could have the same effect.

Mr Bishweshwar was going that evening on a two-day country tour. In his campaign headquarters – the ground floor of a villa: a stripped central room with an empty fireplace, high blue walls with little oblong windows just below the ceiling, worn rugs on the cracked concrete floor, small side rooms enclosed by lattice-work and wire netting – among his workers, some paid (40 rupees a month, £2, for two hours a day), some minor politicians in their own right, whose rustic manner belied the revolutionary promises of the posters sent out from New Delhi, among the barefoot boys sitting on the floor and pasting *Vote Bishweshwar* posters on cardboard, he looked very harassed indeed.

But Mr Mukut had his problems too. Officially he was the candidate of the opposition or Organization Congress. But the Organization Congress had no organization in Ajmer. Mr Mukut was depending on the organization of the Jan Sangh; and Mr Mukut and the Jan Sangh had until recently been enemies. The central executives of the opposition parties had formed an alliance; they had agreed on a division of seats; and Ajmer had gone to the Organization Congress and Mr Mukut.

The Jan Sangh in Ajmer had been planning to put up their own man. Now they had to support Mr Mukut; and Mr Sharda, the president of the local Jan Sangh, who had contested the seat in 1967, didn't like it. He said, "This is a Jan Sangh seat and some Jan Sangh man should have contested. I would have been a better candidate than the man they chose. Have you seen him? He's an old man of sixty-eight, blind, can't see. All the time our people come to me asking why Jan Sangh is not contesting, why I am helping this blind old man."

And it was an unusual alliance. The Jan Sangh, founded in 1951, had grown in strength, Mr Sharda said, because the Congress was corrupt; but for most of this time Mr Mukut was the ruler of the Congress in Ajmer. It wasn't only for its opposition to Congress corruption that the Jan Sangh was known, though. The Congress was non-sectarian; Mr Mukut had a good record as a defender of Muslim rights. The Jan Sangh had come into prominence in North India as the militant Hindu party of the right, rallying Hindus against Muslims, and, within the Hindus, the Aryan, Hindi-speaking north against the Dravidian south. It spoke of the pampering of minorities; its slogan was "Indianization". Latterly, scenting parliamentary power, the Jan Sangh had softened its communal, Aryan line; it had decided that the enemy was Communism; but its communal reputation remained its strength.

"We don't want to take ideas from Russia and Kosygin," Mr Sharda said. "We have a heritage, a culture. We have the Vedas, the first book of the human race. With the Vedas' light other people have developed their cultures. So when we have got such an old heritage we believe that our race is great, is noble. My grandfather, Harbilas Sharda, has written a book called *Hindu*

Superiority. In the 1930s. He has given all the facts and figures to show how the Hindu race is superior to others."

Mr Sharda was in his fifties, small, compactly built, in a striped brown suit. He wore tinted glasses; for all his aggrieved talk of the "blind old man" his own eyes were not too good. Eye trouble, in fact, had made him give up the practice of law and go into business as a commission agent dealing in cement and cloth. He lived in a new concrete bungalow at the bottom of the Circuit House hill, opposite a rock wall plastered with drying cow-dung cakes. He had a glass case of knick-knacks in his drawing-room; bits of vine grew out of whisky bottles, one brown, one green. On the white wall there was a portrait, like a tinted photograph, of Harbilas Sharda, the author of *Hindu Superiority*: a gentle old brahmin with a drooping moustache, in British days an elected member of the Central Legislative Assembly, given the title of Dewan Bahadur (one step below the knighthood), and famous in India as the author of the Child Marriage Restraint Act (still known as the Sharda Act), which in 1930 had banned child marriage.

"My family was the first to revolt against the social evils of the country," Mr Sharda said. But his party was now committed to the protection of the sacred cow, as it was committed to the creation of an Indian nuclear armoury. There was no inconsistency. Like parties of the extreme right elsewhere, the Jan Sangh dealt in anger, simplified scholarship and, above all, sentimentality. It spoke of danger and distress – "Our civilization is in danger," Mr Sharda said – and from present impotence it conjured up a future of power, as pure as the mythical Hindu past, before the British conquest, before the Muslim invasions.

"We want nuclear bomb for the safety of the country. But this is a matter of our all-India policy. I don't talk too much about it to our villagers." The cow was different. "We feel that cow is a very important animal in our country, being an agricultural country, and as such should not be slaughtered. There is a candidate in Delhi, Mr Ram Gopal Shalwala, is fighting only on that. Government should give protection and give good bulls to have a better type of animal. Good arrangements of fodder should also be made, because generally there is famine in this area and thousands of animals die of famine."

He didn't think Muslims would object. "Muslims who live in villages and are agriculturalists like to live as Hindus do. It is only the educated fanatics who want to create this gulf of Hindus and Muslims for their own selfish motives." But later, when we were talking about the way the 40,000 Muslim votes would go, Mr Sharda said in his direct, unrancorous way, "They will be divided. But generally most of the Muslim votes do not go to Jan Sangh."

As I was leaving, a barefoot servant in a torn dhoti brought in the up-country edition of *The Motherland*, the new English-language Jan Sangh daily published in Delhi. The Kishangarh story, and the charge of political murder, was still big on the front page.

The Muslim votes wouldn't go to the Jan Sangh. But Mr Mukut thought they would go to him personally, for his past services. This was on a day of exaltation when, after an evening of well-received speeches, he seemed to think that by allying himself with his former enemies he had left almost no votes for the other side.

We were driving in one of the campaign jeeps from Ajmer to the military town of Nasirabad, through country that had been stripped almost to desert by eight successive years of drought. Between the driver and myself Mr Mukut sat or half-reclined, small, frail, easily tossed about, in a dhoti and a black waistcoat, with his fine head thrown back, his sightless eyes closed, his delicate hands occasionally clutching at air. Sometimes, between sentences, his wide, expressive mouth opened and closed wordlessly, and he was then like a man gasping for breath. His gentle manner and fragility imposed gentleness on all who came near him; and I occasionally felt, as I leaned close to catch his exalted words, that I was rushing a garrulous invalid to hospital, and not racing with one of Rajasthan's master-politicians to a hard day's campaigning.

A leaflet had appeared in Ajmer calling on Jan Sangh supporters to boycott Mr Mukut. Mr Mukut said this was another trick of

Mr Bishweshwar's party; he had, he said, been astonished by the loyalty of his Jan Sangh workers. Mr Mukut spoke, not quite as one who had seen the error of his Congress ways, but as someone who was at last able to speak of the errors of the Congress. The Jan Sangh said that the Congress was corrupt. It was true, Mr Mukut said. "The power corrupted us. Our politicians became Gandhian only in name." But he himself had been helpless; he had never been a minister. And now he saw no moral or political complication in his alliance with the Jan Sangh. His position was simple: it was as a Gandhian that he was fighting the Indira Congress, which was illegitimate, Communistic and westernizing.

"Gandhiji's ideology was quite different from the ideology of Western politicians. The foundation of his political tactics is that means should be as fair as the end." He didn't think this could be said of Mrs Gandhi. He was also concerned about nationalization. "It will ruin the country. All our state-owned enterprises are so badly run." His support of private enterprise brought him close to the hard anti-Communist line of the Jan Sangh. But Mr Mukut didn't appear to be concerned either about efficiency or capitalism. His opposition to nationalization was embedded in an over-riding Gandhian doubt about the machine age. The machine had destroyed the West, as Mr Mukut had heard; the machine would destroy India. "What I particularly admired about Gandhiji was that he went to Buckingham Palace in 1931 in a dhoti."

I asked why that was admirable.

"Because he put the picture of poor India before the world."

"Mr Nehru said that the danger in a country as poor as India was that poverty might be deified."

"Did he say that?" Mr Mukut paused. The idea was new, "western" and perhaps intellectually unmanageable. "I never heard him say that." He opened and closed his mouth wordlessly; and again, head thrown back, eyes closed, he was like a gasping invalid.

We passed the new Shiva temple, still with its bamboo scaffolding, that the peasants had built to celebrate the end of the eight-year drought. It stood white in a desolation of young thorn bushes.

Once there had been woodland here; but towards the end of the drought, at a time of famine, the trees had been cut down for charcoal. And then we were in the military area: barracks old and new in the stripped land, soldiers with rifles on their shoulders running in groups of two or three on the asphalt road.

The main street of Nasirabad was brilliant with stalls of fruit and vegetables. Here we stopped. Many reverential hands helped Mr Mukut out of the jeep and led him, limp-shouldered, limp-armed, between the vegetable-stalls and across the narrow pavement to a dark little office, over the front door of which, on the outside, were dusty framed diplomas from Lucknow University and, on the inside, brightly coloured Hindu religious prints. It was a lawyer's office, with a whole glass-cased wall of Indian law books covered in brown paper, the frame of the case painted yellow, with each section roughly labelled in red.

Mr Mukut said to me, "He's one of my disciples."

The lawyer, a middle-aged man in a chocolate-purple sports shirt, said very loudly, as though addressing the street, "Everything I am I owe to Mr Mukut."

They made Mr Mukut sit on a basket-chair. They brought him tea and a large, fly-infested *cachoree*, a local fried delicacy.

The lawyer said, "Mr Mukut made me what I am. He has served many people here without payment. The people of Nasirabad remember these things."

And Mr Mukut, leaning back, his slender legs drawn up onto the seat, his hands fumbling for the *cachoree* that had been broken for his convenience into little pieces, Mr Mukut opened and closed his mouth, like a man about to sigh.

But the lawyer had pointed the weakness of Mr Mukut's campaign. Some of the people in the office were linked to Mr Mukut by interest. The others were Jan Sangh and they for the most part were small shopkeepers. Even the forbidding, kohl-eyed young man in a cream-coloured suit and pointed black shoes, even he, who was a teacher, came from a shopkeeping family. The Jan Sangh was an urban party; it had no organization in the villages. The only party with a village organization was the Congress. It was that village organization that had to be captured; and Mr Mukut's only weapon was his influence. Mr Bishweshwar's strength was that he belonged to the ruling party; a ruling party had its ways of exerting pressure.

"I will tell you how they won the last State Assembly by-election," the lawyer said. "At that time this area was affected by famine. Rural people were jobless. The government machinery opened famine works in a number of places. And these famine-relief workers were given one slogan: 'If you vote for the other side, famine relief work will be closed down.'" And now the ruling party was again up to their old tricks, this time with the untouchables or Harijans, whom they were bribing in all sorts of ways and especially with loans from the nationalized banks.

A prominent Christian in Ajmer had complained to me that as a result of all the political attention the Harijans were getting out of hand. They were being "brought up" too fast, before they had a proper "footing"; there had been strikes. "I am even afraid to speak harshly to some of them now," the Christian said. I thought that the lawyer might be trying to say something like this in an indirect, un-Christian way. So I asked him, "They're behaving badly then, these scheduled castes?"

"Badly?" The lawyer didn't understand my question. He was a Hindu; he didn't have the Christian's social sense; he couldn't share the Christian's resentment. Caste was not class. No one, however successful, denied his caste, however low, or sought to move out of it; no one tried to "pass"; no one's caste-security was threatened by any other caste. So the lawyer floundered. "No," he said at last, "they are not *behaving* badly. It's just that they're being fooled."

But what did Mr Mukut have to offer? How was he going to balance this powerful appeal of the other side? Was he campaigning, for instance, for cow-protection? Mr Mukut was astonished that I should ask. Everyone in Ajmer knew his record. During his time in parliament he hadn't only campaigned for a ban on cow-slaughter and the punishment of cow-killers; he had also campaigned for free grazing for cows anywhere.

"We are too western-oriented," Mr Mukut said. He was sitting up now, small and neat and cross-legged in his basket-chair. "Go to the villages. Everybody in the village now wants to wear jacket and tie. Look at our own *ayurveda* medicine. It was only after a long fight that we managed to get it accepted, these remedies that are much cheaper than any modern drugs. And then there are the pipelines."

I said, "Pipelines, Mr Mukut?"

"Even in the villages. The pipelines in the villages is going too far. It's all right in the cities. But in villages the healthy water from the well is good enough. But they are taking piped water now to many villages. For our womenfolk this going to the well and drawing water was one of the ways in which their health was maintained. They now have got no substitute exercise for the women. Similarly, we have our own indigenous *chakki* [a quern] for grinding grain on the floor. Now they have substituted these mills run by electric power or oil-fired machines. So now the whole village sends its grain to these mills, with the result that the women are missing this exercise as well. Previously even in cities this grinding with *chakki* was done by small families. But now everything is being westernized. It is morally bad because it tells upon the health and habits of our womenfolk. And unless some alternative employment is found for them it naturally makes them sluggish."

In a famine area! From an election candidate! But Mr Mukut could go into the villages to ask for votes because he was a Gandhian who knew that his own merit was high. He had achieved merit through service and sacrifice. Service for its own sake, sacrifice for its own sake. "Since Mr Kaul and I left the Congress," Mr Mukut said, "there is no one there with a record of service. Mr Kaul was in jail; I was in jail." Democracy, the practice of the law, the concern with rights: one set of virtues had been absorbed into another, into a concept of *dharma*, the Hindu right way; and the distortion that resulted could sometimes be startling.

II

Kishangarh was murdered on Tuesday evening. On Friday evening All-India Radio announced that the police had "worked out" the case and arrested a student. On Saturday the details of the arrested man's "confession" were all over Ajmer, and in the afternoon there were Hindi leaflets in the streets:

LOVE STORY: A POLITICAL OPERA

Bhim Jat, the killer of the Maharaja of Kishangarh, has confessed, and the whole affair is crystal clear. The Maharaja had a farm a few miles from Kishangarh. Bhim Jat and his beautiful sister worked for the Maharaja on this farm. The Maharaja took advantage of the girl's poverty and for a long time had illicit relations with her. Bhim Jat, a youth of nineteen, could not stand this looting of his sister's honour. He took the law into his own hands and with his country-made pistol shot the Maharaja dead.

But politics corrupts the truth and deals in lies. Some politicians immediately called a meeting to mourn the Maharaja's death and with a great show of sorrow tried to tell the voter to take his revenge by defeating the Indira Congress.

Would you vote for a party which plays with the honour of your daughter or sister? There should be rejoicing not tears at the death of these rajas-maharajas whose only princely habit is that they know how to take advantage of the poverty of young girls. Rise and utterly crush these debauched people so that never again will they come to you for votes with the name of Gandhi on their lips. . . .

Has Mr Mukut no shame, to be sitting in the lap of the Jan Sangh, who were once his bitter enemies? The election should be fought on policies. Mr Mukut shouldn't be misleading the voters for his own selfish purposes. Mr Mukut has used the Maharaja's funeral-pyre to cook himself a meal of votes.

Other versions of the story were no less sad. Bhim Jat's sister had left her husband to become Kishangarh's mistress; and Bhim Jat had been ostracized by his caste for the dishonour his complaisance had brought on them all. Kishangarh had given Bhim a house on the farm; he was paying for Bhim's education; he had promised Bhim the farm itself. But then a well on the farm gushed water. In the desert water was money; and Kishangarh, worried about his "de-recognition" and the possible loss of his privy purse, had sought to go back on his promise.

Kishangarh was the name of an eighteenth-century school of painting. Now it was linked with a peasant woman, a farm, a well: a peasant drama, far removed from the princely pageantry of the prize-giving at Mayo College that afternoon. Kishangarh was remembered there, in the obituary section of the headmaster's speech, as a distinguished and popular old boy, like the late Maharaja of Jaipur, "who died in the UK, where he had gone to play polo, his favourite sport".

The boys were exquisite in tight white trousers, long black coats and pink long-tailed Rajput turbans. They sat on the steps of the Mogul-style Bikaner Pavilion, with a view of the cricket field, the blank score-board, the college grounds and, in the distance, the sunlit brown hills of Ajmer. The guest of honour was the Canadian High Commissioner. Prominent among the visitors on the lower steps of the pavilion were some of the princes of Rajasthan: the Maharaja of Kotah, a couple from the house of Jodhpur, and the Maharana of Udaipur, whose ancestor had been the first to respond to an appeal of the Viceroy, Lord Mayo, for funds for a princely public school and had, a hundred years ago, almost to the day, given a lakh of rupees, then worth about £10,000.

In the open area at the foot of the pavilion were the parents, many of them box-wallahs, business executives, some from as far away as Calcutta. All week they had been gathering in Ajmer: India's modest middle class, products of the new industrial society, as yet with no common traditions or rooted strength, still only with the vulnerability of the middle classes of all very poor countries. In the poverty of India their ambition was great, but their expectations were small; they were really very easily pleased. India always threatened to overwhelm them – (those servants at the edge of the cricket field) – as the desert and the peasants and the new politics had overwhelmed Kishangarh and his ancient name.

But the Maharana of Udaipur hadn't come to Ajmer only for the prize-giving. He had been campaigning hard against Mrs Gandhi and her party in a princely freelance way, offering his services wherever they were needed; and he was in Ajmer to give Mr Mukut a hand. He had come in an open dark-green 1936 Rolls-Royce with a chauffeur, an Election Secretary and two bodyguards. He proved his worth almost at once. That very evening, while the Mayo College boys were doing *A Midsummer Night's Dream*, Udaipur addressed a meeting in the bazaar area. His name was like magic. Fifteen thousand people came to hear him.

The next day, Sunday, was the big day. Udaipur was going with Mr Mukut and Mr Sharda on a tour of those districts of the constituency that had belonged to the former Udaipur State. The little convoy started from the red-brick King Edward VII Guest House on Highway 8, not far from the mock-Mogul Queen Victoria Golden Jubilee clock-tower.

It was such an unlikely alliance. There was Mr Sharda, "western" and businesslike in his suit, but with his pastoral Jan Sangh dream of an untouched Hindu world; he was in a jeep, packed at the back with bedding and other supplies. Mr Mukut, the Gandhian and old-time Congressman, but now formally dressed in tight white trousers and a long cream-coloured coat, was in a grey saloon. Udaipur was in his open Rolls, a man in his forties, of medium height and build, with a black beret, dark glasses and dark-blue nylon windcheater. The thirty-six-year-old Election Secretary, very tall, with a paunch, a corrugated beard and glinting black locks, was all in loose white cotton and looked like a holy man. At the back of the Rolls the two khaki-uniformed, orange-turbanned bodyguards sat up high with their rifles: it was like a proclamation of the danger in which, in Rajasthan, princes now lived.

Udaipur was the star. That was accepted. And so briefly did Mr Mukut speak at Nasirabad, our first stop, that by the time my own jeep, after a wrong turning, had got to the meeting-place, he had finished and was sitting cross-legged on the improvised platform, eyes closed, good and quiet and patient at Udaipur's suede-shod feet, like a man accepting his own irrelevance. But Udaipur remembered him. "People ask me, 'But isn't Mr Mukut a blind man?' I say, 'He is blind on the outside, not on the inside. When you go to a temple, mosque or church you close your eyes to pray. You can't see, but you aren't blind on the inside.'"

Mr Mukut sat as still as a man meditating in a temple. But a packed day lay ahead. Suddenly – no speech from Mr Sharda – the meeting was over and the mood of meditation and repose vanished. So quickly did Udaipur and Mr Mukut scramble off the platform, so quickly did they bolt for their vehicles, that I lost them almost at once and didn't catch up with them again until Beawar, thirty miles away.

After Beawar it was desert; and it was desert after Bhim. No irrigated green patches, no trees, no peasants on bicycles; just rock and sometimes cactus, and the empty road. Sometimes a camel, sometimes a peasant in rags with parched leather sandals and a home-made gun: bandit country. But regularly in this wilderness little Rajput groups ran out into the road to stop the convoy and to look for the Maharana they had never seen (a Maharana of Udaipur had last been here in 1938). When Udaipur stood up in the Rolls drums beat and sometimes, unexpectedly, a trumpet sounded.

They garlanded him and dabbed his forehead with sandalwood paste; they sprinkled him with red or purple water (he had dressed for this). Ceremonially, as though he were a god in a temple (and his dark glasses gave him a suitable inscrutability), they circled his face with fire (a blazing lump of camphor in a brass plate). Once a woman fed him some substance with her hand. Here

Udaipur was more than a prince. Here he was *Hinduon ka suraj*, the Hindu Sun, an ancient title of Rajput chivalry that had merged into religion. At one stop a man cried out, "You are our god!" And Udaipur was quick to reply, correctly, "The God that is, is the same for you and me."

Mr Mukut wasn't forgotten. When the Rolls moved on, the Rajputs surrounded the grey saloon. Mr Sharda always waved me on then in his impatient way and so I couldn't tell whether the men of the desert weren't exacting some tribute from Mr Mukut for their devotion to their Maharana.

Early in the afternoon we reached the walled town of Deogarh. There was pandemonium at the main gate; in the middle of the crowd a white horse with a white sheet on its back was waiting for Udaipur. The loudspeaker-man in our convoy became frenzied. "Your Maharana has come. For 1,400 years you have known Maharanas. Now he has come, the Hindu Sun. You have longed for him as you have longed for clouds and rain. Now your Maharana has come." But already, as in some spectacular film, the walled town was emptying; and men and women in bright turbans and saris were hurrying across the desert to the temple of Karni Devi, goddess of the town, where Udaipur was to speak.

Mr Sharda, who was, I thought, a little buttoned-up in the company of his two old political enemies, Mr Sharda whispered to me, "Jan Sangh. All organized by Jan Sangh."

And soon to his desert audience – bright turbans and smiling faces against a background of sand, the walled city and fort, the jagged hills faint in the haze – Udaipur was talking about Mrs Gandhi's threat to democracy and the constitution. Mr Mukut sat cross-legged on the canopied platform. The bodyguards were dusting down the Rolls in the shade of a thorn tree.

Udaipur had changed his beret for a Rajput turban. One man, so many roles. But Udaipur was a good speaker because he accepted all his roles – god, Rajput, democrat – and made them fit together. "I am not a god. I am just a sort of representative. We are all worshippers of Lord Shiva, *Ek Ling Nath*." He was not a politician; he wanted no man's vote. "I am not a supporter of the Jan Sangh. I am a supporter of freedom." The Rajputs applauded that. "We have no policemen here and we need none. We are not like the Indira Congress. There is love between us, because we are one and the same." They laughed at the political hit and applauded the definition of the basis of their Rajput loyalty.

Afterwards, leaving Mr Mukut to the electorate, we went to have lunch in the bare and run-down palace of Udaipur's vassal. Here the election was as if forgotten. The vassal and his infant son glittered in Rajput court costume. A red carpet lay across the dusty courtyard. Drums beat; a smiling doorkeeper took the swords of guests; in an inner room women sang. A bright-eyed old retainer came and recited ancient verses about the duties of kings. Other smiling people – everyone was smiling – came to make obeisance and offer token tributes of one rupee and five rupees.

"You see," Udaipur said in English, his face still stained red and purple, "how *unpopular* we are."

The newspapers were being gloomy about Mrs Gandhi's chances, and the success of Udaipur's tour disheartened many people on Mr Bishweshwar's side. They had no comparable glamour figure. The visit of Mr Chavan, one of Mrs Gandhi's most able ministers, had been a failure; Mrs Gandhi herself wasn't coming. All that Mr Bishweshwar's people could look forward to was the visit, on Tuesday, of Mr Bishweshwar's political patron, the Rajasthan Chief Minister. He was hardly glamorous. He was very much the local party boss, and he was coming less to make speeches than to settle certain internal party disputes which had begun to threaten Mr Bishweshwar's campaign.

The Ajmer Congress was famous for its faction fights. In 1954, when Mrs Bishweshwar's father was politically active, the administration had virtually stalled; and Mr Nehru had written a long and impatient "note" about the local party: ". . . giving us continuous headaches. . . . The government cannot be considered to be an efficient government. . . . The Community Project Scheme in Ajmer was one of the least successful. In fact, for a long time practically nothing was done there." That was the tradition. And after all its further years in power the local party was full of people who thought they had been badly treated and were taking advantage of the election to sulk. Mr Bishweshwar, aiming at independence, and trying to free himself of old intrigues by "creating" new men of his own, had made matters worse. One aggrieved man said, "Mr Bishweshwar is in the position of a man who has stopped believing in the loyalty of his honest wife and has begun to believe the protestations of loose girls."

So now I heard that Mrs Gandhi hadn't come to Ajmer because she disapproved of Mr Bishweshwar, that she remembered how he had hesitated at the time of the party split, and that she was now letting him sweat it out. Other people, with memories of Mrs Bishweshwar's father, said that Mr Bishweshwar's heart wasn't in the election and that he had only been pushed into it by his wife. Everybody agreed that Mr Mukut's workers were more selfless and less mercenary and less given to sabotage. There was a lot of talk of sabotage. One man high in the party told me that of all Mr Bishweshwar's workers, paid and unpaid, thirty per cent were saboteurs.

And it was only then that I heard about the Rawats. The Rawats were originally a caste of animal-skinners. They had been advancing for some time into agriculture, the army and the police. In Jodhpur the Maharaja had decreed twenty-five years before that they were to be considered a Rajput caste. But in Ajmer the Rawats were still low, almost untouchable. They should therefore have been solidly behind the Indira Congress and Mr Bishweshwar. But there had been a crisis. Some weeks before a young Rawat wife in the Nasirabad area had been enticed away by a Rawat Christian convert. The community had been doubly dishonoured, by the adultery (in India an offence punishable with rigorous imprisonment), and by the fact that the enticer was a Christian. There had been complaints to the police, but nothing had been done; and some Rawats felt that Mr Bishweshwar and some of his Christian supporters had connived at the inactivity of the police. A leaflet had been distributed in Rawat areas: RAWATS, BROTHERS! THE INDIRA CONGRESS CANDIDATE BISHWESHWAR NATH BHARGAVA TRIFLES WITH THE HONOUR OF OUR WIVES AND DAUGHTERS. BEWARE OF HIM!

There were 50,000 Rawat voters. Kishangarh, Udaipur, Rajputs, Rawats, and sabotage: Mr Bishweshwar seemed to be in trouble all round that Monday. And this, very roughly, was the assessment of the Ajmer situation that appeared in the *Times of India*. A day or two later a large "human-interest" photograph of Mr Mukut – a blind candidate – made the front page of the New Delhi *Hindustan Times*.

It was from Mr Kudal that I heard about the Rawats. Mr Kudal was a Congressman of fifty and he had a modest ambition: he wanted to be Mr Bishweshwar's Election Agent. The appointment was to be made on Tuesday, when the Chief Minister came; but when I saw Mr Kudal, late on Monday evening, he had heard nothing at all and was in a state of some nerves. He said, "I very much fear that the intelligentsia is being cleverly weeded out all over India from political life."

Mr Kudal was a lawyer. He lived in a lavatorial lane off Highway 8, in a large three-storeyed house built in the Rajasthani style with galleries around a central courtyard, and with an iron grille at the top to keep out intruders. Narrow enclosed concrete steps took you up past his law offices and his servants' rooms to the flat roof and his pink-and-red sitting-room. Upholstered chairs were pushed against three walls and there was a glass case with figures made from shells, plastic models of Hindu deities, and other knick-knacks. It was a little like a waiting-room, with all the chairs, but Mr Kudal had many visitors. He kept in touch with the constituency; he had prepared himself for the job of Election Agent.

He was worried about the Rawats. He was less worried by Udaipur's tour. "These public meetings are just *tamashas*, excitements. Nothing." Elections were won with votes, and vote-getting required work. "By work I mean the direct approach to the voters. Taking them out of the houses and sending them to the booths. I will tell you as a zealous worker that all will depend on the work we put in in the last two or three days." And in that lay Mr Kudal's promise and his threat.

He said, "I could swing the election in certain districts without leaving this room. It would take me a week. If I went out on the road it would take me two or three days."

I asked him how.

"I am a man of the masses." It was something he had worked at. He was a brahmin and a townsman and he said he had wasted a lot of time on bridge and chess before he had thought of service to the poor. He had gone out then "among the lowest sections of the community – the Harijans and the serpent-charmers". Not many people had done that; and it was well known in Ajmer that Mr Kudal had a lot of influence in certain low quarters. "That is why people get worried when they hear that Kudal has joined the fray."

So on this last evening Mr Kudal rehearsed his case, and his slightly desperate attitude was that, ready as he was to serve, he was also perfectly prepared to let Mr Bishweshwar stew in his own juice, that if the Chief Minister and Mr Bishweshwar wanted his services, if they cared at all about things like the snake-charmer vote, they would have to seek him out the next day. Mr Kudal himself intended to do absolutely nothing the next day. It was the festival of Shivratri; he was a devotee of Shiva; for him it was to be a day of temple, prayer and meditation.

Early in the morning, too early, Mr Bishweshwar came to the Circuit House to look for the Chief Minister. He looked even more harassed than I remembered. He was with a gang of rustics in dusty dhotis, brown waistcoats and Gandhi-caps. Pointlessly, like a swarm of midges, they bustled back and forth about the spacious lounge, following Mr Bishweshwar's nervous lead. When Mr Bishweshwar stood still, they all settled down on the carpet, the way the Circuit House servants did when they thought no one was about. After some fearful jabbering, four or five people speaking at once, the same things said again and again, they decided that the Chief Minister wasn't in the Circuit House and was probably somewhere else. And suddenly they all swarmed out again.

But the Chief Minister did come. And he must have had a hard day. He was still at the Circuit House at 7.30 that evening, when he should have been down in the city addressing a meeting at Kesarganj. It was just as well. Shivratri, the weekly service at the Hanuman temple, the Flower Show and the illuminations in Shah Jehan's lakeside gardens had drawn the holiday crowds; and there were only three or four hundred people – government officers, Muslims, people proving their loyalty – at Kesarganj. For an hour we were deafened by music, songs and election jingles. The crowd grew. And when at last the Chief Minister arrived, with all his party notables, I was glad to see that Mr Kudal had been called out of his retreat and was with them.

After a day spent on personality squabbles the Chief Minister now dealt only in principles. *Garibi Hatao:* nothing about Rajputs and Rawats; not a word against Mr Mukut; hardly anything about Mr Bishweshwar. Mr Bishweshwar didn't speak. Like the figure of the wife in some Egyptian sculpture, small at the feet of her lord, like Mr Mukut at the feet of Udaipur, Mr Bishweshwar sat still and modest at the feet of the Chief Minister. He leaned back on his arms; his paunch showed to advantage; and I thought I had never seen him so relaxed.

"He has every reason to look relaxed," Mr Kudal said, as we drove to Nasirabad with some of his workers the following afternoon. "Yesterday at 9.30 a.m., after he saw the Chief Minister he came and surrendered before me. He and his wife and his sister, his wife with tears in her eyes. I told him, 'But you, Bishweshwar, must know that I was always helping you, because I believe in the principles of Mrs Gandhi, and not because of any affection I bear to you.'" So, indirectly, Mr Kudal announced that he was the Election Agent. Then he added, "Now is the time for onslaught."

But first we stopped at the new Shiva temple, and Mr Kudal, grateful devotee of Shiva, paid his respects to the lingam, which was set in the ground in the centre of a concrete lotus with a serrated rim. The yellow clothes of the images were damp with a sweet substance and black with sated, drugged flies.

"Here at Nasirabad," Mr Kudal said, when we were on the road again, "I will introduce you to Mr Mukut's and Mr Bishweshwar's staunchest supporters. They are both my closest friends and they will both offer you a cup of tea. Sometimes I contest these elections like sports."

"Like a hobby," a worker in the back of the jeep said.

And at Nasirabad the news was as bad as Mr Kudal could have wished. Mr Jain, the plump little jeweller ("High Class Military Novelties and Gold Ornaments") who was also the Treasurer of the Ajmer Rural District Congress Committee, seated us against bolsters on his porch, in the cosy little space – at once his office and his day-bed – between the showcase and the front wall, gave us tea and *cachoree*, and told us that the way things were going Mr Bishweshwar would be lucky to get thirty-five per cent of the town vote and fifty per cent of the village vote. "They are neglecting the old workers. The new workers they've brought in drink and go to hotels and abuse the opposition and they think they're winning votes."

The lawyer who was Mr Mukut's Nasirabad man – his office was just across the road – gave the same figures. "Oh yes," the lawyer said in his booming voice. "Things are going right for Mr Mukut. Because of somebody. You can say it is because of me. And the Jan Sangh. And Mr Mukut – he's a great asset. And the poor personality of the opponent. All these things have combined."

We left Nasirabad and drove off into the desert.

"Depressed?" Mr Kudal said. "I'm a warrior who knows no defeat."

A worker in the jeep said, "Mr Kudal can turn the tables."

"I'm a man of the masses," Mr Kudal said. "I will take you now to a village where very few people go. The Harijans there have built a Shiva temple and dedicated it to me. When I went to work among them they were an alcoholic community. I made them take the pledge. It wasn't easy. It took months."

Sunset in the desert: neem trees and Australian dogwood black against the ochre sky. And then, on an eminence, a walled village, a high gateway, a dusty road, a temple, and a crowd around the jeep shouting, "*Indira Gandhi ki jai!* Long live Indira Gandhi!" It was as Mr Kudal had said: he was known here. Babies were shown to him, children re-introduced; boys read out the inscription on the temple gateway to show how well they could read now. And Mr Kudal, tall, bald, one of his legs shorter than the other, walked among the Harijans with his awkward gait, blinking fast behind his glasses. Without any Gandhian trappings, he was a dedicated man; and it was moving.

We went on in the dark to a village where Mr Kudal said he wanted to do "some CID work". I recognized the village as Saradhna. I had been there with Mr Bishweshwar and I remembered that he had been promised "unanimous" support. But Mr Kudal doubted whether Mr Bishweshwar would get forty per cent of the vote. Saradhna was a village of Jats; a Jat political party had recently emerged, hostile to Mrs Gandhi; and the previous evening Mr Mukut and some of the leaders of the Jat party had held a meeting at Saradhna.

"CID, CID," Mr Kudal said to his workers when we stopped. They went to the tea-stalls and we sat silent in the jeep. Our presence couldn't have been all that secret, though. Cups of tea were brought out to us. A villager came and whispered that only seventy-five per cent of the village was for Mr Bishweshwar. "He is only giving me butter," Mr Kudal said in Hindi. But another villager came and whispered that Mr Bishweshwar couldn't expect more than ninety per cent; and the workers, coming back from the tea-stalls, said eighty per cent.

So it seemed that the caste-appeal hadn't worked at Saradhna. And I began to wonder whether Mrs Gandhi hadn't simplified Mr Kudal's labours; whether she hadn't lifted this mid-term election high above the local politics Mr Kudal understood and

5

enjoyed; whether in Ajmer the choice wasn't between Mrs Gandhi and the Jan Sangh in some areas, between Mrs Gandhi and Udaipur in other areas, and between Mrs Gandhi and poor old Mr Mukut everywhere else.

No drama on the road, then, for Mr Kudal. But when we got back to Ajmer we found that someone had been distributing leaflets accusing Mr Kudal of sabotage.

Mr Kudal had said that Friday was going to be a hard day. But by the time all our workers had come and we had ordered food from the bazaar it was half past eleven; and when we got to our first village it was time to eat. We sat in the rough little council-hall in the middle of a million furious flies. The workers ate off newspaper, Mr Kudal and myself off dry peepul-leaves; and the kulaks, the local vote-catchers, who had been waiting for us, waited on us. Their manner was penitential, and Mr Kudal hinted that he had come to rebuke them. They received their rebukes in private, after we had lunched.

The lunch had been heavy; the new famine road – part of the network built during the famine – was smooth. Mr Kudal fell asleep. We passed a village. Mr Kudal woke up and said he was sorry he had missed it, but he would send some of his workers there by bus that evening. We came to another village. A water-channel, freshly dug in the sand, barred our path; and Mr Kudal decided to leave that village as well to his night workers.

"Well," he said later, "you're seeing the Nasirabad district. You've heard the assessments of both sides. So when the results come out you will know it is entirely the result of this" – he waved at the road and the boundless desert – "this movement. The result of this onslaught."

At the next village – more a little town: a low-caste wedding procession in the dusty main street, a brass band in spectacularly tattered uniforms – we had cardamom tea in a cloth-seller's shop and Mr Kudal talked to the Muslim village headman. Nothing more was needed, Mr Kudal said; by evening everyone would know that Kudal was out campaigning for Indira and Mr

Bishweshwar. "They know that after the election they will still have to come to me." The statement worried him, and some time later he said, "I have helped these people. I have handled their cases for them without fee."

At the village after that we didn't leave the jeep. People saw us arrive, but the only man who came to us was a quarry-owner in a jacket and pullover. He said to Mr Kudal in English, "The people need *guidance*."

"He is not for us," Mr Kudal said afterwards. "He employs a lot of labour and he is going to spoil thirty per cent of the vote. But I don't argue with people three days before an election."

Public meetings were to end in Ajmer at five on Saturday afternoon. But canvassing and private meetings could continue; and I heard from Mr Mukut's son, who was also Mr Mukut's election agent, that Mr Mukut and Mr Bishweshwar were to debate that evening before the Rotary Club of Beawar. A Rotary Club seemed an unlikely thing for a place like Beawar to have. But Beawar also had a Communist group. And it also, as I now learned, had one of India's most famous astrologers, Professor B. C. Mehta. Professor Mehta was a "commercial" astrologer: he specialized in market fluctuations. His cable address was MEHTA.

I heard all this from Professor Mehta's thirty-year-old lawyer son while we were waiting that afternoon for Mr Mukut at his campaign headquarters. Professor Mehta, being only a commercial astrologer, hadn't issued any statement about the Ajmer election. But young Mr Mehta was so confident of Mr Mukut's victory and was so obviously welcome at campaign headquarters – "His father's an astrologer," Mr Mukut's son said, introducing him – I felt there could have been no astrological discouragement. And Mr Mukut, when he appeared, in spotless white dhoti and koortah, with a black woollen waistcoat, was like a man touched with glory. The gentleness which he imposed on all who approached him now also held a little awe.

It was a long drive to Beawar. We got there at nightfall and found that nobody knew anything about a Rotary Club debate.

Somebody said that Mr Bishweshwar had got cold feet; but sabotage was sabotage, and all we could do was sit in the front room of the local hotel and drink coffee. I asked about Professor Mehta. The young hotel-owner said the Professor was not only his adviser but also a personal friend. He went out to telephone and came back with the news that the Professor was coming over as soon as he had finished his supper.

"From the beginning I've had faith in astrology," Mr Mukut said. "Every year I have a reading on my birthday. On the 30th of January I entered my sixty-ninth year and I had a reading then."

He wouldn't say what he had been promised. And when I asked whether Professor Mehta was his astrologer he gave his crooked long-lipped smile and didn't reply.

He became reflective. "An election has three stages. There's the excitement of the campaign. Then there's the tension. Then the reaction, whatever the result."

"What are you prepared for?"

He opened his sightless eyes. "*Anything.*"

But then he was restless; he wanted to leave; and he was led out to his car.

Professor Mehta was a small fat clean-shaven man of sixty in trousers and shirt. He had the distant manner of an overworked physician who has heard everything. He was unwilling to speak. As soon as he understood what I wanted he began to write, very fast, on a foolscap sheet: *Mrs Indira will win her own election by more than 50,000 votes. But she won't be able to get full majority in Centre. . . .*

I feel that after the busyness of the headquarters, and after the excitement of the drive, the mood of Mr Mukut's men changed there, in the stuffy little room of the Beawar hotel, when Mr Mukut's face clouded at the thought of the sabotaged evening.

On Sunday morning some of his supporters had premonitions of defeat. They came to me, as to an impartial witness, with stories that Mr Bishweshwar's men were distributing liquor in

two wards of the city, and with the warning that the next day
there would be leaflets, purporting to come from Mr Mukut,
saying that he had withdrawn, that he had all along been for Mrs
Gandhi.

Premonitions of defeat. And in the morning the disaster was
clear. Outside every polling booth on the road to Nasirabad there
was a decorated Indira Congress tent, where young men sat with
electoral rolls and waited to receive voters. At half past ten, the
sun already blazing, some of Mr Mukut's tents were only just
going up; and in some places there were no tents and sometimes
not even tables. Mr Mukut's son, defeat on his face, spoke of
sabotage. Outside one booth two of Mr Mukut's workers stood
forlorn, separate from the crowd; one of them shrugged and said,
"Harijan area".

In Nasirabad one young man was close to tears. The Congress
had ruled in Rajasthan for as long as he could remember; it was
rotten and corrupt and had at last seemed about to wither away;
now Mrs Gandhi had preserved it. "You've won, you've won,"
he said to Mr Kudal; and Mr Kudal, sympathetic to the young
man's pain, blinked fast.

The Congress had not withered away. Its organization had
remained intact and was behind Mrs Gandhi and Mr Bishweshwar.
The Congress hadn't really split. There had only been defections,
sufficient to provide acclamation and crowds (deceptive in a constituency with half a million voters) and what Mr Kudal had
called *tamashas*, excitements. In Ajmer the Opposition or Organization Congress, on whose behalf Mr Mukut was standing, was a
phantom party.

But Mr Mukut also had the Jan Sangh. The Jan Sangh was
strong in Ajmer City, and a bonus was that the poll there was
usually high, seventy per cent as against fifty per cent in the rural
areas. With a good majority in Ajmer City – dependent on a good
poll – Mr Mukut might still be in the fight. But it was in the Jan
Sangh areas of the city that Mr Mukut's disaster was most plain.
In Naya Bazaar, the area of small traders, a Jan Sangh stronghold,
the poll at one o'clock was under forty per cent; and Mr Mukut's

election tent, without a table (and the formality that imposes), only with a long bench, was overrun by small children and already looked abandoned.

The Jan Sangh voters were abstaining. It was the possibility Mr Mukut had always discounted. By allying itself with other parties, by supporting Mr Mukut, its old enemy, by softening its racial-communal Hindu line, the Jan Sangh had compromised its right-wing purity. It had ceased to be a crusade; in the eyes of its supporters it had become as "political" and tricky as any other party. And later that afternoon, when the news everywhere was that Mr Mukut was losing, some of those Jan Sangh abstainers were to go out and vote against him.

At half past four, half an hour before the booths closed, there were three people in Mr Mukut's campaign headquarters: a wizened old secretary at a table with a telephone that was now idle, a thin black-capped accountant in a dhoti who sat with his legs drawn up on a straight-backed chair, and a boy. Someone came in with a bill. The black-capped accountant, without changing his posture, considered the bill and spiked it. I stretched out an inquisitive hand towards the spike. Wordlessly, the accountant spun the spike away from me to the boy, who put it in a corner of the paper-littered floor.

Mr Bishweshwar, surrounded by his workers, sat in a basket-chair on the open concrete porch of his villa headquarters. He was in a state of great, laughing excitement and he was shouting into a telephone. Most of his workers were in trousers, shirts and pull-overs. But Mr Bishweshwar was in his politician's costume of homespun dhoti and koortah, the white panoply that spoke of Gandhian merit and, now, of its political rewards, all the things that went with being a member of parliament: the flat in New Delhi, the two free telephones, 51 rupees a day during parliamentary sittings, free first-class rail travel throughout India (with priority in reservations), and 500 rupees a month.

It was some time before I saw that Mrs Bishweshwar was also there, still and withdrawn, standing on the open porch as on a stage, draped in a dark-green sari, her head bowed and modestly covered in the presence of so many men: like a sorrowing classical figure, a symbol of downtrodden Indian womanhood.

Ten days later, after the remoter districts had voted, the count took place. The weather had turned, the heat was beginning; and on Highway 8 there were handcarts with little conical heaps of green and red powder for the gaieties of the Festival of Spring on the following day. The counting was done in a marquee in the Collectorate yard. Neither Mr Bishweshwar nor Mr Mukut was there. "The commander-in-chief doesn't have to be at the front," a counter said.

And Mr Mukut was spending this, the longest day of his political career, in his flat. It was going to be worse for him than we had expected. In Ajmer City – the counting was done district by district – he had only got 19,000 votes; Mr Bishweshwar had 43,000.

I said to Mr Mukut's son, "So Professor Mehta advised you wrongly?"

"He didn't *advise* us wrongly. His calculations were wrong."

Mr Bishweshwar was at his campaign headquarters. He was used now to his victory; he was at peace, but tired. The election had been a strain; he didn't share Mr Kudal's delight in the "sports" side. He had suffered at that moment when important people had seemed about to defect. He had been badly frightened by the Rawats, and he hadn't forgiven that damaging leaflet. "I'm going to sue. Let them apologise and so on. There's a lakh or two there."

But he had suffered mostly because of Mr Mukut, in whose shadow he had lived for so long. I asked whether he thought they might now have broken for good. He said, "I don't know. I went to see him yesterday. He didn't talk to me." And Mr Bishweshwar was anxious to show that he too, though young, had a record of service and sacrifice. He hadn't been to jail, like Mr Mukut; but because of his social work he hadn't found time to marry until he was thirty-two. "From the beginning I was interested in social service. I was scoutmaster in Government College. I don't know why, the poorer sections always attracted me. Since 1952 I have devoted myself to the peasantry."

He made it sound like a hobby. He had modelled himself on his uncle; he too was half Gandhian, half politician, and claimed the right to exercise political power because he had earned religious merit. And Mr Bishweshwar might so easily have been on the other side, against Mrs Gandhi. "It was a testing time for me," he said, speaking of the Congress split, "the choice between principle and personality." In the end he had managed to combine both: Gandhian principle and Mrs Gandhi's personality.

All afternoon his lead lengthened. At last it reached 66,000. Mr Mukut, in the days of his glory, had never had such a majority. The caste issues had nowhere mattered. The Kishangarh affair hadn't mattered; nor had the Rawat enticement. Only Udaipur's tour had had some effect. In that remote district, where he was a god, Udaipur had cut Mr Bishweshwar's lead to just over 3,000. The electorate had everywhere voted for Mrs Gandhi and *Garibi Hatao*; they had voted out of their common distress and need.

At about half past three Mr Bishweshwar and his wife came to the Collectorate. They were both in homespun, he in white, she in blue. He was smiling quite helplessly; she was abashed and delicate. As they walked up the middle of the marquee all of us at the District Magistrate's table rose. Someone ran up with a garland of gold and silver tinsel: it was for Mr Kudal, the triumphant election agent. The second garland, of marigold and white champa flowers, was for Mr Bishweshwar.

Outside, the crowd grew. And when, just before the results were announced, Mr and Mrs Bishweshwar left, going out the way they had come, the counters, who hadn't saluted their arrival, stood up with palms joined in the gesture of greeting and respect. The brass band, waiting outside, struck up *Colonel Bogey*. There was a float with the cow and calf in white. Men in a packed jeep scattered coloured powder on the crowd: the Festival of Spring, occurring one day early. And copies were being distributed of a one-sheet "extra" of the Hindi *Rajasthan Patrika*:

BISHWESHWAR GETS HUGE MAJORITY
Nephew Crushes Uncle

I thought I would go to Mr Mukut.

"I will come with you," Mr Kudal said. And when we were in the car he said, "I must come with you. Terrible. A man who has controlled the destinies of this district for two decades, to be defeated now by his nephew, his own creature."

In the top floor flat the unlined curtains were drawn in the front room and Mr Mukut sat cross-legged and still on his narrow bed. His eyes were closed and his head was held to one side. He was in clean white cotton, and the white was momentarily shocking, like the colour of death and grief. Half a dozen men, among them the black-capped accountant, were sitting silent on a spread on the terrazzo floor. Mr Kudal didn't speak; he went and sat on the floor with the others.

Mr Mukut's son came out and offered me a chair. He bent over his father, said, "Bapuji," and gave Mr Kudal's name and mine. At first Mr Mukut didn't move. Then, abruptly, he turned his head to face the room and, in a terrible gesture of grief, beat the back of his open hand hard on the bed.

No one spoke.

Mr Mukut's son brought out tea. He pulled the curtain open a little way: the barred, wire-netted window, the sunlight on the white wall of the terrace, the brown hills. He hung a brown waistcoat on his father's shoulders and the effect of the white was softened.

"They were canvassing votes for Indira," Mr Mukut said, "not for the candidate. Nowhere was the candidate in the picture." He hadn't yet accepted his defeat; he still dealt in the politics of personal merit. I asked whether he and Mr Bishweshwar might be friends again. He said, "I don't know. He came here yesterday. But he didn't say a word to me." He turned on the transistor and the six o'clock English news from Delhi was of Mrs Gandhi's landslide victory all over the country, of the defeat everywhere of old Congressmen who had miscalculated like Mr Mukut.

5*

"There are no morals now," Mr Mukut said. "The Machiavellian politics of Europe have begun to touch our own politics and we will go down."

Mr Kudal stood up.

"As election agent I have to make an appearance in the procession," Mr Kudal said, when we were outside. "Otherwise my absence will be misinterpreted."

We caught up with the procession in the bazaar. Men in open lorries were pelting everybody with little balls of coloured powder. "Give me seven minutes," Mr Kudal said, and disappeared into the crowd. When he came back his clothes and hair and face were satisfactorily stained with red. Red the colour of spring and triumph, and sacrifice.

III

Looking Westward

Mr Matsuda's Million-Dollar Gamble

Daily Telegraph Magazine, 14 July 1967

In June 1966 Mr Morihiro Matsuda, in his own words "a petty citizen of Japan, uneducated and anonymous", made history of a sort when he took four pages of The Times and New York Times for a "personal message" to the world. Mr Matsuda said – among many other things – that he had a plan for bringing about peace in Vietnam in a day or, at the outside, three days. He would not reveal his plan until he had "unrestricted power of attorney, on a blank sheet of paper" from the President, Secretary of State and Defence Secretary of the United States and from the Prime Ministers of Japan and Great Britain. "Please give me, Morihiro Matsuda, any and every authority to conduct world politics for just one day." It was expensive to advertise, Mr Matsuda said; it would take him ten years to save up again the £10,000 he had spent; but it was his duty to express his thoughts. He wanted no one's charity or "goodwill money". "The important thing is, it is a mistake to send £1 or £5 to Matsuda and expect him to do all the work to realize world peace. . . . Peace must be earned by courage and effort of everyone's conscience." Four months later Mr Matsuda advertised again.

HIS TWO four-page advertisements in The Times and New York Times last year – Idea for Peace in Vietnam – were not Mr Morihiro Matsuda's first extended writings. In 1963 he published, also at his own expense, but only in Tokyo, his Bible of Wisdom. This book, about 60,000 words, is what its title says. It is an attempt at a personal scripture, the work of a sage or aspirant-sage who is as yet without disciples or an amanuensis. Many of the ideas in Bible of Wisdom were restated in the advertisement. These ideas – about happiness, neutrality, the MM (Morihiro Matsuda) method of fasting, the merit of meditation in one's coffin, the construction of a profit-making Paradise – crowded out the Vietnam issue, and suggested that Mr Matsuda was aiming at more than the cessation of a single war.

The English version of the MM *Bible* is typewritten and offset and looks like the annual report of a small company. On the back of the title page, below the copyright notice, there are comments from "men of distinction": "the keenest pleasure", "nonsense", "clamour", "Bible of Bible", "threshold for culture". All these comments were composed by Mr Matsuda himself. *Bible* was offered to the public, in Japan and abroad, with the assurance that "if this book zooms into best-sellerdom I should like to use all the profits for the establishment of the Paradise." The Paradise is to be a mixture of holiday camp, monastery and factory. Mr Matsuda estimated its construction costs at £10,700,000. The selling price of *Bible* was seven shillings. In four years not a copy has sold anywhere.

Mr Matsuda feels he has done better with the advertisements. Most Japanese periodicals have written about him – he had the file out to show. Some have been hostile, but Mr Matsuda doesn't mind. He expected greater sympathy abroad, and he feels he has got it. *Epoca* magazine in Italy gave him five pages – Mr Matsuda's copy was worn from his brisk, flat-handed turning of the pages. *Life* gave him only two pages; but they called him a saviour.

And the letters. Mr Matsuda jumps up, making the small room smaller, and slides back a frail wall panel. He is a body-built five foot nine – he was in the body-building business until recently – and his gestures are as abrupt and large as his voice is deep. He takes out bundles of letters from a cupboard and dumps them all together over the magazines on the low table. Six hundred letters, each still in its envelope, each envelope neatly guillotined: another detail that reminds us of a fact which is obvious but not easy to grasp: that in spite of the setting, the low ceiling, the mats, the low table, the fragile partitions, all the daintiness of the Japanese house of school geography books, Mr Matsuda comes from an industrial city and is a businessman, a natural user of office equipment.

He looks on the letters as trophies. The number pleases him, but he hasn't read them all. It was news to him that one encouraging letter, on Claridge's paper, was from a Russian princess. He gave two deep grunts of pleasure when he heard, and held his head on one side. Then he recovered and said that the nobility couldn't really understand his ideas.

He has received little money. Just after the first advertisement American readers of the *New York Times* sent him 250 dollars. But there was a report in a Japanese weekly that Mr Matsuda was hoping to get a dollar from each reader of the *New York Times*; and Mr Matsuda refused the 250 dollars. He said he wasn't a beggar. Since then he has been sent only 300 dollars. He has kept this money, and intends now to keep whatever he gets. It won't be much. Over the months the letters have grown fewer; now he gets no more than one or two a week. But two Chicago newspapers have invited him to the United States. This was the call Mr Matsuda was waiting for. Once he is in America and suitably sponsored, he thinks he will make a million dollars.

Mr Matsuda is a businessman. He wouldn't say he has gambled; he would say he has invested. The advertisements cost £23,000. To find the money, he has had to sell his house and his block of fifteen flats. To give himself time for his movement, he has made over his mail-order body-building business to his former employees. They loan him £100 a month; this keeps him going for the time being. He lives now in a £25-a-month rented house in a muddy new road almost at the eastern limit of Tokyo. The houses here, in varying shades of blue, are diminutive and choked together; they have tile roofs and walls of finely corrugated tin; even the blossom gives no grace.

Mr Matsuda has no regrets. As a sage, his subject is happiness; as a businessman, he knows he has done the right thing. His routine has not greatly changed. His fishing tackle lies in the outer, mat-less room of his house, in a clutter of toys, cardboard boxes and body-building catalogues. This fishing is an aspect of his routine he has publicized; in his advertisement he even dramatized himself as someone with "the brand of the simple fisherman". In fact, he took up the hobby when his *Bible* failed; and in spite of difficulties – more and more barbed-wire fences – he continues to fish for four or five hours every morning on the Edo river. He has also maintained his sexual activity. Sexual vigour is one of the bonuses of his fasting; he says he enjoys sex "just in the way that children play".

To ask whether he thinks he has behaved fairly towards his two children or – sexual activity apart – towards his wife, his seventh, who reportedly disapproves, is to raise an irrelevant moral question. Mr Matsuda says he hasn't done a good thing or a bad thing. He has simply invested; and his sacrifice, or the fact of his sacrifice, now as widely reported as he expected, is part of that investment.

Mr Matsuda needs money. Without money he will not be able to do anything. He certainly won't be able to stop the Vietnam war. It comes from his theory of neutrality: once every man's interests are recognized, disputes vanish. It must be recognized, for instance, that the Vietnam war is kept going by American industrialists. But it must also be recognized that these industrialists have a point. Their fear of a recession if the war ends must be taken seriously. This fear must be allayed. Mr Matsuda thinks he can do it. He will protect Wall Street; he will develop America. That, no less, is his present aim. But first he must make a million dollars.

This is how he will do it. He will go to Chicago, to deal with the newspapers that have invited him. Then he will give lectures to the university about happiness and the seven degrees of beauty. He might also make a model of his indestructible motor car – no more deaths in road accidents – and sell the development rights. From Chicago he will go to New York. He will rent a room in the Time-Life building. Then he will go to the Patent Office and register his ten patents. He has a genius-creator or logic-trainer from which he expects much; he also thinks he will do well with a *go*-game, a type of Chinese chess. His rights established, he will return to the Time-Life building, take the lift to his room, and settle down to work. He might begin with a fast. The normal MM fast lasts for thirty days. In New York he will give them one of thirty-five days. The fast will startle America; it will be taken up by newspapers and his name will be known.

Then he will launch his necklace scheme. He will have necklaces manufactured in quantity and he will get the banks to distribute them. The necklaces will be sold for 10, 50, 100, 1,000 dollars. If the Vietnam war ends through his efforts in one hundred days, these necklaces can be returned and the buyers will get three times what they paid. So he will get America to invest in peace. If the war doesn't end – well, people will have their necklaces. Mr Matsuda calculates that he will make a million dollars from the sales of the MM necklace. All this money he will use for the cause, to advertise, to develop, to reassure Wall Street.

Mr Matsuda is not taken seriously in Tokyo. He is uneducated, a self-confessed black marketeer of the late 1940s, and he is Korean. In Japan the Koreans are immigrants, and immigrant stories attach to them. Their appearance is different, their faces being flatter and less accented than the Japanese; their food is different; they have a reputation for boisterousness and violence; and it is said that a Korean can be recognized by his smell alone. This – being a Korean – is not the only category Mr Matsuda falls into. In Japan, a land still of order, where class, character and mood are printed on the face for all to read, Mr Matsuda can also be recognized as the uneducated businessman. The main characteristic of this type is that it is made illogical by easy success. The grasp of cause and effect is weakened, and is replaced by a belief in good fortune and the rightness of decisions made under its influence. "It is essential," *Bible* says, "to start or invest in business when one's own fortune is strong. . . . See the waves on the sea. There are no similar waves because energies come from various directions." The successful businessman, energized, lifted above his fellows, can even say: "Show me the map of the country now and I will tell you where to drill for oil and where to dig for gold."

His confidence is total and business becomes confused with the religious impulse in a breathless exaltation. The businessman on whose shoulder the god of good fortune sits can cry with Mr Matsuda: "I am my own lord and master throughout heaven and earth."

Mr Matsuda's face can be read as honest, open, generous. Although in *Bible* he says that it is part of the highest wisdom, he is not such a master of the "reverse meaning" of words as he thinks. In both his advertisements he threatened to burn himself. But he wasn't serious; he wanted only to make a sensation. In the second advertisement he said he had been offered a job as a writer at 500 dollars a month. But that was only to appease the *New York Times* who, in their concern for Mr Matsuda, might otherwise have turned down his advertisement. In both cases the deceit is transparent. Mr Matsuda is no writer. And death – especially if accidental, and if imposed by man on man – is the one thing he hates and fears.

He wants to conquer death. He wants to live one hundred years. He wants to leave some memorial of his passage. Through all the reverse meanings of words and all the confused thinking, this is the impulse that can be discerned. This is what he has compounded with his business instincts and raised to religion. "I think I will die a painful and fearful death. I wonder why I alone must be tormented with such thoughts. . . . To me my death is the most sorrowful thing in this universe."

Now the fear is in the background. America and a million before him: a spectacular and much-ridiculed investment prospering: the god sits with Mr Matsuda. And he has conquered death. Every year for the last ten years he has done a thirty-day fast. It is his custom then and at other times as well to meditate in his coffin. It is a plain coffin of expensive Japanese cedar; ten years ago it cost £80. It is not equipped with the winking lights Mr Matsuda would like, to remind him of the pyre. But his imagination supplies that. So he keeps in touch with his fear and his private victory, which is also his luck.

*

It is with a vision of this victory that *Bible* begins. The detail is cinematic; the chapter is unlike anything else that Mr Matsuda has written.

The narrator – unidentified, but he is Mr Matsuda – finds himself in a group of a hundred students of the Juvenile Classification Office at Ueno railway station, the terminus in Tokyo of trains from the north. The students board a train and after an agreeable lunch get off at a country station. An hour's drive in a waiting bus takes them to a building marked "Goseiin Headquarters". In the information office there are five cameras behind the counter; in front of the counter, facing each camera, there is a chair. Each student pays, sits, and is photographed. Each student is then given a gown of white silk and shown a casket. The caskets are more than six feet long but weigh less than five pounds; they are made of corrugated cardboard and printed paper scented with Japanese cypress. Each student shoulders his casket and the white procession begins to climb the hill to the temple. From time to time the students put down their caskets and refresh themselves with orange juice. It is dusk when they get to the temple. They are perspiring and hungry; they place their caskets in a designated place and in that very place, seated on cushions, they are fed. Then they take off their white robes. In the valley below lights flicker. Like the evening lights of childhood, the narrator thinks: the lights of lonely farmhouses, fireflies, lights bringing to mind tales of ghosts. But these are the lights of industrial Japan, of automobiles and motor-cycles in the rush-hour.

The temple bell sounds four times. The students from the Juvenile Classification Office hurry to the stage in the main temple. Below a chandelier sits a man they know well. He is Mr O, a millionaire and a powerful politician. He wears a white gown and is flanked by lighted candles; before him, on a low table, two black-framed photographs of himself are set face to face. Incense burns before the photographs, and there is a dish of sacrificial rice.

"Please put on your white gowns again," Mr O says. "And get into your caskets."

Waiting, Mr O studies his photographs.

The narrator gets into his casket and once more smells the cypress-scented paper. The electric lights of the temple go out. Only the candles on either side of Mr O continue to burn.

"These caskets await all of you," Mr O says. "Even if you live for fifty years more. Deduct one third as sleeping time and another third as working time. That leaves you only six thousand full days. You cannot then say that you have girl friends or children or parents. The casket will be waiting. You cannot then say that you were not loved by your parents or that they were poor and other people were more fortunate or that your life was spoiled by treachery. There is only calcium in the urn. There is no such article as affection. You say you were born. I say a puppy was also born; the cause is the same. Do not think that your parents are divine. Learn the attitudes of the West. They are right to think of you Japanese as sentimental twelve-year-olds. Learn non-attachment. The youth of the West do not seek assistance from their parents. Learn independence. See the nobility of work rather than its burden. Get off the merry-go-round of avarice. Now please get out and burn your caskets and white gowns."

The lights go on. The air is frosty. The caskets and gowns are set ablaze, and the temple bell sounds ten times. The blaze dies down. Dying, it is reflected in the little mirrors hung on the surrounding trees. The narrator thinks he has never experienced anything more sublime; and he sees how foolish he has been to ignore death out of his fear of it.

"Please polish with the ashes the thing you were holding."

The narrator picks up the brass casket-knobs from the warm ashes and polishes them until they glitter.

"That part of you which was idle and pointless has been burnt away," Mr O says. "That part of you that knows death, and is meaningful, survives."

When the narrator goes back to the main temple he finds his own photograph, also in a black frame, on the same table as the photographs of Mr O – the millionaire, the politician.

The framework of the vision is perhaps derived – a Japanese photographer who read a draft of this article was certain that it was – but Mr Matsuda denies any inspiration and even denies that he is dealing in fantasy. The vision came to him, complete, one day in 1957 when he was meditating in his coffin during a fast. It passed through his mind; it existed. It is personal. So it no doubt is. The meditation on death is a Japanese common-place; but Mr Matsuda's conclusions were needed by him alone. If death is the final futility, it also mocks affections and renders painful relationships painless. It ridicules complaint and excuse. Death lifts a man out of himself and his affections. If death is the equal end of all, then it touches human achievement with true grandeur. The true futility, the puppy-existence, is the life of the man who at the end can only say that he has raised a family. Death makes achievement urgent. Death, so far from darkening the future, enhances it. It is the past that death abolishes.

The name Morihiro Matsuda, the repeating initials of which Mr Matsuda has turned into a flourish, is Japanese. Mr Matsuda took it when the Japanese Government, as an integration measure, required Koreans in Japan to take Japanese names. Mr Matsuda's original name was Sun Tokwan. He was born forty-five years ago in a riverside village some two hundred miles north of Pyongyang. His father worked as a labourer for a timber company and earned about 65 sen a day (100 sen make a yen and a yen was then worth about 2s). There were four children, and the whole family lived in a hut less than ten feet square. They ate pickled meat and pickled fish every day at every meal, with the cheapest sort of Tibetan wheat as an occasional extra.

Mr Matsuda was not strong as a child and wasn't sent out to work like his brothers. He went to the church school. He liked the church better than the school. The boys teased and beat him. He didn't fight back; he had no friends or protectors; and when he got home there was no one to console him. His mother was out most of the day, looking for food for the pigs she kept; she managed to sell three or four a year. There were fights at home, too, when Mr Matsuda's father came home drunk. But his father never beat him; his father always handled him gently. It might have been because he was weak or because he looked exactly like his father. More frightening than school or drunken father was the picture of hell-fire in the house of the Roman Catholic priest next door.

Mr Matsuda's interest in Roman Catholicism faded as he grew older. He read a fair amount; he especially liked *Resurrection* by Tolstoy and Gide's *La Porte Etroite*. When he was twenty he thought he would go to Japan and try to get into a college. One brother, who was now running his own iron foundry, gave him 100 yen for the journey; his other brother, who had already emigrated, met him at Tokyo Central Station. Mr Matsuda failed two entrance examinations. He was an uncompromising candidate. He thought of himself as a "unique existence" and didn't see why he should learn foreign languages. He laid aside the black student's uniform, the only clothes he had brought from Korea, and became a labourer.

He remained a labourer all through the war. But later, in occupied Japan, there were opportunities for a Korean citizen. An acquaintance urged him to go into black-marketing. It turned out to be simple. His first deal was in sugar. He took a taxi to the barracks of the 7th Cavalry Division and loaded up with 500 yen's worth. Within hours he had sold the sugar for 900 yen. After six months of trading he had made 100,000 yen, at a time when a house could be built for 1,000 yen.

"Adequate food and clothing make people learn graces" – the observation is in Mr Matsuda's first advertisement – and now he gave himself a holiday. He went to an inn in the Chiba Prefecture, which adjoins Tokyo, and idled in luxury for a year. When the money was exhausted he began dealing in soap and rubber on the black market in Hokkaido. He used the profits to start a *sushi* (raw fish) shop in Asakusa in downtown Tokyo. He employed a woman in the shop. She was ten years older than he. She became his first woman, and they lived together for three years. Then he began to manufacture pin-ball machines. He lost his money, the *sushi* shop and the woman.

But it didn't matter now. From now on money was easy to the

Korean labourer's son, himself a labourer; and women were easy, to the man with the "foolish Korean face" who had had his first sexual experience at twenty-three in a brothel. The miracle had occurred: good fortune had come to Mr Matsuda, proof of what he had known for some time: that he was a "unique existence".

He had used the words in his first advertisement, and they interested me. They held less and more than simple arrogance; they were a description of the man of destiny, the man who felt himself marked. I wanted Mr Matsuda to go back to his first apprehension of this fact about himself, back to his childhood, the boy in straw shoes in the Korean winter when the river froze over.

I had spoken too quickly. I was misinterpreted.

"Yes," Mr Matsuda said. "I was born without the sense of smell. And I was born with one breast missing."

The interpreter broke off. Mr Matsuda continued to talk. He put his hand on his gabardine windcheater, over his breast, and made a gesture; his face was twisted with remembered pain. But now I had misinterpreted. He was still answering a question about his childhood. But he had gone beyond his defects; the look of pain was for his first experience of beauty, when he was five. His mother wanted him to wear a kimono with buttons – it was the modern style. He had rejected the buttons; he had insisted on ribbons.

Thirty years passed before he had a second experience of beauty. Then he was experimenting with fasts and the coffin, defeating death; and it was during a fast that his eyes had been caught by a Japanese sign. His breast ached at the beauty of that sign and in his delirium he found himself playing with the size of the characters, now making them tiny, now making them enormous. Out of this experience arose his theory of beauty, which is in *Bible*. The beautiful is the manageable; to be beautiful, terror has first to be tamed.

We had been talking for almost four hours. The interpreter and the stenographer were tired; I was tired. Mr Matsuda was still fresh. His wife brought in glasses of Coca-Cola. Mr Matsuda ignored her and she looked at no one. I tried to read her face, especially for that disapproval about which I had heard. But her face told me nothing; and Japanese to whom I later showed her photograph said it was a Korean baby-face, characterless.

Presently, putting on our shoes in the outer room, we went outside ourselves. It was still raining. In the muddy road there were groups of heavy-thighed schoolboys coming back from school: black peaked caps, black Prussian uniforms, thick-soled white canvas shoes. Mr Matsuda led us over boards laid on the mud in his yard to the unpainted corrugated-iron shed just at the back of his house. We went past the kitchen; in the open doorway an aproned woman stared expressionlessly at us.

"The wife?" someone in our party asked in a whisper.

"No. She was wearing a green dress, if you remember."

The coffin was in the shed, with much household junk. It was unvarnished; it stood on its end on a stack of scantlings. It had stain marks and looked old; at the top of the lid there were two roughly-made panels that swung out on hinges. Mr Matsuda lifted the lid away and was anxious to get in, to give us a photograph.

Later he drove us back to central Tokyo in his Japanese estate car. It was a new car – a replacement for a Buick, as I understood: part of the advertisement sacrifice – but it had been casually handled. The seats were grubby and there was litter on the carpets. As he drove he spoke, and now he didn't even wait for the interpreter. Leaning back in the driving seat, he spoke without pause; his harsh voice rose and rose. He was speaking of his American trip again, outlining all his plans and hopes. Traffic was heavy. Beyond our closed windows, fog, fumes and rain: eastern Tokyo a worse-than-Midland townscape, in tin.

Mr Matsuda wanted our second meeting to be at the Tokyo Press Club. He knew it well; he had spoken there twice. But I also knew that he was on the look-out for a press agent for his American trip, and I said it would be better if we met at my hotel. He said he would bring his wife to drive him back home.

He might want to do some drinking, and in Japan the police are fierce about people who drink and drive. In *Bible* Mr Matsuda describes himself as a drunkard; sage-like, he makes a fuss about what he considers his unlikely addiction. In the end his wife didn't come; but he had a beer. He brought the copies of *Epoca* and *Life* with him, and the letter he was sending off to the princess in Claridge's.

I wanted to hear about the necklace scheme again. I didn't think I had got it right. But I had. I said I thought he would sell more necklaces if he promised to pay up if he *didn't* stop the war. He didn't agree. Americans had contributed millions for the cause of peace; and if *Life* and *Time* and the *Reader's Digest* publicised his mission, he was sure he would do well. The necklace scheme, besides, wasn't his idea. It was *Life's*. They wanted to sell necklaces and they had asked him to help. But he didn't want to be employed by *Life*. He just wanted to sell the MM necklace; he thought *Life* would co-operate. I said it was more likely that there would soon be two new necklaces on the American necklace market. He laughed, and added independently, in English, shaking his head over his beer, "America many, many money."

"What will you do if you fail, Mr Matsuda?"

It was a foolish question.

"I can't fail."

So far, in the unfamiliar hotel, he had been subdued. But the beer reanimated him. He jumped up, walked to the bookstall and bought the latest issue of *Life*; his attitude to that magazine was already proprietorial. He came back to the table and, reading my face, said to the interpreter, "I see I have astonished him. But let him think of Columbus and the egg." It is one of his favourite stories; it occurs twice in *Bible*.

Admiration assists Mr Matsuda's misconception of the West he proposes to save by conquest. In *Bible* Mr Matsuda even attributes to the West the attainment of the Hindu-Buddhist ideal of non-attachment. He can find philosophical balance in the protest demonstrations of "English gentlemen". As *Bible* says, "They never denounce the policeman crying severally 'Damn tax-eaters!' On the contrary, they are taking pleasant lunches sitting and singing with placards putting erect." This idealism is to be admired; it also appears as something that might be exploited. It has led Mr Matsuda into absurdity. But he is too removed for comedy. Equally, there is no tragedy or pathos in his present adventure. His situation – a favourite English word in Japan – holds its own cure.

I asked a middle-aged Japanese, a man of culture, what he thought would happen to Mr Matsuda.

"Our businessmen of the Matsuda type and at the Matsuda stage," he said, "are not crazy in any medical sense. They just feel they are bound to win. But if they fail and fail and fail again, they can take the hint. They will know when good fortune has left them. Then they usually become ordinary again."

Mr Matsuda will die.

In 1970 Time Magazine *reported that Mr Matsuda – now separated from his wife – was working as a lorry-driver in Yokohama.*

Steinbeck in Monterey

Daily Telegraph Magazine, 3 April 1970

A WRITER IS in the end not his books, but his myth. And that myth is in the keeping of others.

Cannery Row in Monterey, the one John Steinbeck wrote about, disfigures a mile of pretty Californian coastline. The canneries used to can sardines; but the sardines began to disappear from Monterey Bay not long after Steinbeck published his book in 1945; and today all but one of the canneries have closed down. The cannery buildings remain, where they have not been destroyed by fire: white corrugated-iron buildings, as squat and plain as warehouses, backing out into the sea over a low cliff, braced by timber and tons of concrete which now only blasting can remove. Some are abandoned and show broken windows; some are warehouses; some have been converted into restaurants, boutiques, gift-shops.

The old Row has gone: the stink of fish and fish-fertilizer, the cutters and packers who could work up to sixteen hours a day when a catch was in, the winos, the derelicts who slept in pipes in empty lots, the whores. It was what Steinbeck wrote about but transmuted. What remains is like a folk-memory of community, wine, sex and talk. The tourists come for the memory. The name, Cannery Row, was made official in 1958, long after the sardine went away; before that it was Ocean View Avenue. And today, in Ring's Café next door to the Steinbeck Theatre in Steinbeck Circle – the whole complex on the site of a former cannery – the new shop-keepers and business people of the Row are meeting to talk about what they might do to get the tourists in in 1970.

1970 is the bicentennial of the founding of Monterey by the Spaniards. Some people in Ring's remember the centennial of

1947; that was the centennial of the American seizure. The main
street of Monterey (today a wasteland, awaiting renewal) was
painted gold and there was dancing in the streets. History in the
Monterey Peninsula is this sort of fun. Steinbeck wrote angrily
of Indian servitude and American land-grabbing; but there is a
mixed-up myth here of a gay and gracious Mexican past, of
heroic Spanish missionary endeavour, and numerous Indian
slaves, all converts, happily accepting the whip for religious mis-
demeanours. In the dereliction of Monterey every adobe from
Mexican times is preserved and labelled; there is even a movement
to have the first Spanish missionary, "the first Californian",
canonized. The American seizure is celebrated on the Fourth of
July with a costume pageant devised by the Navy League and the
Monterey History and Art Association: old-time señoritas and
Yankees listening companionably to the proclamation of
annexation.

Ring's café has been in Monterey for some time, but on the
Row for just over a year. Like many new places on the Row,
Ring's honours the fishing past with a fishing net in its windows
and wooden fish caught in the net. The proprietor is an old
advertising man; from his café he publishes *The Monterey Foghorn*,
a four-page satirical sheet whose cause is Cannery Row, gaiety
and youth. Ring's offers "beer, skittles and vittles"; it says it is
"under no management" and has "the world's cuisiest cuisine".
There are paintings; the Peninsula is full of artists. At the top of
the inner wall a trompe-l'oeil painting continues the braced
timber ceiling of the cannery. And above the bar, among other
posters, is one advertising "Doc's Birthday".

This was an event that Ring's staged last year, to bring to life
and perhaps to perpetuate something in the book. "Doc" was the
marine biologist in *Cannery Row*, the educated man around whom
the others idled. Mack and the boys gave a party for Doc's
birthday, and the party went predictably wild. Doc was a real
person on the Row, Doc Ricketts; *Cannery Row* is dedicated to
him. Steinbeck lent him money to buy the low unpainted wooden
lab which is squashed between two cannery buildings and will

now, as a men's club, be preserved. In 1948 a Southern Pacific locomotive ran into Doc's motor-car one evening on the level-crossing just above the Row, and Doc was killed. On the bar of Ring's, below glass, is a large photograph of the accident: Doc on a stretcher in the grass, the wrecked Ford, the locomotive, the crowd.

Fact, fiction, folk-lore, death, gaiety, homage: it is unsettling. But it is how myth is made. Doc as the tallest "character" on the Row: it is as unquestioned now as the myth of gaiety. No one in Ring's can say why Doc was such a character. He was nice to everybody, they say; he drank a lot; he liked the girls. It is the book, of course, and Steinbeck. But the book itself recedes.

There are about thirty people in Ring's. Solid bald men; younger men in dark glasses; middle-aged ladies in suits; an intense young woman in a check suit and matching deerstalker cap; a mother of two, with the yawning two; a Chinese lady. The solemn young man with steelrimmed glasses, drooping moustache, leather waistcoat and patched jeans is one of the Peninsula's artists; he and his wife run an ambitious boutique called Pin Jabs. He used to cycle up to the Row from Monterey in the old days. But most of the people here are new. Many have read *Cannery Row* and say they adore it; but some have not read any more Steinbeck.

The chairman, a gentle, slow-speaking sculptor of sixty-four, is one of the few people now on the Row who knew Steinbeck. He is a long-time Californian and knew Steinbeck in the 1930s, in the days of failure and poverty, when "if you didn't know about his background you wouldn't have known he was a writer". Steinbeck never spoke about his work; he was, outwardly, like the people he mixed with and wrote about. But the sculptor remembers the writing of the last page of *The Grapes of Wrath*. The novel ends in a black night of flood, when, the world a void, her own baby born dead, her family scattered, Rose of Sharon offers her breast to a lost and starving old man.

"I happened to be in his house that night. A little house he had then in Los Gatos. It was about three o'clock. I'd gone to bed and I heard him call out, 'I've got it! I've got it!' I got up, everybody else got up, and he read out this last piece. The only piece I ever heard him read out."

The sculptor is willing to forget Steinbeck's later books; for the early, Californian books, "when he was like in his own place", he feels the deepest affection; and his attitude to Steinbeck comes close to piety.

He rises now, calls the meeting to order, and asks for ideas for Cannery Row pageants or "projects" that might get financial support from the Monterey Bicentennial Committee and so get the tourists in next year.

"The only project we have so far is getting perhaps one of the old tanks and making a little house of it and having explanatory material there about the family that lived there." The Malloys of *Cannery Row* set up house in an old locomotive boiler, crawling in through the fire-door; they rented out subsidiary pipes to lodgers; but then Mrs Malloy began to cry for curtains and nagged her husband away. "Only thing we have so far. We need projects. I sure need your help."

"I've just finished *Cannery Row*," a young woman says. After such a flourish, what? She suggests "a little kind of walking tour. With a map. Have the different spots, like Doc's place, what was there then, what's there now. . . ."

"I suppose some kind of designation on the buildings."

"We don't want to get too historical."

The girl in the deerstalker suggests a tour of the surviving cannery.

"You mean the sequence of the machinery. Where the fish came in, where they went out. . . ."

"What we want is a brochure like the Hearst Castle – "

"This isn't a Hearst Castle. This is spread out a little."

" – simultaneously bringing out the historical aspect."

Speech is slow, lingering. The ideas come slowly, linger, fade. A Steinbeck film festival. Steinbeck plays. The hiring of a "colourful character" to wander about the Row. Each shop featuring one Steinbeck book.

"If there could be a trade fair," the girl from Pin Jabs says.

"We have a lot of vacant lots. A lot of the action of the book took place in vacant lots, and – "

"Things happen in the vacant lot, and we get no activity at the other end. We want something that will give *complete* activity from A to Z."

"Something more like Doc's Birthday. Let Cannery Row be Cannery Row, and downtown be downtown."

"You're talking about something that's got to have some life going in it for three, four months."

". . . dancing in the streets."

"For three, four months?"

". . . in the empty lots. Every two hours have a different band."

"Trouble is, we talk about sunny California. But it gets pretty cold at nights."

"They could have like a pass to Cannery Row. It could cost five dollars and they could get a drink in the different places. A pass. The Gold Key of Cannery Row."

"You don't want to scare off the elderly."

The mother of the two rises with the two, now quite stupefied. She says she has to go. But she wants to say one thing. She is a mother of two, plump and pretty and perfectly serious; she gets respectful attention. They've got to raise money for the advertising, she says; and she has a couple of suggestions. "Like have a carnival down here or something. Whole day." She loses her audience. She suggests auctions. "The restaurant people could auction a meal." The restaurant people don't twitch. "The other people could auction – "

There is a decent pause after she and the two leave.

"We're talking about auctions and things. We're talking about nickels and dimes."

They are not tycoons, these people who have invested in the Cannery Row name; they are a little like people infected by the atmosphere which they are promoting. They call themselves "the little people". The big people are off-stage: the owners of the cannery buildings, investors in real estate, to whom the rents and a percentage of the profits go. Older, non-tourist businesses might go on. Like the Natural Science Establishment, which for more than a decade has been offering embalmed cats, among other things. "We can make immediate shipment of any quantity. All our embalmed cats are shipped in waterproof plastic bags." But for the last six or seven years the little people have been coming and going with their boutiques and batiks. Where is yesterday's "Den of Antiquity"? Can "Antimacassar Factory and Psychedelic Tea Cozies" depend on its sense of fun? Not all ventures on the Row last; at least one sculptor has hanged himself.

In fifteen years, when the leases begin to run out, the high-rise hotels will go up on this reclaimed bit of pretty Californian coastline. But by that time the Cannery Row myth, which the busy little people have created, will have grown hard.

Myths grow fast here. California, of the sun and the fruit and the cool Pacific shore, is where Americans go when they have been weakened by America. And the twenty-five or thirty square miles of the Monterey Peninsula are special. "It seems," says Wesley Dodge, one of the new "big people" of the Row (he's made eighty times his investment in cannery buildings and machinery), "it seems like there's always been a group or something here that's anti to what the mass is interested in." There have been beatniks and hippies. ("Hippies have money," the girl from Pin Jabs says, with respect and hope.) In the old days it was the bums with their "bindles", riding the freight cars to the Peninsula from all parts of the country.

And not only bums and beatniks. Many years ago a visiting Hindu yogi reported that the vibrations at Pacific Grove, to the west of Monterey – it begins where Cannery Row ends – were as good as anything he had found in the Himalayas. The leading bookshop in Monterey, among the restaurants and gift-shops on Fisherman's Wharf, is mystically inclined. And something of mystic exhilaration remains in the ordered pinewoods and timber lodges of Asilomar, a noted conference centre, where even on this Fourth of July weekend they are gathering for a Philosophical Roundtable.

Bang! Boom! With AURAS *flashing, sparkling and colorful as Fourth of July skyrockets, here we are* CELEBRATING *our latest Conference series get-together.* WELCOME EACH AND EVERYONE!! *We think we've a joyous and full-filled* PROGRAM, *so once again please write down those* DREAMS, VISIONS, IMPRESSIONS *and share them with all of us along with that* SPECIAL PAST LIFE COSTUME *for our* BIG PARTY NIGHT JUBILEE.

The Roundtable's cause is reincarnation. But the thin young girl from San Diego, whose sister was in it first, says that the aim is "to bring back like the people to God". Her eyelids are coloured green; her painted eyebrows slant upwards in a waving line. The weekend costs 45 dollars.

Pacific Grove also has a famous festival in honour of the Monarch butterfly; a legend has been worked out which involves a lost princess and her sorrowing Indian subjects. Just to the south of the vibrations and the butterflies is an area of golf courses and country clubs dedicated to *Treasure Island*. Stevenson came to Monterey as a young man and used the topography of part of the Peninsula in that book; everything is appropriately named. And then there is Carmel-by-the-Sea.

If Monterey, just two miles away, is Mexican, then Carmel is English. Everything in Carmel is small. The houses are small, the signs are small, the shops are small and their windows display the littlest things. The smallness goes on and on; it becomes tininess, it becomes grand; it is tininess on the American scale. On a main street a cluster of rustic doll's houses with geraniums outside the tiny windows turns out to be an expensive motel. There are crooked little roofs, crooked little gates. A shop is called Hansel and Gretel, a house The Wooden Shoe.

Steinbeck called them "the Pixie people of Carmel". There was a vogue here in the 1920s for doll's houses for real people. There are no street lights in Carmel, no postal deliveries; the houses have no numbers; and there is a fiercely protective city council. The whole elfin English thing has become confused with an ideal not so much of literature and art as of the literary and artistic life, of culture flourishing in a certain "atmosphere" and

6

expressing itself in a separateness from commercial America. The place is a raging commercial success. Four million tourists come every year; people come back again and again. There are one hundred and fifty shops and boutiques. Every block of the rustic shopping centre is cross-hatched, sometimes on more than one level, with arcades, each with its directory of linked wooden slabs hanging from a wrought-iron standard.

Carmel deals, above all, in art. In galleries that look like those in Bond Street, in glass-fronted studios that are like film-sets, answering every concept of the glamour of the artistic life, waves break on rocks in sunlight and moonlight, at sunrise and sunset; Monterey cypresses bend before the wind in every twentieth-century idiom. "Verdult Art Gallery presents a showing of Dutch Master Paintings by William Verdult." "The immediate acceptance of her work by the public brought her to the decision that the painting profession was to be hers and her speciality in the art field was to be the ever present challenge of an ever changing sea." "While in high school, Garcia worked . . . for Ed Ricketts, the noted marine biologist and true-life model for 'Doc' in John Steinbeck's novel, *Cannery Row*. . . . Although primarily an impressionist, Garcia's style has ranged from realism to abstraction."

In the setting, it is the quantity of this art, the confidence of it all, and again the quantity, that unsettle the visitor. It is as though, at its geographical limits, a culture is parodying itself: rich middle America, middle in everything, paying its holiday tribute to art, the idea of artists and freedom, and buying prettiness.

At Seaside the blacks are starting a boycott of something. At Fort Ord, just a couple of miles away, soldiers in green fatigues are training for Vietnam. Beyond that, the endless level lettuce-fields of Salinas, the bitter landscape of stoop-labour. But America ends where the Monterey Peninsula begins. On the Peninsula all is fairyland.

To be received into fairyland: it is a strange fate for Steinbeck, the novelist of social conscience, the angry man of the 1930s, the propagandist for the unions, the man who always scoffed at the myth-making capacity of his Peninsula. Probe among the shopkeepers and you find that Steinbeck didn't care, after Doc's death, what happened to Doc's lab. Look up the files of the *Monterey Peninsula Herald* and you find that in 1957, when there was some talk of preservation, Steinbeck, writing from Manhattan, where he had moved, was for pulling the whole Row down.

Or perhaps, he wrote, the canneries "should be kept as a monument to American know-how. For it was this forward-looking intelligence which killed all the fish, cut all the timber, thereby lowering the rainfall. It is not dead either. The same know-how is lowering the water-table with deep wells so that within our lifetime California will be the desert we all look forward to."

This is the sort of anger Monterey forgives and forgets. It is true that during the war the annual sardine catch suddenly doubled, to nearly a quarter of a million tons. But it is better for legend that the fish of Monterey should be as mysterious as the butterflies of Pacific Grove. It is better to say, as the lady from Carmel said, that "the sardines just *flipped* their tails and went away".

Steinbeck himself bears some responsibility. His sentimentality, when prompted by anger and conscience, was part of his strength as a writer. Without anger or the cause for anger he writes fairy-tales. He has the limitations of his Peninsula. He yielded to the success of *Cannery Row*; he wrote a sequel, *Sweet Thursday*. He parodied his charm; he turned the Row into fairyland.

Don Westlake's mother worked in a cannery from 1936 until 1950. Westlake himself began to work part-time in the cannery cafeteria when he was twelve. He graduated from the local high school in 1952; he is now in his early thirties. Westlake's mother and stepfather, Californian for five generations, left Monterey for Oregon last year. Westlake himself now lives in San Francisco and is a public relations man for a pharmaceutical firm.

He is tall and lean, easy of manner, the image of the healthy, educated Californian; and his Cannery Row background comes as a surprise. But it is Cannery Row that has driven him, as, he says, it has driven many of the sons of those "Okies" who worked in the Row.

"They weren't all Italians and Poles. Many people don't know that. Okie: that was the worst insult in the world. It was to be just next to an animal. But you have to be careful nowadays. The sons of those people are the leaders of California. You use the word in distinguished company and you notice strange looks." Not all broke away. "Some of the boys I knew fell into their parents' way of life. Some have been to jail. As far as I'm concerned they could burn the whole Row down. It's all right for the tourists. But they and Steinbeck are romanticizing something that wasn't there. Living in pipes and boilers. That wasn't funny. Those people were human derelicts. They had nowhere else to live."

Westlake talks less with anger than with distress. He talks like a man who will never exorcize a personal hurt.

"And the place used to *stink*. Not only the fish. The heads and tails they cut off and turned into fertilizer. Every cannery had its fertilizer plant. The fish came in in the morning. There were no sonic devices in those days. You could tell where the sardines were only by the phosphorescence at night. Every cannery had a special whistle, and when the catch came in the cannery would blow one whistle for their cutters and a later one for their packers. When you heard your whistle you would get up and drive down to the Row. We lived at Seaside; it was always the lower-class, working area.

"The girls would stand at a long trough, in front of what looked like a tractor-tread. They would drop one sardine in each tread. You would start at three in the morning and go on for twelve, fourteen, sixteen hours, until the packing was finished. In the thirties the girls were paid by the can. Sometimes they got no more than 25 dollars a week. During the war, when the unions came in, they were paid by the hour.

"Something you don't hear much about now is the fish poisoning. The pilchard sardine has a toxin to which some people are allergic. The hands then become red and raw and pitted and scaled like a fish. Blood poisoning can make the hands red right up the arm. Some people lost fingers through the gangrene. In those days the only cure for this fish poisoning was to soak your hands in epsom salts. My mother never had it badly. But you would see these frightened people soaking their hands in epsom salts. They were frightened because if their hands went bad they wouldn't get any more work for the rest of the season. And when the season was over there was no work for anyone. It was a boon to Monterey when the canneries were forced to close down and the people who were being exploited were forced to leave. Though most of those refugees from Monterey are still in packing. Fruit packing, in the valleys."

The only place Westlake remembers with affection is the Bear Flag, the brothel Steinbeck wrote about, one of six on the Row at its wartime peak.

"It was my favourite hang-out when I was five. Some nights my stepfather and I would drive up to meet my mother and we would have to wait until the packing was finished. The girls would take me in then from the car. I can't remember what they looked like. All I remember is they were big motherly types. I was always warm and comfortable when I was there."

"Sentimental?" says Wesley Dodge, the post-cannery millionaire on the Row. "You going to be sentimental about whores? They're talking about things I didn't participate in. I didn't participate in the whores."

Dodge is a fat, pink man with glasses. He is sixty-four and says he is too old to be happy; but he smiles easily. His office, in a converted cannery, is where the women's lavatories used to be. "Twenty on that side, twenty on this side." The purchase of this particular cannery was one of his coups. "Flause was asking 240,000 dollars. I said, 'Mr Flause, I don't want to give you a price. We are too far away. Mr Flause, all I will give you is 70,000 dollars.' I called on the man every day for two years. I never mentioned price again. I would go around the cannery with him, inspecting the machinery. And he would turn the

motors on, just to keep everything in order. One day he put his
foot on a pump and it fell over and he said, 'Dodge, you've just
bought yourself a cannery.' I paid a deposit, and as I sold the
machinery, I paid him."

If the idle canneries had come up for sale all at once, Dodge and
his associates mightn't have been able to buy the seventy per cent
of Cannery Row they did buy. But the cannery owners held on,
hoping that the sardine might come back. For a time some canned
anchovies, labelling them "sardine-type". "The canneries dropped
over nine years. One by one."

It was as a dealer in second-hand machinery that Wesley Dodge
came to the dying Row. A Fresno man, one-eighth Cherokee,
self-educated, used from youth to working "from can till can't",
he had already made and lost two fortunes, in fruit in the 1930s,
in a private airline in the 1940s. His knowledge of the second-hand
machinery business came from his own love of machines and
from "watching other nationalities", mainly Jews. "I am one of
the few Gentiles in second-hand machinery." The secret is to buy
well. "Everybody in America is a salesman. I learned to be a
buyer. If you buy right, selling's no problem." He sold Cannery
Row machinery all over the world. "Apple-canning, fish-
reduction, tallow plants which take chicken waste. I didn't
necessarily sell back to the fish business." They sometimes got
more from the machinery than they paid for the cannery.

And there was Dodge's interest in ocean property. "All my
life I wanted to own ocean property. There's no ocean in
Nebraska. Does that mean anything to you? No ocean in
Oklahoma. There's an Atlantic Ocean, there's a Pacific Ocean.
In between there's no ocean. In my commercial life anyone that's
owned ocean property had it made."

There was a stripped cannery to be seen, the last. We drove
there in his Cadillac.

"It's air-conditioned," he said, as I fumbled with the car
window.

It was almost dark in the cannery building; the corrugated-iron
roof looked higher inside. Small motors with fresh grey paint on

their casings covered half the concrete floor. On the other side, no longer in sequence, under polythene, were the big, complicated machines. Moving lightly, he undraped, touched, felt, explained. Here, still looking new after twenty idle years, were the "tractor-treads" into which the girls – now scattered, and always women – dropped the sardines one by one, for hours; here was the sardine gut-sucker; here were metal arms so finely balanced that only full cans would depress them to that track which led to the capping machine.

"There's about 80,000 dollars here," Dodge said. "I live this machinery. Machinery isn't difficult if you *live* it."

It was time for a drink. Dodge himself, after many years of whisky, eighteen to twenty shots a day, now drinks only orange juice and Seven-Up. We went to the Outrigger. It was on the sea side of a converted cannery, past gift-shops whose walls dripped pink bougainvillaea. Three gas jets on tall metal poles flared at the entrance. A spotlight picked out rocks in the sea. We entered a carpeted green grotto, of Polynesian atmosphere, with a waterfall, and stepped out into openness: the old cannery pier, carpeted, re-timbered and glassed-in. We were on water, in the middle of the bay, the lights of Seaside and Monterey curving far to the right. After the desolation of the Row, the beauty of rock and water was abrupt. It was the future.

"The square-foot value of the property will be many times greater than when Steinbeck was here," Dodge said. He pointed to where a basket-like metal frame rose out of the sea. "The old hopper. That's where they unloaded the fish. They were pumped in through a pipe into the cannery."

From the high-rise, resort future of Cannery Row Dodge has withdrawn. For two million dollars, paid in cash, he and his associates have sold out to a San Francisco millionaire. "He is seventy-five, but he has a different idea of his life than I have of mine." Dodge feels he has had a full business life; even while on the Row he went back into fruit, where he had failed thirty years before, and "made a lot there, a lot". Dodge, who has no children of his own, is interested now in educating the children of his relatives and friends. He would like to support a hospital or some kind of research; but he is concerned to make his money work. "You don't get the true value of your dollar with a foundation. You are just paying the salaries of the top men."

Later, driving down the Row back to the centre of Monterey, he slowed down beside an empty, fenced-in lot. "Frank Raiter's place. A real Cannery Row character. Over eighty, worth several millions. His cannery burned down two years ago. But every morning he comes here and sits in his – not a Cadillac, the one next to a Cadillac, I forget – and reads the *Wall Street Journal* for a couple of hours."

The Row bent and straightened again. It was just here that Doc Ricketts died in 1948 – the scene under glass in Ring's café. Dodge talked about Steinbeck. He never met him; he spoke to him once, on the transatlantic telephone, to get permission to use his name for the Steinbeck Theatre.

"He hurt California terribly. I like *Tortilla Flat*, I like *Cannery Row*. I know those paisanos without knowing them, if you know what I mean. But he wrote *The Grapes of Wrath*. I've no background of being able to say this book's better than that one, but it hurt me to read *The Grapes*. It wasn't factual enough. You know what an Okie is? They moved here in *hordes*. Thousands. Thousands a *day*. I was making five to six dollars an hour, packing fruit. When they came they worked for fifteen cents, twenty cents. Fifty cents a day. Any amount a day. And I was out of a job. We had problems in 1932. They came and compounded our problems. But Steinbeck wrote *The Grapes*. It's something that people look at us as, as Californians. And he sold a lot of books. You can't assess the damage."

New York with Norman Mailer

Daily Telegraph Magazine, 10 October 1969

NORMAN MAILER ALWAYS campaigned in a correct dark-blue suit. Towards the end he cut his hair short. A week or so before election day the Mailer campaign staff lost some hair as well. The hefty thirty-year-old campaign manager shaved off his little beard, and the sideboards of others were abbreviated. Angry young necks showed fresh and clean; plain dark ties closed up open shirts. The first order, the one that had got rid of the manager's beard, had come from Mailer himself; it had worked its way down; and for three or four days in this last week the candidate and his staff were partially estranged.

"There's been some degree of role-confusion," one shorn young man said.

They were still loyal at headquarters, but they said they were loyal to the campaign, the cause, the ideas. They spoke less of "Norman"; they spoke of "the candidate" and they made the election sound like a day of sacrifice. Where someone had pinned up *Get Ready for the Norman Conquest* someone now chalked an anti-Mailer obscenity in red, but shyly, not using the name, only the initials.

Campaign headquarters (Senator Eugene McCarthy's last year) was a large grimy room on the second floor of a decaying building on Columbus Circle, above a couple of cafés and a sauna establishment. The lift didn't always work; it was safer to go around the corner to the staircase, where rubbish was some-times left out on the landings in plastic sacks; New York in places is like Calcutta, with money. The headquarters room was divided into offices by low flimsy partitions, which for various reasons were knocked down one by one as the campaign progressed. The furniture was sparse, trestle tables, old folding chairs, duplicating

6*

machines; there was printed paper everywhere, on walls, floor, tables.

The helpers moved in little cliques within the larger club. Sometimes, when girls brought their babies strapped to their backs in aluminium frames, it was like a hippy encampment with its familial privacies and self-satisfied dedication. During the days of the estrangement privacies vanished; and, like amateurs miming dejection in a low-budget film, the helpers huddled round a table behind the last partition and tried with the help of some beer-cans to give the impression to correspondents – at first ignored, but then welcomed – that they were drinking heavily.

It had been an ambiguous campaign – professional-amateur, political and anti-political. *The other guys are the joke*, a Mailer campaign button said. But now it was possible to feel that the estrangement was also a cover-up for doubt, perhaps panic. A fortnight before, a New York writer, no friend of Mailer, had told me that Mailer's campaign would be as self-defeating as Goldwater's had been in 1964. Mailer, like Goldwater, was a licensed figure. The media would cheer him on, but only in this role. After a time Mailer would begin to suffer from a lack of serious attention; it would get worse as the campaign went on; and at the end Mailer's ideas, however good, would be discredited and Mailer himself would be running for cover.

It didn't work out like that. But this was the gamble Mailer was taking, at the peak of his reputation. Mailer never stopped complaining about poor press coverage; but he got a lot, and it became more and more serious. On election day 41,000 registered Democrats voted for him. A good sale for any writer; and for Mailer the seven-week politician, a triumph. The blue suit, the walking tours, the handshaking: Mailer's instincts had been right. The display of energy and campaigning orthodoxy – the politician's simple self-satire – had helped to establish Mailer's seriousness.

At the same time the campaign had never ceased to be an intellectual entertainment. Through all the repetitions and simplifications Mailer always rang true. He never lost his gift of the phrase, that made so many of his comments sound like epigrams. "Anonymity creates boredom." "Crime will be on the increase as long as it's the most interesting activity." "You will need more and more police to keep more and more bad government in power." To the end he was good in the direct interview. His replies then – after what looked like a flick of the tongue against the top teeth, as though a piece of chewing gum was being hidden away – were abrupt, swift and pithy. The writer's imagination, ceaselessly processing and ordering experience ("You are always writing that novel about yourself," he told me later), could at any moment pass inspection.

"If you win the Democratic nomination, which Republican would you like to run against?"

"Marchi. He says he's a conservative. I call myself a left conservative. We could have an extraordinary discussion about the meaning of conservative principles. Many people who call themselves conservatives are right-wing reactionaries. Which is a different thing altogether." Next question. And this was at the last press conference, when Mailer was tired with words.

He was least effective in the later, non-controversial TV tournaments, where each candidate did a one-minute joust in turn. The politicians won then. Though using words, they appeared to be dismissing words, even their own; they made it plain that they genuinely wanted power and knew what that power was. Mailer's words were part of Mailer. As a writer and politician he carried a double burden; and the ridiculous part of his gamble – so private, so public – was that irresponsibility in either role would have led to the disaster that many had seen coming.

The ideas were big – New York a dying city, alienation its major problem, a complete political reorganization the only hope, with New York as the fifty-first state, more directly controlling its own funds, and the more or less autonomous city districts developing their own life-styles. There were attractive elements of fantasy: no cars in Manhattan (the city-state ringed by a monorail), free public bicycles, and a monthly sabbath, a Sweet Sunday, traffic-less, when "nothing would fly but the birds".

The platform was like an anguished intellectual statement, and the publicity in the beginning had been a writer's publicity: rallying approval from the *New York Times* in a ponderous, punning editorial; the prizes for *Miami and the Siege of Chicago* and *The Armies of the Night*; a reported million-dollar contract for the new book about the Apollo moonshot.

The first meeting of the campaign, in Greenwich Village, was an intellectual-social occasion. It was rowdy. From press reports it appeared that Mailer was attempting a re-make of *Armies*. A false start – this was admitted later – but a writer's false start: the new book often begins like a repeat of the one just finished. Then the campaign changed. It found – what it had lacked – a political issue. It became political; it acquired substance.

The City College of New York, CCNY, which had been having its racial troubles, formulated a dual-admission policy: half of its places would be reserved for students from disadvantaged communities. There was an uproar. The disadvantaged would be black and Puerto Rican; Jewish students would suffer; standards would be lowered. Every mayoral candidate, Democratic and Republican, spoke out against the plan. Only Mailer and his "running mate" were for it. The campaign that had begun as an entertainment now seemed dangerous to some. "The Jews here regard Mailer as a sinner": this was the message from a Mailer worker in the Bronx. A poll showed opinion eight to one against dual-admission; and for the next few days, for five or six or more times a day, Mailer worked hard to show that what looked irresponsible had logic and was socially necessary. After a week there was a compromise; CCNY said they would take only four hundred disadvantaged students, not fifteen hundred; the issue faded. But the campaign had proved itself.

In the early days Mailer could say of a rival: "If I didn't make a vow to use no obscene language, I would say that Wagner was full of an unmarketable commodity." This was the Village Mailer. At the end he said of Wagner: "He's the lead hobby horse in a wooden field." This was funnier; it also made more political sense. On election night, the fight lost and won, the cheering crowd followed Mailer from headquarters across Eighth Avenue to his car. They were also cheering Mailer's wife and Mailer's mother, both of whom had taken part in the campaign. The politician as family man: to this extent the campaign had become orthodox.

Three weeks before, Mailer had told a television reporter that running a campaign was like writing a novel. The same confidence was required; there were analogous problems of creation. "Your brains are working all the time. The writer works on a world, brings it to a resolution; and that world changes him. When a writer finishes a novel he is a changed man."

If Mailer had a political base, it was his glamour as a writer. But glamour also stood in his way.

At the annual dinner of the Village Independent Democrats the two speakers were to be men who had worked with Senator Eugene McCarthy and the late Senator Robert Kennedy. McCarthy, Kennedy: these were the magic names not only of the left, the protesting, the liberal, but also of those asserting an intellectual separateness and therefore content to lose. "I know a man who supported fourteen losing candidates," a visitor from the Lexington Avenue Democrats said. Mailer was going to lose, but the Lexington visitor wasn't prepared to admit Mailer as one of his losers. The ideas were good, but Mailer belonged to another area of American glamour.

Benign now, still powerfully built rather than "unwillingly fat" (his own words), a little tired after a day spent on a campaign paper, blue eyes twinkling in a harassed, mobile face, Mailer was undeniably a presence among the Village Independent Democrats at their pre-dinner cocktails.

"I've talked to Mr Mailer," a forty-year-old woman said. (Over severe, separating foundations, her neckline plunged and plunged.) "And he says I can follow him around in the press car and I want to go everywhere he goes." Her escort, led by the hand, smiled neutrally.

Banning, the campaign manager, listed the evening's engagements. They were to end about midnight.

The woman hesitated, then chose the dinner.

Schwartzman, the nineteen-year-old student on the Mailer advance staff, said, "She probably said she was a freelance and writing a feature. You do get types like that. Now the agency girl, that's more my type of writer. A little tall, but still."

The agency girl, blonde, tanned, cool in a flaming red sweater, had just joined the campaign. She too was writing a feature. In the car afterwards she got out her notebook.

"Why haven't you gone to Vietnam, Mr Mailer?"

"I don't want to get killed."

"I was there for two years. I wasn't killed."

"That is a horrible and obscene war. I would have done something. I would have got killed."

Banning leaned over the front seat to talk of campaign plans. Mailer sat forward, and the two men discussed walking tours and the wisdom of campaigning in certain East Side bars. Mailer didn't want to campaign in bars. It would mean either doing a lot of drinking in one place or getting in the way of a voter who wanted a drink.

The agency girl said, "Do you think you have enough of a political record, Mr Mailer?"

Mailer turned to her and smiled. "As a man who's been married four times – take this down – I say to politicians never run on your past record."

While her pen worked, Banning talked about an article on the campaign in *Life*. "On Wednesday it was four pages. On Thursday it was two. On Friday it was one and a half."

Mailer said it was hard on the writer. "That's why *Life*'s going broke."

"People say," Banning said, "*Life*'s going broke because of what they're paying you for your moonshot article."

Mailer smiled at the agency girl. "Perhaps they're trying to rebuke me."

"Perhaps," the girl said, "I should get you angry. Mr Mailer, why do you talk so much?"

It was the sort of newspaper feature the campaign was attracting.

We were in the lower East Side. A "surviving" area, Mailer called it affectionately: decaying red-brick houses, narrow shops with dirty windows, an occasional empty lot.

"If you are Lithuanian," a man said on the steps of the East Midtown Reform Democratic Club, "how come your name is Mailer?"

"Lithuanian Jew," Mailer insisted. "On both sides."

It was a small hall, panelled down one side and decorated with KLM posters, bunting and the Stars and Stripes. There were about forty people on folding metal chairs.

"By the look of you," Mailer said, "I can see you are not a soft Democratic club. Let's have the questions. I can see that the person who asks the first question is going to be in as much trouble as me."

The question was about the fifty-first state. "You think the Governor of New York would let you or anybody else get away from them?"

"We all know what breaks up an unhappy marriage. It's a smart Jewish lawyer. I submit that I am the smartest Jewish attorney in town."

The mood didn't last. A woman asked about CCNY. She sat next to a tweed-jacketed man who might have been her husband; they both looked like teachers. "Why don't you send them all to Harvard and give them all a really *good* education?" This was the Jewish backlash; she was speaking of the blacks and Puerto Ricans.

"You know you are just giving expression to your prejudice. Harvard's my old college – "

"That's why I said it."

"Let's assume that Harvard's going down the drain – "

"You're putting words in her mouth!" the man shouted.

"Our universities are to education what the *New Yorker* is to literature. A minor organ with a major function." Laughter cleared the air. "Pardon this digression. No one should trust a speaker who strays from the point." He addressed the man: "You recognize the unhappiness with which you speak?" It was a direct, gentle inquiry.

"I do," the man said. His response was like a reflex; his tone was confessional.

A moment of stillness: the man and woman, for all their passion, and the respectable jauntiness of their "budget" clothes, were older than they had first appeared.

It wasn't a perfect solution, Mailer said, exploiting the moment. But it was better that the colleges should make some adjustments rather than be destroyed altogether. If the blacks hadn't been betrayed so often, if opportunities had been given them, "you would have had blacks as mean and as ugly as any – " His mischievousness was like the other face of anger; he was deliberately destroying the mood.

"You are asking the kids to pay for it!" the woman shouted. "Let him talk!"

"The kids will have," Mailer said, above the voices calling for order, "the exhilarating existential experience of going to school with black people."

That was the end. And, unexpectedly, there was applause, Mailer walking smartly down, arms held out wide, palms open, like a wrestler about to charge.

The next halt, a fund-raising one, was at a place called the Electric Circus in the Village. It was a good name. In the stairways and corridors blue, red and mauve neon strips reflected on walls that might have been papered with aluminium foil; and at the end of this neon fantasy was a wide white hall, packed with the young. It was a paid-up Mailer crowd. But Mailer, solitary before the microphone, appeared irritated. "You are here to see me work, is that it?" The questions were too sympathetic. "When we win, which would give all of us great concern – " But there was little of that. It was as though, out of his security here, Mailer had committed himself to frowns and silences and was waiting to be provoked. "Now listen. I'm much more conservative than most of you people here. I'll work for and support your neighbourhood, but I don't think I'll approve of it."

After that, ten minutes at the League of Women Voters in the public library opposite the Museum of Modern Art. An anti-

Rockefeller art-student demo going on outside that: a swift exchange of literature, campaign with campaign. And then a confusion of causes: Badillo, one of Mailer's rivals, coming out of the library with his staff, Mailer going in with his, everybody with leaflets for everybody else.

"Everywhere I go I see Badillo buttons. I feel Badillo's staked you guys."

"Norman, Norman," the Badillo supporter said. "That's not a nice thing to say."

A meeting with the East Side Democrats was on the schedule. But only the wife of the campaign photographer was there, in a belted pink mackintosh. She had been waiting on the pavement a long time; the club room was locked. The busy campaign, unexpectedly isolated, reassembled; and then Banning told us to hurry over to the West Side Democrats; we were already very late for them.

"Advance did a fine job," someone in the second car said.

"I've been talking to taxi-drivers," a foreign reporter said (he had joined us at the Electric Circus). "They may know about *The Naked*. But they don't always know who the author is."

"I was talking to an old Jew in Brooklyn yesterday. I told him about Mailer. He said, 'Isn't he the guy stabbed his wife?' Nine years, and he's talking about it like he'd read it in the paper that morning."

"He probably gets his papers late."

They talked about the agency girl.

"You think she's for real, a writer?"

"With looks like that she could be anything. But she's a groupie. She's only going for the big man."

We weren't late for the West Side Democrats. A dingy first-floor hall overlooking Broadway, photographs of Robert Kennedy, old Eugene McCarthy stickers, the Stars and Stripes. A mixed crowd of about fifty, some Puerto Ricans, a couple of blacks. One of Mailer's rivals was still talking.

". . . I tell you one thing we can do real fast to get better crime control. . . ." This was Congressman Scheuer, spending half a million dollars to come last in the primary, below Mailer.

Mailer entered, his hair frizzing out now. The TV lights blazed on him. Heads turned; hands were shaken.

". . . get police out of all station-house and routine jobs . . . all non-crime-control functions. . . ."

The applause wasn't for the Congressman. It was for Mailer, withdrawing after his false entry. Presently, through the mêlée, the Congressman walked out, smiling, a private figure.

But they were a dull audience, and because they were dull, Mailer tried. Irony, to begin with. CCNY was being taken over, he said, by the same Communist plot Mayor Wagner had talked about some years ago. The audience remained vacant. "That was a joke." He told an Irish joke in an Irish accent. Silence. "Now that I've lost this club – " The laugh came; the audience relaxed. Mailer talked for twenty minutes; it was the best speech of the evening.

In the morning there was a story in the *New York Times*.

> "Campaign" by Mailer Upstages
> The Once Festival in "Village"
> . . . First, however, the audience at the last in the current Electric Ear series of multimedia affairs at the East Village rock hall witnessed a psychodrama of another variety, "The Campaign", starring Norman Mailer. . . . While TV cameras captured the bizarre scene, Mr Mailer urged statehood. . . .

And at the Overseas Press Club they were gloomy. Neither the *Times* nor the *Post* nor the *News* had sent a man to the press conference that morning, when Mailer and his running mate – Jimmy Breslin, a popular columnist, a heavy, dark-haired Irishman of menacing and explosive appearance – were to present a paper on housing. Banning had brought a boxful of copies; he found only about fifteen takers, radio and TV people, who always served the campaign well, some foreign reporters, and the agency girl, now in green. The TV cameras and the lights played on her for a little. She remained cool. Out of a cross face Mailer smiled.

A reporter asked for a statement on the "integrity" of the New York press.

"The simple statement," Breslin said, "is that no one's here. They'll begin to listen when they hear shotguns on Park Avenue."

"Electric Circus," Mailer said afterwards, looking at the *Times*, which Banning had folded over to show the story. "I didn't like the name. I didn't like the building."

"It was a horrible building," Banning said.

"How much did we get out of it?"

"A couple of hundred bucks."

"Not worth it."

"I was talking to an AP man," Banning said, explaining the poor attendance at the conference. "They had a list up in the office. 'These stories we will cover this morning'. And another list. 'These stories we will not cover this morning'. We'll call *another* press conference tomorrow at the *same* time. *That's* the way to test them."

I was beginning to recognize Banning's style in drama. It might have been his diplomatic training; he had served for some time in the American Foreign Service. Or it might have been his later work in broadcasting. ("I couldn't tell you even today," he said after the campaign, "whether politics or show business is my first love.")

About thirty reporters came the next day. The agency girl wore cream. The *Times* sent a man; so did the *Post*. There had been a lot on the TV networks the previous evening – the interviews, so casual, given an extra, separate reality when slotted into the news programmes on the small screen – but Mailer was still complaining.

"We have to bludgeon our way into a newspaper office to get a small piece. They are trying to make our campaign ridiculous and up to a point they have succeeded. We have made mistakes on the way; we have played into their hands."

Tempers were shorter; there were fewer jokes. Mailer looked

tired and aggressive; it was a face that suggested defeat. But he
might have been acting: his face was so mobile, his moods so
quick.

Two hours later, at his Wall Street rally, standing below the
statue of Washington on the steps of the Old Treasury Building,
he was a different man. Hands now in trouser-pockets below the
buttoned jacket, now in jacket pockets, he appeared to strut, like
a boxer in the new respectability of a suit, confident of his public
spread out in rows on the wide steps, filling the famous narrow
street below. The sound system was bad. All the words were lost,
including Breslin's threat about the shotguns on Park Avenue.
But the scene was dramatically right.

A stranger coming on Wall Street at that moment with a
knowledge of America gained only from films would have found
in the scene a familiar glamour. He would have seen the man up
there as every type of American myth-figure: boxer, sheriff, bad
man, mobster, even politician. It was the setting: the famous
street in the famous city, the buildings, the flags, the rhetoric and
history in the Washington statue. And it was also Mailer: his
sense of the city, perhaps, his sense of occasion.

But when I talked to Mailer a week after the election I found
that his own memories of the Wall Street rally were vague; the
details of the campaign, of particular scenes and particular words,
had blurred.

"You don't operate as a writer. You don't see what people are
wearing. You are aware of people only as eyes, a type of response.
It's more like being an actor."

II

The day after the Wall Street rally, after many more meetings,
speeches, ceremonies, questions and answers and statements,
Mailer said, "I've become duller. Steady, serious, duller. I've
become a politician."

He was in shirtsleeves in headquarters. The grimy windows

were pushed open; the afternoon was thundery. He had just
given a twenty-minute "in depth" TV interview; and it was part
of the wastefulness of campaigning: that excellent interview, and
the events of the week, would make about five minutes on the
network's Saturday news.

He had discovered, he said, that politics was hard work. Sleep
was the thing he dreamt about and he understood now how sleep
could be the politician's sex. "Someone should do a Freudian
analysis of this thing, being a politician. It's all a matter of orality.
It's the most oral people who get along. My tongue feels like a
hippopotamus's. It's all a matter of tongue and lips. It's so strange
for me, so different from my practice as a writer. I used to feel
that if I talked about something I had lost it. I would go out to do
an article. When I came back and my wife asked me what I
thought about it, I wouldn't talk. That's why I feel I couldn't do
a book about this."

"What do you think about him?" Schwartzman asked me
afterwards.

It was a question Mailer sometimes asked his staff after a
meeting; it was a question the staff often asked reporters they had
got to know. It was the burden of glamour: Mailer's staff required
him never to fail, even in a short exchange with a reporter.

"Friday's a fun day," Banning said. "He's going to the races at
Aqueduct."

"Fun?" I said. "You mean no campaigning?"

"There are going to be 70,000 people there."

The special express trains funnelled them in from Manhattan
and Brooklyn; and from the platform, level with the floor of the
coaches, they poured down the covered ramp to the stand, spoiling
the symmetry of the arrangement only when they broke out into
the sunlight – the wide car-parks glinting like the open sea – to
get to the two-dollar gates. First on the covered ramp (leading to
the five-dollar gates) and then in the sunlight, Mailer and his
party stood, facing the rush: Breslin, the columnist, more
popular than Mailer here, Mailer in light check trousers and a

blazer, smiling shyly, Mailer's wife, small, an actress, in a sober olive outfit, now part of the campaign.

The crowd swirled past them. But, like pebbles on a smooth beach, the campaign party was a disturbance, and disturbance built up around them: swift handshakes, an exchange, a little crowd, enough for the cameras, and even a little sound off-camera. "I've been thinking about this guy. I wanted to see him. He's in favour of dual-admission." "You haven't got a ghost of a chance, ya bum!" Then the party, going through the five-dollar gates, were taken up the escalators to the concourse, where they were soon untraceable.

I fell in with a young man, equally lost, from Liberation News Service. He was hairy and hippyish and aggrieved. He had had to fight his way into the campaign car that morning and he hadn't even had an interview with Mailer. He showed me a transcript he had made of his conversation with Banning.

"Banning: Look, we need coverage from you New Left nuts like a hole in the head. . . . You got to get votes from a lot of strange places to win in this town. . . . He needs support from the left like he needs a shit haemorrhage."

"Mailer isn't offering an alternative to American politics," the man from Liberation News said, as we walked through the crowd, looking for the campaign. "He's offering only a distorted version of the old style."

The bright green centre of the track was patterned with flowers; in the distance the jets rose one after the other from the permanent kerosene haze over Kennedy Airport.

"The trouble is that Mailer sees himself as an existential hero. In America, where action is frowned on among intellectuals, the existential hero would say, 'The worst thing in the world is boredom. We must create drama by our own actions.' Mailer creates this excitement, without giving an analysis of why that world is boring and dull. He says, 'It is boring and dull, but it will be interesting if I inject myself into it.'"

Existential: it was a Mailer word I was beginning to learn; it explained much of what I had felt about the campaign, its glamour and ambiguity. He was only nineteen, the Liberation News man, but the fluency of the American young no longer surprised me.

"What is most important is that when Mailer is defeated it won't be said that he's been defeated by the unworkable and corrupt New York City system. It will be said that it was his individual failure. As a critical man he will have lost a marvellous opportunity of exposing the undemocratic nature of American politics."

It was easy to see why Banning didn't want him around. Just then, though, the Liberation News man very badly wanted to see Banning: he had forgotten a roll of exposed film in the campaign car.

We ran into one of the TV cameramen. I asked him how he assessed the day's campaigning.

"Oh, we'll make it look bigger."

"Is that official policy?" the man from Liberation News asked.

"We make everything bigger."

Outside the restaurant – Mailer having a slow lunch inside – we saw Banning, brisk and businesslike. His beard barely lifted; he ignored us.

"He *hates* me," the man from Liberation News said, and looked down at his soft suede boots.

I wanted company back to Manhattan. I gave the man from Liberation News some of my notes and persuaded him to forget his exposed film. The train was full of boys and girls, red from the beach. Everyone in the Mailer campaign spoke of the sickness of the society. But to the visitor no city appeared richer in pleasure, and more organized for it. And Mailer's trip to the races made a three-column spread, with a photograph, in the *New York Times*: that was the reality of our afternoon excursion.

"The thing about this campaign," the girl in headquarters said, "is that it's fantastically seductive." She was twenty-four, thin, with a sharp little nose. "These boys here on the campaign are all like Norman. They have the same tremendous ego and this makes them fantastic to be with. They're so fantastically alive every minute. Hardly anybody else is." She herself came from New Jersey. "I had to leave because I was like a freak there. I am like" – she sighed, and her eyes widened behind her tinted granny glasses – "well, a socialist." After the campaign she was going on to do some summer work for GI Resistance. "It'll be idealistic to say it's because I have a brother in Vietnam. It's more like, well, being addicted."

"I don't know how the whole concept of doing your own thing became so sacred," Banning said when the campaign was over. "I don't know whether it's American or just youthful. I know how vicious the establishment is. I am 20,000 dollars in debt – well, say 15,000. But maybe I'm not as disillusioned as everybody else. Maybe everybody is uptight. Notice the difference between the Kennedy kids we had and the McCarthy kids. The Kennedy people want to win. The McCarthy-oriented types are addicted not just to lost causes but to a concept of lost causes. They just want to make a statement and stand around being right. 'I know what is wrong, I'm noble.' This I don't buy."

McCarthy types, Kennedy types, the New Left, the addicted, the Mailer-glamoured, the election-glamoured (bullhorns, loud-speaker cars, sticky labels): even with the heroic pattern-figure of Mailer, the wonder was that the campaign held together and looked professional, that the strains didn't show more.

The reporters came and went. The press became better and better. Dustin, who was in charge of Advance, told me that the article by the agency girl had come out. "They must have cut a lot," he said. There were occasional muted reports of internal trouble: a public outburst because of some carelessly displayed posters; an amateur art show not opened, Mailer's wife going instead to speak the nice words Mailer couldn't bring himself to speak. Then Banning lost his beard.

The gloomiest day in headquarters was the Friday before the election. A Harlem rally had been planned for that day. But Clarence 27X Smith, a Black Muslim of some local renown, was

shot dead in a lift in the morning (New York always organized
for drama, as it was for pleasure), and Mailer cancelled the rally.
In headquarters they felt that Mailer had let them down; the
show ought to have gone on. The cast and band of *Hair*, I was
told, had been recruited and were game; black bodyguards
could have been hired for a hundred dollars.

"Don't ask Banning too many questions," I was told. "He'll
hit you like Norman."

Banning, tie-less, jacketless, with a beer-can, was dejected and
acting tough. He said there was "an atmosphere of political death"
over the campaign. I asked for the schedule. He mimicked my
pronunciation. "Stick around," he said. "You'll hear." It struck
me for the first time that he would have a good microphone voice.

"It isn't all Norman," the girl from New Jersey said. "Half of
this is that it's all going to end on Tuesday and everybody on the
campaign's got to go back to not having power. Everything else
is going to go on. This stops on June 17, this closeness and inti-
macy with people who have become your whole life. And these
boys, they fight with Norman, but they go to the meetings. And
when Norman gets up there and tells it like it is, they all dissolve
and you can tell it in their eyes. It's why they come the next day."

Banning wasn't in the office the next day. But Dustin and his
wife and some others were, and after lunch we drove through the
rain to Macy's department store, where – but no one was sure –
Mailer was campaigning among the shoppers. All we saw from
the car were some very young volunteers offering damp leaflets;
they didn't know where Mailer was.

He and Mrs Mailer were inside the store, as it turned out, until
the guard asked them to campaign outside.

When we walked round the block we found them. Girl
volunteers were asking people, "Have you met Mr Mailer?" And
the Mailers were shaking hands. Mailer looked worn, preoccupied, working only with his eyes; his hair, cut shorter, looked
greyer. Mrs Mailer was as composed as always. "I am an actress,"
she said later. "This is the biggest audience I've played to." A
blind man stood beside Mailer, rattling his coins in a green cup

and tapping his stick; his eyelids were sealed over hollow sockets so that his face, without expression, was like a dummy's.

It was an extraordinary, smiling scene. The Mailers smiled; the people whose hands had been shaken smiled, and they waited, smiling, to see others have their turn. The girl volunteers smiled; we were all smiling.

"It's *good*," Dustin said, his gloom vanished. "We could win." Dustin had been a Kennedy man.

Mailer, getting into the car, called Dustin over. A girl volunteer turned on me with big eyes. "I'm *crazy*!" A minute ago she had been demure. "I *love* him! I've read *all* his books. This is the first time I've *seen* him! I *love* him!" She sat down hard on the table with the campaign buttons. "I'm *crazy*!"

Dustin came back, exultant. "He wants a motorcade." Dustin liked motorcades.

Later, at the Sullivan Street fair – old brick houses with fire-escapes, the street muddy and littered, remote Italian women sitting with bandaged ankles and legs beside foodstalls and toy-stalls, sausages grilling over charcoal – Dustin and Mailer talked again.

"Look at them," Dustin's wife said. "Don't you think they look a little alike, with the hair?"

On Monday, at the last press conference, Mailer bounced back to form after a tired, constricted TV appearance the previous day. Banning was there, friendly again, in a suit, stage-managing again. The four motorcade cars were waiting outside. A German producer said, "The film on Germany is finished. It was shown Saturday night." A girl with a foreign accent was told that press seats were reserved for the New York City press. Mailer, Mrs Mailer and Breslin sat in the third car. Banning was in the loud-speaker car at the front; he was to do the talking.

"*Mailer-Breslin and the fifty-first state. You've had the rest. Choose the best.*"

It was the motorcade slogan. The story was that it had been suggested to Mailer by a Negro. Banning didn't like it, but he was speaking it with conviction. On Broadway there were some waves and shouts. But Harlem, with its sullen privacies, where garishness and dereliction appeared one and indivisible, was silent. In the South Bronx the advertisements were in Spanish; and Banning – a new talent revealed – spoke in Spanish: ". . . *dos coches atrás, en el carro abierto. . . .*" His accent was good. But there was no response from the pavements. The motorcade slowed down in the traffic, merged into it.

Mailer signalled from the open car. Banning ran to confer, then came to us. "OK, we'll meet up at 50th Street and Sixth Avenue, in front of the Time-Life Building. We're just going to shake hands and cut the horseshit with the motorcade." Banning hadn't liked the idea of the motorcade. The motorcade broke up; and in silence, without loudspeakers, the cars raced separately back to Manhattan.

The reception outside the Time-Life building was very good. Mailer, with his vision of New York as two cities, spoke passionately for the disadvantaged. But his best audience was always the middle-class, the educated, the bohemian, the people who held him in awe.

They had laid in the beer in headquarters. The TV cameras and monitors had been installed. The last partition had gone, and at the end of the room they had built a platform, against a wall decorated with the campaign posters (already souvenirs, already being taken away by collectors). The mood was good. It was a victory mood, and victory meant not coming last.

"It's been important to me," Banning said, summing up the campaign. "Mailer's obviously going to be important to American history. He'll either be a force for enormous destruction or he'll be one of the great builders. He clearly is going to do something more than write *The Armies of the Night.*"

In the evening the hall began filling up: the media people (the TV reporters grave, aware of the envy of the young), the volunteers from the boroughs, a number of strays. There was a girl in half-Mexican, half-Hindu hippy costume sitting on the floor before a red candle. She had missed the point; she had also under-estimated the crowd. The girl from New Jersey turned up with a Negro. Banning, dashing and unexpected in a pale-blue silk neck-scarf, stood on the platform, like an actor in the lights, and repeatedly called for order. The results began to come in. They were as expected. Mailer was running above Congressman Scheuer, with five to six per cent of the votes; Breslin was doing even better in his contest for the Presidency of the Council: he was getting ten per cent. There was applause and stamping.

Banning said that the building would collapse. "If you have the death wish, don't wish it on other people."

They were rebels, and the moment was high. But they were also Americans, careful of the self in every way, never reckless. They began to go.

At about midnight Mailer, Mrs Mailer and Breslin came, cameras and lights preceding them. Through handshakes they walked to the platform.

"We can hardly claim victory," Mailer said. It was their joke; victory was what they were celebrating. "Listen. You've been terrific. We've run further on less. We've spent one-tenth of what Wagner spent. I've got five per cent of the vote; he's got thirty. So we've done twice as well as he." He was mischievous, the hero restored to his followers. Banning stood beside me, dissolving; it was as the girl from New Jersey had said.

The TV lights heightened colour, deepening the beauty of Mrs Mailer. Mailer's eyes showed as the clearest blue. The posters on the wall glowed. It was a narrow hall, the platform central, and on the monitor screens the scene was like something out of a well-organized film. So that this last moment of glamour linked to that other, on the steps of the Old Treasury Building in Wall Street.

One notice hadn't been forgotten. *Anyone interested in GI Resistance work this summer please sign name. . . .* There had been four signatures in the afternoon; now the sheet was full.

I had lunch with Mailer a week later. He had spent a few days

in Cape Cod; he had been to the Frazier-Quarry fight the evening
before; he was editing a film that day; he would soon have to
start working on his moonshot articles. "That's going to be a
strange assignment. The astronauts won't talk to me. They're
writing their own book." His writer's life was catching up with
him again.

Politics seemed far away. But he was sensitive to the charge
that he had split the liberal vote and helped the cause of the backlash. He thought that many of the people who had voted for him
wouldn't have otherwise voted. He didn't think he had done well
enough; he had lost some votes in the last week; not enough
people had been reached. It astonished him that people who had
shaken his hand and had been friendly hadn't voted for him.

He said again that, becoming a politician, he had become duller.
But he understood now that politicians were serious when they
spoke of "service". A politician had to serve, had always to give
himself, to his supporters, to the public. It was his weakness, for
instance, that he couldn't answer when people asked him whether
he would clear their streets of garbage. He remained loyal to his
ideas – the fifty-first state, power to the neighbourhoods – but he
thought that perhaps another candidate, even someone very dull,
might have done better politically with them.

Dull: it was the recurring word. It was as though, during the
campaign, Mailer had redefined his writer's role by negatives.
He couldn't assess the value of the campaign. "If you don't win,
you change very little." Perhaps some of the ideas would survive:
time alone would show. "Or it might just be a curiosity. Perhaps
four years from now, at the next election, someone might say,
'Remember when that writer ran for Mayor?' "

Jacques Soustelle and the Decline of the West

Daily Telegraph Magazine, 26 January 1968

FROM A DISTANCE Jacques Soustelle appears to be two men. There is the exiled politician whose cause, *Algérie française*, Algeria is France, has been destroyed. And there is the ethnologist and scholar, the imaginative interpreter of ancient Aztec life, whose first book, published when he was twenty-three, was *Mexique, Terre Indienne*: Mexico is Indian, you might say. Both careers have been remarkable and both are likely to continue. In the serenity of the last two or three years of exile, Soustelle has become a prolific scholar again. *Arts of Ancient Mexico*, published in England a few months ago, has been recognized as a major work. And he is still only fifty-five: he will not be a political exile forever.

Serenity is Soustelle's own word. It is one of the unlikely things that have come to him in his exile which, when it began in 1962, was "dreary and dangerous". He was then on the run, a figure of newspaper melodrama, alleged to be plotting in Italy, Portugal, Vienna.

Early in his exile he was denounced to the Italian police by a newspaper reporter who spotted him in a Brescia hotel. The name Soustelle used then was Jean Albert Sénèque. It "amused" him. (The Stoic philosopher Seneca, when he was very old, was accused of conspiring against the Emperor Nero, and was required to commit suicide.) But exile presently became less amusing. Soustelle was expelled from Italy, banned for a time by Switzerland and West Germany. After someone tried to kill de Gaulle in August 1962, French government agents became active all over Europe. During a carnival dance at a Munich hotel in February 1963, ex-Colonel Argoud, another exile, was kidnapped; he was found in Paris the next morning, badly beaten up, in a van near Notre Dame. After this Soustelle dropped out of the news. When, a year later, he was arrested in a Lausanne hotel and expelled from Switzerland, he was using a more commonplace name: Jacques Lemaire.

"Two attempts were made to kill or kidnap me. The first time I didn't know. The second time I knew. A clumsy attempt had been made to bribe someone with $100,000. We played hide-and-seek for a few days. Then I shook him off."

Now the pressure has lessened. France is still closed to him but he can move about freely outside. General de Gaulle is reported to have asked recently after Monsieur and Madame Soustelle and to have sent his good wishes to M. Soustelle through a common acquaintance. Mme Soustelle still lives and works in Paris. She, too, is an Aztec scholar. She and Jacques Soustelle were married in 1932, when he was nineteen; they have no children. They keep in touch; Soustelle confirms the Paris story that the language of the Aztecs is their secret language, which they use, or used, on the telephone.

Last March, Soustelle was a candidate in the French elections in his old constituency of Lyon. Election would have given him immunity. But he would have been arrested if he had entered France to campaign; in that month a traveller saw his name prominent among the list of proscribed people at Orly airport. Soustelle sent over a tape-recorded speech. He came second with 8,000 votes. Some people think that Soustelle should have gone to France then, that his arrest would have been a one-night affair. But Soustelle is cautious. Though he is open now to interviews and no longer feels he has to sit facing the main door of hotels, he still requires meetings to be arranged through his lawyer. And the lawyer sits in on all conversations. It is a remnant of the theatre that has surrounded Soustelle since his flight from Paris to Algiers in May 1958, when his aim was to use *Algérie française* to bring de Gaulle back to power. He was reported then to have escaped from Paris – where he was being watched – in the boot of a car.

He says it isn't true; and all that high adventure now seems so unlikely as, among the flowers and carpets of a grand hotel in the slack season, Soustelle breaks off to consider the wine list or to ask a solicitous waiter for a packet of Players *médium*. The pronunciation is for the waiter's benefit. Soustelle's own English is brisk, complex, colloquial. The occasional French words he uses – *éveilleur, acharné* – are those for which there is no ready English equivalent.

Photographs emphasize Soustelle's heaviness, his double chin, the firm set of the wide mouth, the rimless glasses and the dark pouches under the assessing eyes. But the face is mobile; eyes and lips are easily touched with humour. He knows about wine and will talk about it, but precisely: "I know the vineyard", "I know the owner". He draws your attention to the cigarettes he smokes. They are Players; they hold a story. In Lyon in 1927 Soustelle won an English essay competition. The prize was a fortnight in London. He stayed in a house near Clapham Common. He travelled a lot on the Underground, and it was from a machine in an Underground station that he bought his first packet of cigarettes. They were Players; he has smoked them ever since.

His manner is like that of a university lecturer who knows his own reputation and will not be drawn beyond his own subject. "If you have nothing to say to him," his lawyer says, "he has nothing to say to you." Soustelle is not interested in ideas for their own sake. He always appears to speak from a well-prepared position; and this is more than an attribute of exile. He gives the impression that he came to terms with himself a long time ago, perhaps even in his precocious adolescence, and that his areas of interest have been defined by his experience: his scholarship, Mexico, the war, Algeria. He still seems able to survey his experience with wonder; he seems continually to process and refine this experience as it expands within its defined limits. It is the method neither of the scholar nor of the politician, but of both together; and it comes close to the method of the novelist, making art of egotism, creating a private impenetrable whole out of fragments which from a distance might appear unrelated.

Consider the Players cigarettes. Soustelle is conscious of them as a link with his adolescence, his early academic brilliance, his first trip to London – and the Elgin Marbles. In that fortnight he spent much time among them in the British Museum. They made him want to go to Athens; and it was only last spring, in the serenity of exile, that he was able to go. He was overwhelmed; he had expected Greek monuments to be on a smaller scale. And there was another surprise. He had always liked Roman monuments; he found he didn't like them as much in Athens: they seemed so crude. The visit helped him to clarify his ideas about the United States and the "provincialization" of Europe. And these ideas have come directly from his experience as a scholar and politician.

Europe has been provincialized because she has withdrawn from the "wide spaces" of Africa. Civilizations are limited in space as well as in time; and this withdrawal, like the Roman withdrawal from Dacia and Britain, is "the first sign, the first wrinkles, of old age". Rome incorporated Gaul; France ought to have incorporated Africa. Instead, France yielded to the "idol" of decolonization and the pressures of mercantile capitalism and converted the low cultures of black Africa into a *poussière* of petty dictatorships.

"They will use what France left there to the last tractor, to the last bolt, to the last little teaspoon. After that, as in Tripolitania, they will let the goats graze where wheat formerly grew."

True decolonization would have come from incorporation, with equal rights and an equal advance for all. But this was rejected; it was too difficult.

France has failed and has retreated across the Mediterranean into her own "hexagonal" territory not through defeat – militarily Algeria was a French victory – but through decadence, through bourgeois selfishness, *les week-ends et les vacances d'été et d'hiver*, and through racialism: the unwillingness of the French to accept that Africans, Arabs, Berbers, and the Maltese, Spanish and Greek *colons* of Algeria might also have been made Frenchmen.

All civilizations have perished; even their ruins will go one day; there is no pattern and no goal. But it is Hegelian nonsense to say that the world's history is the world's justice; the stoic must always fight. Ideas which do not lead to action are just dreams; action without an "ideological orientation" is only nihilistic opportunism.

So, until the serenity and release of exile, Soustelle the scholar-politician has been trapped in his dual role. The politician is only a part of Soustelle; and his political views, when separated from his experience, can be simplified and used by people to whom they give comfort. Like de Gaulle himself in 1958, Soustelle can be all things to all men.

All Soustelles must originally have come from the area around Soustelle, a hamlet in the Cevennes which today has a population of about one hundred, many of whom are named Soustelle. Jacques Soustelle was born in Montpelier and grew up in a semi-rural suburb of Lyon. He never knew his father; his mother remarried when he was ten; his stepfather, "a very good man", was a motor mechanic and worked at his trade until recently. The family was Protestant. Jacques Soustelle was an only child in a house which at one time held a grandfather and three aunts, one of whom managed the household. During the first war his mother worked in a post office; later she worked in an office. "We were not lumpen-proletariat. But we were proletariat."

It was his class teacher, "a very good man", who suggested to Mme Soustelle that her son should look beyond the *certificat d'études* and go to a lycée. He was the first of those teachers, those very good men, as Soustelle today remembers them all, who helped and guided and arranged the scholarship examinations which led to Paris and the École Normale Supérieure when he was seventeen, the *agrégation* and the diploma in ethnology three years later. "By the time I was twenty I had sat twelve competitive examinations. I wasn't very good in mathematics, but I came first in everything else." In Paris he had also ghosted a Fourier anthology and some detective stories, to supplement his scholarship money; and he gave lessons.

He had always read a lot, and his interests had set early. He read natural history and history; even as a boy he liked reading about the Roman Empire in its third-century decline, "that majestic and terrible spectacle"; and a taste for Jules Verne had led on to books of travel and books about exotic peoples. In Paris his thoughts turned naturally to ethnology after he met three scholars who were outstanding in the subject. Paul Rivet was one of these. Rivet was director of the Musée de l'Homme, then the Musée d'Ethnographie. Soustelle worked in the Musée de l'Homme for half the day, among the artefacts of the people he studied. To him these artefacts were works of art and not quaint; and through them he felt linked to the makers. He had developed the almost religious feeling that the finest and most comprehensive study was Man. About this time some dancers from New Caledonia came to Paris, and Soustelle was able to spend an evening with them. He remembers it as a privilege, part of his luck.

The peoples of Oceania – visited for the first time in 1945, when he was de Gaulle's Minister for the Colonies – were then his special interest. But Paul Rivet had visited Mexico in 1930 and had come back enthusiastic about the Otomí tribe, about whom little work had been done. Rivet said he would send Soustelle out to Mexico, where there was a French cultural mission, if Soustelle became *agrégé*. Soustelle shifted his interest to Mexico. And Rivet was as good as his word. The *agrégation* results came out in August 1932; in October Soustelle and his wife – they had not long been married – sailed for Mexico.

The Soustelles worked among the Otomí in central Mexico. They also worked among the very small tribe called the Lacandones in the south-east. In the rainy season the Soustelles went to Mexico City. There they fell among Mexican intellectuals; they became friendly with the painter Rivera. "There was still something of the post-revolutionary fervour, a general awareness of the Mexican past. I remember that someone even organized a *velada*, a vigil, in honour of the old Aztec god Quetzalcoatl. On the other side there were people, sometimes of Indian ancestry, who thought that the Indian past was bloody and barbaric and should be forgotten. Of course I took the Indian side. But Mexico can be neither Indian nor Spanish. It is what it is: Indian and Spanish."

The Aztec universe, as Soustelle has described it, was fragile and unstable. The world had been destroyed more than once before and was going to be destroyed again. Destruction could be stayed only by a continual offering of human blood. "I never thought of human sacrifice as a barrier to my understanding of the Aztecs. I was imbued very early with the idea of the relativity of human morals." In Soustelle's writings this sacrifice becomes the tragic, ennobling, wearying act of men determined to keep their world going. But destruction came. Between 1519 and 1521 the Spaniards smashed the head and heart of the developing civilization. If the Atzecs had been left alone, Soustelle thinks, they would have taken Mexico into the equivalent of the Meiji era in Japan. And, strangely, in his writings there is little anger at the destruction, and little regret for what might have developed. "The Spaniards couldn't have acted otherwise. And we mustn't forget the efforts some Spaniards made to record and defend; or that they made possible the society in which Indian life was to reawaken."

It was this Mexican experience – so large, so complete: grandeur, destruction, decadence, incorporation, new life – that Soustelle sought twenty years later to apply to Algeria: the equation of Mexican Indians, who had only Mexico, with Arab guerrillas, who could look to a vast Muslim world, which had once just failed to overrun Europe itself.

Soustelle was in Mexico, vice-president of a conference of Americanists, when the war broke out. He took a Dutch ship to Ramsgate and made his way to France to join the regiment in which he had done his military service in 1936. He had nothing to do for some months. Then he was recruited into the Ministry of Information which the Daladier government was establishing. He was sent back to Mexico and was there when France fell. He

was prepared then to be an exile forever. He thought he would go
to Canada and serve in a French Canadian regiment. But a friend
in the British Consulate told him that there was a French general
in London who was setting up an organization. Soustelle sent a
cable to London; after three days he got a reply from one of de
Gaulle's aides.

He was asked to stay on in Mexico for a little to organize
support for the Free French from the local French community.
Then, in a ship full of New Zealanders and Australians, future
pilots, he went to England. "At Liverpool, where we docked, I
had a lot of trouble to prove that I wasn't a dubious character.
But it was all right at Carlton Gardens. By some chance de
Gaulle's ADC was an old schoolfellow of mine from Lyon. I met
de Gaulle that very day. Two or three days later I was invited
to dinner." Then, as always later, de Gaulle's manner was one of
icy formality. De Gaulle was fifty, Soustelle twenty-eight; it was
the beginning of an association that lasted eighteen years. "The
great qualities in him which attracted me can still be seen today,
but only in caricature."

Soustelle was put in the "foreign service" section and sent back
to Latin America once again. Later, in London, he was National
Commissioner for Information with the Liberation Committee.
When the Allies landed in North Africa he became Secretary-
General for Action in France. His job was to pool the resources
of the Free French Intelligence with those of the Vichy Deuxième
Bureau, which had fled to North Africa after the German occu-
pation of Southern France; and to supply the French underground.
"We ran short of French banknotes, and in the end we were
dropping little pieces of paper signed by Mendès-France promising
to pay after the liberation. The winter of 1943-4 was horrible.
So many people one knew disappeared, were killed or committed
suicide. Such a waste of life. I don't think the underground in
France would have lasted another year."

The liberation came, and disillusionment. "Everything just
went back to what it was before. We overestimated the importance of the Resistance. You know, it was just point something

per cent of the population that took part. I suppose the First World War was the beginning of the end for France. Fewer people were killed in the Second War. But France was occupied and we became hopelessly divided. We fought against one another in Syria and Dakar. And we didn't show sufficient restraint after the liberation. It would have been difficult, I know."

General de Gaulle presently withdrew from politics. But Soustelle stayed on. His academic career continued. In 1955, the year he published his master-work, *The Daily Life of the Aztecs*, he became – with de Gaulle's blessing – Governor-General of Algeria, where, on 1 November 1954, the insurrection had broken out, with seventy separate incidents.

In time the insurrection tied down 500,000 French troops. When it was over in 1962, the French had lost 14,000 men, the insurgents 140,000; 3,000 European civilians had been killed, 30,000 Arabs.

In the legend, which has lasted, Soustelle underwent a conversion in Algeria. The sight of a massacre, it was said, unhinged him; overnight the reforming pro-Arab liberal became a supporter of *Algérie française*; and his head was finally turned, so the legend goes, by the adulation of the *colons* among the crowd of a hundred thousand who gathered to cheer him off at the end of his two-year term. The massacre story is in Soustelle's favour, but it is the part of the legend he most vehemently rejects. His aim in Algeria had always been integration, on the Mexican pattern. To hand the country over to a terrorist faction would have been irresponsible, illiberal and stupid. Integration would not have been easy. It would have taken time and money, but he was prepared to use the newly-discovered resources of the Sahara to create this new Algeria. In 1958 integration was more than a possibility. But de Gaulle wasn't impressed. And to Soustelle all that has followed has been betrayal and destruction. "Destruction is not a style: it is the negation of all styles." The million *colons* have left; one Algerian dictatorship has been replaced by another. Arab Algeria sinks; an idea of France has been destroyed.

*

Soustelle's political career so far has been contained within two periods of exile. The scholar whose nationalism was aroused before the war by the German threat has known only political defeat. The defeats grew bigger even as his political authority grew. The fall of France has been followed by the fall of the French Empire. The vision of the Paris-Algiers-Brazzaville axis shrank to the vision of France stretching from Dunkirk to Tamanrasset, the Touareg town in the Sahara. Now there is only France. But if Algeria went yesterday, Corsica and Brittany might go tomorrow: it is the logic of bourgeois indifference and decline. The third world that France now seeks to lead is a chimera; de Gaulle's personal rule has taken France away from her friends. France, Soustelle feels, has been politically neutered. A fresh disaster is being prepared.

Dealing with defeat, the scholar, so exact in his own discipline, turns to the generalizations of emotion. He sees technical progress coinciding with moral and aesthetic decay. "Our civilization has had no style for a century." "A civilization which is exhausted no longer attracts." And his imprecise fears have now gone beyond the ruined idea of France to Western civilization itself. No capable enemy, no overwhelming external proletariat is yet visible. But that proves nothing.

These propositions are all debatable. Perhaps what is missing is a definition of the civilization that is threatened: perhaps such a definition will show that at the heart of the despair lies a patriotism that has been both nourished and wounded by defeat, as by a drug. Soustelle's main concern now is to return to his country. Inaction need not be ignoble. "I might abstain from political life. But I can't admit being ostracized after twenty-seven years in the service of my country." This is part of the serenity of exile and it may go when exile ends. The certa⁚ y of total defeat, the defeat that leaves no more battles to be fought, is its own dangerous solace. It can commit a man to hopeless duty and quixotic action and release him from the fear of failure.

This playing with the idea of defeat appears also to come from the Soustelle who makes art out of his experience and who now, in exile, has discovered all the consonances of this experience. The politician has known defeat; the ethnologist has studied a defeated people (a recent letter has told him that the Lacandones are in danger of extinction); the study of ethnology itself derives from a civilization that is on the defensive. The pattern, too neat, belongs to art. It is art, though, that comes close to self-indulgence. Even the stoicism is like romance: one of Soustelle's favourite historical tableaux is the second-century philosopher-emperor Marcus Aurelius holding the Germans on the Danube.

This romance, which holds the fear of the sudden unknown destroyer, can be taken beyond the scholar's discovery of the nervous Aztec world, awaiting Cortés. When he was a boy in Villeurbaine in Lyon, Soustelle liked to read the Roman histories of Ammianus Marcellinus. In a footnote in his last book, *Les Quatre Soleils*,* Soustelle retells a story from this historian. On a day in AD 241 the citizens of Antioch were at the theatre. Suddenly one of the actors broke off and said: "Am I dreaming? Or are those Persians?" The audience turned. The archers of King Sapor stood on the topmost terrace; their bows were drawn.

* *The Four Suns*, translated by E. Ross, André Deutsch, London, 1971.

IV

Columbus and Crusoe

Columbus and Crusoe

The Listener, 28 December 1967

THE ADVENTURE OF Columbus is like *Robinson Crusoe*. No one can imaginatively possess the whole; everything beyond the legend is tedious and complicating. It is so even in Björn Landström's book, *Columbus*, which makes the difficult adventure as accessible as it can be made. The text itself is a retelling from the usual sources. The maps and illustrations are more important. The maps make medieval ideas of geography clear. The illustrations, a true labour of love, are numerous and exact: ships, the islands, the people, the weather, the vegetation, and even the Flemish hawk's bell which delighted the natives until it became a measure of the gold dust the discoverer required them to collect.

In the legend Columbus is persecuted by many enemies; he goes back to Spain white-haired, in chains, and he dies in poverty and disgrace. It is Columbus's own picture: he had a feeling for theatre. His concern for gold exceeded his sovereign's: he expected to get a tenth of all that was found. The chains were not necessary; he was begged to take them off. He wore them for effect, just as, after the previous disaster, he had returned in the Franciscan habit. That disaster had its profitable side. He had sent back slaves, as he had always intended. He claimed, or his son claimed for him, that he had got rid of two-thirds of the natives of Hispaniola in two years; the remainder had been set to gathering gold dust. (This was an exaggeration: he had only got rid of a third.) Even after his disgrace he fussed about his coat-of-arms, appropriating a red field for the castle of Castile, as on the royal coat-of-arms. He complained to the end about his poverty, but one of his personal gold shipments, again after his disgrace, amounted to 405 pounds. His father was a weaver; his sister married a cheesemonger; his son married a lady of royal blood.

And at his death Spain hadn't gained very much. Mexico was thirteen years away; and the Indies, the source of his gold, where he thought he had discovered the Terrestrial Paradise, had become, largely through his example, *anus mundi*.

It is a story of extended horror. But it isn't only the horror that numbs response. Nor is it that the discoverer deteriorates so steadily after the discovery. It is the banality of the man. He was looking less for America or Asia than for gold; and the banality of expectation matches a continuing banality of perception. At the heart of the seamanship, the toughness, the avarice, the vindictiveness and the brutality, there is only this:

> 16 September. Here the Admiral says that on that day and all succeeding days they met with very mild breezes, and the mornings were very sweet, with naught lacking save the song of the nightingale. He adds: "And the weather was like April in Andalusia."
> 29 September. The air was very sweet and refreshing, so that the only thing lacking was the song of the nightingale; the sea was as calm as a river.

This is from *The Book of the First Voyage*, when he was at his most alert. The concrete details are deceptive. The sea and its life are observed, but mainly for signs of the nearness of land; just as, at the moment of discovery, the natives are studied, but only by a man "vigilant" – his own word – for gold. "Their hair is not curly . . . they are not at all black." Not an anthropological interest, not the response of wonder – disappointment rather: Columbus believed that where Negroes were, there was gold. Beyond this vigilance the words and the perceptions fail. The nightingale, April in Andalusia: the props of a banal poetry are used again and again until they are without meaning. They are at an even lower level than the recent astronaut's "Wow" – there is nothing like this pure cry of delight in Columbus. After the discovery, his gold-seeking seaman's banalities become repetitive, destroying romance and making the great adventure trivial. A book about Columbus needs to have pictures, and this is why Mr Landström's book is so valuable.

The medieval mind? But Queen Isabella wrote during the second voyage to find out what the climate was like. April in Andalusia wasn't enough: she wanted pictures, and the romance. Marco Polo, whom Columbus had read, dealt in romance; and Amerigo Vespucci, after whom the continent is not unfairly named. Vespucci thought it worth mentioning that the natives of the islands and the Main pissed casually into the hot sand during conversation, without turning aside; that the women were wanton and used a certain animal poison, sometimes lastingly fatal to virility, to increase the size of the male member. Perhaps he made this up; but though he too was vigilant and his own voyage ended in profitable slave-trading, he sought in the tradition of travel-romance to awaken wonder at the fact of the New World.

The facts about Columbus have always been known. In his own writings and in all his actions his egoism is like an exposed deformity; he condemns himself. But the heroic gloss, which is not even his own, has come down through the centuries. When the flagship ran aground at Haiti on the first voyage, the Indians were more than helpful: they wept to show their sympathy. Columbus was vigilant: he noted that it would be easy to subdue this "cowardly" unarmed race. This was what he presently did. Mr Landström suggests that it was unfortunate and not really meant: it is the traditional gloss. On the third voyage Columbus thought he had discovered the Terrestrial Paradise. Mr Landström, again following the gloss, says that Columbus wasn't very well at the time. But it was just this sort of geography that had made him attempt the Ocean Sea.

In this adventure, as in today's adventures in space, the romance is something we ourselves have to supply. The discovery needs a hero; the contempt settles on the country that, in the legend, betrays the hero. The discovery – and it would have come without Columbus – could not but be horrible. Primitive people, once exposed, have to be subdued and utilized or somehow put down, in the Indies, Australasia, the United States, Southern Africa; even India has its aboriginal problems. Four hundred years after the great Spanish debate, convened by the Emperor, on the treatment of primitive people, Rhodesia is an imperial issue. The parallel is there; only the contemporary debate, conducted before a mass-electorate on one side and a dispossessed but indifferent primitive people on the other, is necessarily more debased.

There is no Australian or American black legend; there is at the most a romantic, self-flattering guilt. But the black legend of Spain will persist, as will the heroic legend of Columbus. The dream of the untouched, complete world, the thing for ourselves alone, the dream of Shangri-la, is an enduring human fantasy. It fell to the Spaniards to have the unique experience. Generosity and romance, then, to the discoverer; but the Spaniards will never be forgiven. And even in the violated New World the Spaniards themselves remained subject to the fantasy. The quest for El Dorado became like a recapitulation of the whole New World adventure, a wish to have it all over again; more men and money were expended on this in twenty expeditions than on the conquest of Mexico, Peru and New Granada.

Robinson Crusoe, in its essential myth-making middle part, is an aspect of the same fantasy. It is a monologue; it is all in the mind. It is the dream of being the first man in the world, of watching the first crop grow. Not only a dream of innocence: it is the dream of being suddenly, just as one is, in unquestionable control of the physical world, of possessing "the first gun that had been fired there since the creation of the world". It is the dream of total power. "First, I made him know his name should be Friday, which was the day I saved his life. I called him so for the memory of the time. I likewise taught him to say master, and then let him know that was to be my name." Friday is awkward about religion; Crusoe cannot answer. Power brings problems. Crusoe sees some cannibals about to kill and eat a man. He runs to liberate. But then he stops. What is his right to interfere? Is it just the gun? Some Spaniards are to be rescued. How will his freedom and power continue? How will they obey? Where do sanctions start in the empty world? They must sign a contract. But there is no pen, no paper: a difficulty as particular and irrational as in a nightmare. It is from more than a desert island that he is rescued. The issues can never be resolved.

Later Crusoe makes good, in that very New World, but in the settled, beaten-down slave society of Brazil. The horror of the discovery, of being the first totally powerful man in the world: that happened a long time before.

The Ultimate Colony

Daily Telegraph Magazine, 4 July 1969

BRITISH HONDURAS IS the last British territory on the American mainland, and the present Governor ought to be the last. But this is uncertain. After five years of internal self-government, with a Premier and ministers, complete independence is still difficult. The problem is one of succession. Guatemala says that British Honduras is hers and should be returned to her. American mediation has failed. In British Honduras itself the Opposition has grown strong on the charge that the government is preparing to sell out to Guatemala. The government says it isn't. But it cannot act. It requires independence to prove its point, and independence will come only when the point is proved.

The Governor who is there, withdrawn, waiting to hand over, is Sir John Paul. His service before this was in West Africa, in Sierra Leone and the Gambia. British Honduras is his last colonial posting. He is fifty-three; his own future is uncertain. He is no longer a pensionable officer and he has as yet no job in England to go back to. In British Honduras he has little to do. He assents to bills in the name of the Queen; he is head of the Civil Service; he handles external affairs. His only direct responsibility is defence – there is a small British garrison – and public order – he shares control of the police with the minister concerned.

"Security and stability. Very important, but rather boring. One doesn't really have a full-time job. One tends to be a little isolated and divorced. Quite rightly: the country runs itself. One doesn't want to impinge."

The Governor's tact is like sensibility, an expression of a natural cool melancholy. He is a tall man, heavy but still athletic. During office hours he wears a white shirt and a tie, no jacket: the dress expressing the ambiguous formality of his job.

"So long as it's a dependent territory the Governor can't be an anomaly. But he can have damned little to do. It's even worse when you're a Governor-General. There's even less to do. I had a year of that in the Gambia. I saw that the only way of getting out was to write a republican constitution. I did so. We put it to the electorate and they rejected it."

White water-skis and fishing rods lean against the wall of the Governor's office, airy and light. A half-open umbrella hangs from the grey steel safe. There is a wall-map: this all but empty British territory – 9,000 square miles, 100,000 people – incongruous in Latin America: Mexico the industrial giant to the north, Guatemala of the high mountains, the political assassinations, the temperate flowers and fruit, the Spanish and Mayan architectural antiquities, to the west and south. The wire-netted windows of the Governor's office show the sparse gardens of Government House, the two tall royal palms. Just beyond the garden wall is the Caribbean, not blue here, thick with catfish, restless scavengers of the waters of this city built on swampland.

The Empire here was never grand. It began as a seventeenth-century coastal intrusion on the Spanish American Empire. The territory doubled its size in the last century. But it was acknowledged as an intrusion and was never settled; it never became a land of plantations. The first interlopers came with their Negroes to cut logwood; their successors went further inland to cut mahogany. The mahogany forests have all been cut down. Bush remains, and scattered little bush communities: Maya Indians, who move among the mighty ruins of their civilization like any other degraded immigrant group; Black Caribs, transported from the West Indian island of St Vincent, considered by Negroes to be very black and ugly, with a bad smell; Spanish and mestizo refugees from Yucatan; and, in the last ten years, some thousands of Mennonites, a Bible-reading German-American sect, who have transformed many square miles of tropical bush, bought at fifteen shillings an acre, into the landscape of pioneer America. The descendants of the Negro log-cutters, now two-thirds of the population, and confirmed lovers of city life, live in the over-crowded coastal capital, Belize City.

From the air Belize City is an arbitrary white huddle at the edge of a sodden land where forests occasionally reflect the sun as a pale white disc. The coastline is untidy with drowned islets, like darker cloud shadows; during the 1961 hurricane one "exclusive" American-owned islet, the cause of some local resentment, sank with its three cottages. Corrugated-iron latrines overhang the wide, slow canals of the city; in one night-club tourists are invited to feed the catfish.

In this city to be buried in "a good dry hole" is to be lucky. In the late afternoons Negroes in jackets and ties – famous throughout Central America for their immunity to disease – walk behind the hearses to the cemetery just outside the town, waving white handkerchiefs. Afterwards they stand relaxed and emblematic among the higher tombstones, chatting, waving in the dusk. It is like a ceremony of bewildered farewell at the limit of the world. But they are only keeping off the mosquitoes and sandflies.

In Belize City the Union Jack is the flag of Negro protest against the Guatemalan claim. The Negroes of British Honduras were not plantation slaves. They were foresters. And though until recently some private houses in Belize City could still show their old slave punishment cells, with the original chains, the Negroes look back with pride to the days when, securely British, they fought shoulder to shoulder with their proprietors against the Spaniards.

"If you mention slavery here," the Negro leader of the Opposition says, "people would stare at you and wonder what you are talking about."

The Guatemalans say jokingly that Guatemala should take back British Honduras and Britain should take back her Negroes. The Mexicans have a joke like this too: Mexico will take British Honduras, Guatemala will take the *negritos*.

The Vice-President of Guatemala, one of his country's leading intellectuals, doesn't find the joke funny. He doesn't want the Negroes, and he is frightened of Mexico. Mexico too has a claim, to a good half of British Honduras; but Mexico will act only if Guatemala does. The Guatemalan Vice-President despairs. He is an Indian and a patriot; he thinks that Guatemala has lost British Honduras, her twenty-third department, that the land has been spitefully spoiled by the British, who packed it out with Negroes and now require neither the land nor the Negroes.

"We have no Negro problem. A Negro has only to square his shoulders, and ten of our Indians will run. We are a weak race. The British brought over those Negroes from the Congo, Angola, the Sudan. They can work well in the heat; our Indians can't. Negroes don't fall ill easily. Malaria doesn't touch them. When the Negro mates with the Indian he produces the *sambo*. That is a race that quickly becomes degenerate."

But Vice-Presidents change; the Guatemalan claim can at any time become a Guatemalan crusade. Nothing will happen, though, while British Honduras remains British; and the question of who will get the Negroes will remain academic so long as there is a Governor and the Union Jack flies over Government House, not as protest, but as a sign of a continuing order.

Government House is a white two-storeyed wooden building that looks like a large private house. It has only three – enormous – bedrooms. Its neutral style conceals its age. It was begun in 1815, and is not like the Government Houses of the later Empire. It has been neglected for periods and has been through many hurricanes. The tidal wave that followed the last, in 1961, covered the main floor and disfigured the central mahogany staircase, the building's only notable feature.

"It was all much grander in the Gambia. There had been East African governors before. They had, I think quite rightly, very strong views about how a Governor should be looked after. Most beautiful garden too. But of course this house suits the resources of the country."

Government House costs the Government of British Honduras

£11,000 a year. That covers everything: the monogrammed china and silver, bought through the Crown Agents in London; the three stewards, Lloyd, Garnett and George; Leone, the cook, Adela, the laundress; the two secretaries in the Governor's outer office; and the Governor himself. The Governor's ADC is an adjutant in the local Volunteer Guard.

"He's part-time. There's very little formality about this job now. The flag is lowered at 6.30. The police sentries do it. In the Gambia it was done with ceremony, with sounding – what do they call it – the Retreat. We did it once here and I must say I thought it was jolly impressive. We had a presentation of insignia and we had three hundred and fifty to four hundred guests and the flag was lowered and they beat the Retreat. But it taxed our resources so much we haven't done it since.

"We have receptions every month or so. Generally. It's the one place where everybody can meet. It's not a criticism, but people here tend to mix with their own group. My wife does the whole thing herself. I have no housekeeper. So when I am on my own the entertaining is restricted.

"We had a fine new car. It's just been smashed up. Brand-new Austin Princess, possibly a write-off. Most infuriating. It's been sent to England for repairs. So we are reduced to a 1962 Rover."

The Governor has a Land-Rover for touring. His tours are official, but muted and almost private: the Premier of British Honduras has made it clear that he doesn't like official public "confrontations" with the Governor.

"He's very sensible. One can only talk piously."

The Governor has been to the Assembly only once. He has only once seen, and can no longer remember, the locally designed costume – black coat, white lace cuffs, white cravat, long red gown – which the mace-bearer, a former stevedore, complainingly wears. The Assembly has been adjourned and adjourned: the Governor has never made a Speech from the Throne.

"Not that this concerns me," the Governor says.

The Governor has taken up painting again. "It keeps me out of mischief." His Gambian watercolours – precise, meticulous, limpid – hang on the grey walls of Government House among old official photographs, a tarnished oil painting of the Berkshire downs and a view of the Thames.

"The Governor," the Premier says, "is like St John the Baptist. He gets smaller every day. Government House isn't Government House. Government House is the Premier's Office and the Assembly."

Next to Government House is the Premier's official residence. It is an inelegant wooden bungalow, white with blue facings – the colours of the Premier's party – and a red tin roof.

In the dining-room there is a larger-than-life portrait of the Premier, done by a local artist from a photograph. It shows a youthful, mischievous man of fifty in glasses and wearing an open-necked shirt. The mischief is in the eyes and the mouth; the lips are welted and look bruised and parched. The artist had trouble with the mouth, and managed to hit it off only while listening to the Premier's voice on the radio. The Premier is heard every morning on the programme called *Wake up and Work*. The Premier is a man of mixed race: Maya Indian, European, some seepage of African. He looks white; this painting makes him black.

The Premier, the Honourable George Price, does not live in his official residence. He lives in his old family house in the run-down centre of Belize City. The unpainted house, on tall stilts, had been weathered black. It is blank and shuttered behind a high fence; and it has no front steps.

The Premier goes home early. He is unmarried; a neighbour cooks for him. He receives few visitors at home and he seldom takes home official papers. He reads novels – Thomas Mann is a favourite – and theological works. He says his prayers before going to bed. He is up at five and goes to Mass at 5.30. He does not worry through to political decisions; they come to him after the night of prayer and rest; and he is in his office punctually at eight. He has no grey hairs.

When he was a young man George Price studied for the

priesthood – the disturbing mouth is that of a self-willed priest – and even his enemies say that neither age nor power has changed him. He is not interested in money; he is known to give away money; his outer office is always full of suppliants. His official car is a Land-Rover; he ceaselessly tours the empty country, greeting, checking. Then, abruptly every day, the public life ends.

"Mr Price is not like the rest of men," the leader of the Opposition says. "The rest of us have wives and families, recreations. Mr Price has a one-track mind. He wants to get rid of the British but we believe he is quite willing to replace the British by the Guatemalans."

"This is a subtle thing," the Premier's second-in-command says. "The subtlety is that if Guatemala takes over, Mr Price has less to lose. Mr Price's complexion and racial make-up have given some credence to this belief."

"It usually is a good way," the Opposition second-in-command says, "to parade as a religious person. Who's Price trying to kid? Price has long dreamed of a glorious Latin-Catholic Central American Empire."

"Price doesn't look it," the Guatemalan Vice-President says, "but he is a Negro. If he was a Maya Indian and a patriot, as some people say, he wouldn't have got mixed up with all those Negroes over there."

Once, when he was only a nationalist agitator, the first in British Honduras, the Guatemalan claim was useful to George Price. Now, as Premier, he is trapped by the claim; it erodes his power.

"I don't think anybody felt the life was going to come so quickly to an end. After Ghana one could do nothing about it and one wanted to do nothing about it."

A visit to Trinidad in 1934–5 was the Governor's first glimpse of a colony. It made him think of a career in the Colonial Service.

"I liked the *ambience*, the friendliness of the people. Mark you, in those days there were far fewer opportunities for people like myself in the industrial or commercial world, for people who had

– it tends to be a dirty word – a public school education." The Governor was at Weymouth in Dorset. "Long since defunct."

"I applied to join the Colonial Service before the war. I was at Cambridge, came down in June 1939. Thought I might as well have a regular commission and get properly involved instead of hanging around getting pushed around. I was a prisoner most of the war. I was in the Royal Tank Corps. Captured in Calais in 1940. After the war I was seconded as ADC to Sierra Leone. When I was released from the Army I joined the Colonial Service and became a District Commissioner. I had great difficulty getting rid of my regular commission. Not because they particularly wanted me – I'm sure of that – but on principle. . . .

"The work of a DC was one of the most fascinating jobs you could ever have. You were virtually on your own in those days. You got very attached to the people. We all felt a sense of participation. One talks of colonialism now. . . . People tend to look at Empire in the context of the last fifty or one hundred years. But I think it fair to say that without Empire over the centuries there wouldn't have been the spread of knowledge. Africa is the most contentious example, I suppose. I feel there must be something on the credit side. This is no criticism of the local people. They were prisoners of their own circumstances. . . .

"It was the most rewarding part of my life. You were very clearly defined. One knew exactly, in one's modest way, what one was trying to do. You weren't humbugged too much by what we used to call the Secretariat. We were alone much of the time. Pretty early evenings, no electric lights. We had small children. That kept us pretty busy. We used to read a lot. One spent a lot of time on tour. Of course, in those days one walked, seeing what was going on."

On the stroke of eight the Land-Rover sweeps up the short drive to the portico of Government House. The Premier, tall and slender, in an open-necked braided Yucatan-style shirt, bounces out after his aide.

"Morning, Excellency!"

The Premier likes to use titles and he always appears to put them between inverted commas.

It is the day of the Premier's weekly tour; the visiting writer will go with him. The Governor, in white shirt and tie, is there to greet the Premier. The formalities are brief and urgent. The aide runs to close the Land-Rover door, and soon we are on the road.

"Marnin', Miss Virginia."

When the Premier waves he abandons conversation and concentrates; he is like a man giving a benediction.

Nine men are standing around a small patch on the main road. The PWD lorries have broken down again. The Premier makes a note. Later we pass PWD mounds of earth.

"Jarge Price, clean the road!" someone shouts.

We stop often.

"Marnin', marnin'."

The Premier strides ahead in his flapping shirt, loose tan trousers and big black shoes. The aide runs, to protect the Premier against enraged dogs. The muscular young Negro driver stands beside his vehicle, chewing gum, tall, in boots, tight jeans and jersey, dark glasses.

"Marnin'. It's Jarge Price, the Premier. Lemme see your kitchen. Lemme see wa' you cook this marnin'."

He lifts lids, examines breakfast plates, gives his benediction. And we bolt for the Land-Rover.

When George Price left the seminary, for financial reasons, he found a job with a local self-made timber millionaire. He stayed with him for fourteen years as secretary and travelling companion.

"We travelled everywhere. I remember one day at a hotel in Chicago putting a value on the people around the dining table. I made it 300 million dollars. When you mix with people like that all the time you can't feel too much envy. I very early on had the feeling of *sic transit gloria mundi*. Turton had all this money. But he was a sick man. . . .

"Whenever I went into a bank I used to feel: you are entering the temple of the capitalists. I suppose I used to say it sometimes.

Turton didn't always like the things I said. I was quoting to him one day from the 1931 Encyclical – I think it was *Quadragesimo Anno*. About relations between employer and worker, the living wage and so on. He listened and I thought I was getting through. At the end he said, 'Jarge, the Pope doesn't know a shit about business.'

"It was Turton who made me go into politics. He said, 'You will go into politics.' He made me run for the Belize City Council in 1944. I lost. Now if a doctor said to me to give up politics, I wouldn't.''

But politics do not stand still. The colonial politician who is the first leader and educator is also the man who most speedily makes himself out of date. Politics as the vocation of the failed priest, the empty land as the parish: it no longer answers. The Guatemalan claim has made the politics of British Honduras artificial and static. Development, like independence itself, recedes. The Premier has been to these villages too often before; he is no longer a man with news.

"They don't seem to be looking for a messiah," the Premier's second-in-command says. "They seem to want participation. Or collective leadership. I think Mr Price senses this change in the country. He has recently enlarged his cabinet."

"I am getting old," the Premier says. "I am not a fighter as I used to be."

"One's career has changed quite completely from the way one envisaged it," the Governor says. "One of the ironies is that most of the time one's been working oneself out of a job. I've been extremely lucky. Very few left now, out of the old Colonial Service. Infinitesimal number really."

The world intrudes. The sons of people once content with the Premier's benediction go away to study and come back and curse both parties. They talk of Vietnam and Black Power. They undermine the Negro loyalty to the slave past.

"The whites are buying up the land. English colonialism tried to condition the black man against using the land. There was a concerted effort by the English colonialists to have their black slaves remain log-cutters. It became a sort of phallic symbol to the black to be a log-cutter."

The politics of British Honduras have always had a racial-religious undertone: the Negro-Protestant town, the Roman Catholic country. Now race threatens to make the old politics even more irrelevant. The Premier, white below his carefully maintained tan, a political vanity, is especially vulnerable.

The Governor gets a report on the latest Black Power meeting. "They pulled in one hundred and fifty last night. I must say I couldn't make head or tail of what was said."

We are having drinks around the small new pool at the side of Government House. The sea breeze is moist.

"Do you think he'll have lunch with me?" the American Consul asks. He is concerned: the local spokesman for Black Power, who is just twenty-one, went to an American university on an American government scholarship. "I wish someone would give me 12,000 dollars to send my son to college."

The Consul is friendly, intelligent. He has had some experience of British colonies in transition. He "watched" the affairs of British Guiana at a time when the Jagan government was being overthrown by Negro racist riots and an American-supported strike.

The United States has an interest: it is the true issue of imperial succession.

The Governor, anxious to be active again, thinks of his own future.

"There is no obligation on the part of the government to find another job for me. I don't know what the future holds. But we've been lucky. The big concern was the education of one's daughters, and we are more or less at the end of that tunnel."

The Governor will leave the Colonial Service with an affection for the countries he worked in, but with no great nostalgia. He will remain concerned about the debasing effect of tourism on backward countries, and all that these countries have to do.

"Take the Gambia. You couldn't get people to go to school in some areas. Most awful waste of manpower. Those people, as of now, they've not a hope in hell, and they'll be living for, what, sixty, seventy years."

The Governor will also be taking back a memory of the midnight handover in the Gambia: the Union Jack coming down, the lights going off and coming on again, the new Gambian flag in place, the handshakes from the Gambians, delighted but also managing in that moment to express a personal concern for the Governor.

The flag that came down that midnight is in the Governor's Hampshire cottage. It was hung out of the window to celebrate his daughters' success in the A-level examinations.

The Premier plans to build a retreat in the cool Mountain Pine Ridge region.

"Mr Price knows how to survive," the Premier's second-in-command says. "He's a natural politician. I don't see the demise of Mr Price."

But in the clerical mischievousness of the Premier, which can at times be like arrogance, and in his daily routine, there is already more than a hint of withdrawal. He will fight to the end. But he also tells his supporters, "My day will come. I will go."

He has never cared for the things of the world. But for most of his life he has been immersed in them, and he often reflects on the strangeness of his career.

"I have this recurring dream. I am in church. Someone is saying mass – Turton, my old employer, or Pinks, one of his managers – and I wonder why I, who would so much like to be up there, am not, and that old sinner is."

St Kitts: Papa and the Power Set

The New York Review of Books, 8 May 1969

AFTER MORE THAN twenty years as a folk leader, one of the Negro shepherd-kings of the Caribbean, Robert Bradshaw of St Kitts – "Papa" to his followers – is in trouble. Two years ago he became the first Premier of the three-island state of St Kitts-Nevis-Anguilla. The state had a total area of 153 square miles and a population of 57,000. It has since become smaller. Anguilla has seceded and apparently gone for good, with its own islet dependencies of Scrub Island, Dog Island, and Anguillita: a loss of thirty-five square miles and 6,000 people. There is discontent in Nevis, fifty square miles. In St Kitts itself, Papa Bradshaw's base, there is a dangerous opposition.

The opposition union is called WAM, the opposition political party PAM. WAM and PAM: it is part of the deadly comic-strip humour of Negro politics. These are still only the politics of kingship, in which there are as yet no rules for succession. It is only when leaders like Papa Bradshaw are in trouble, when they are threatened and fight back, that they become known outside their islands; and it is an irony of their kingship that they are then presented as dangerous clowns. Once Papa Bradshaw's yellow Rolls-Royce was thought to be a suitable emblem of his kingship and courage, a token of Negro redemption. Few people outside knew about the Rolls-Royce; now it is famous and half a joke.

The folk leader who has been challenged cannot afford to lose. To lose is to be without a role, to be altogether ridiculous.

"Papa Bradsha' started something," a supporter says. "As long as he lives he will have to continue it."

Bradshaw prepares to continue. The opposition are not allowed to broadcast; their supporters say they do not find it easy to get jobs. Men are recruited from the other Caribbean islands for the police. The St Kitts army, called the Defence Force, is said to have been increased to one hundred and twenty; Papa Bradshaw is the Colonel. There are reports of a helicopter ready to police the island's sixty-eight square miles.

It has been played out in other countries, this drama of the folk-leader who rules where he once securely agitated and finds that power has brought insecurity. In St Kitts the scale is small, and in the simplicity of the setting the situation appears staged.

Think of a Caribbean island roughly oval in shape. Indent the coastline: beaches here, low cliffs there. Below the sharp and bare 4,000-foot peak of a central mountain chain there is forest. Then the land slopes green and trimmed with sugar-cane, uncluttered with houses or peasant allotments, all the way down to the sea. A narrow coast road encircles the island; it is impossible to get lost. The plantation workers live beside this road, squeezed between sugar-cane and sea. Their timber houses are among the tiniest in the world.

All the history of St Kitts is on this road. There, among those houses on low stilts, whose dirt yards run down through tangled greenery to the sea, Sir Thomas Warner landed in 1623, to found the first British colony in the West Indies. Here, in the barest opening in the sugar-cane, are two rocks crudely carved by the aboriginal Caribs, whom the English and the French united to exterminate just there, at Bloody River, now a dip in the road. Sir Thomas Warner is buried in that churchyard. Not far away are the massive eighteenth-century fortifications of Brimstone Hill, once guarding the sugar-rich slave islands and the convoys that assembled in the calm water here for the run to England. The cannons still point; the site has been restored.

In the south-east the flat coastal strip broadens out into a little plain. Here, still set in the level green of sugar-cane, are the air-strip and the capital, Basseterre. There is one vertical in this plain: the tall white chimney of the island's single sugar factory.

The neatness and order is still like the order of the past. It speaks of Papa Bradshaw's failure. He hasn't changed much. His fame came early, as an organizer of the sugar workers; a thirteen-week strike in 1948 is part of the island's folk-lore. But Bradshaw's plantation victories mean less today to the young. They do not wish to work on the plantations. They look for "development" – and they mean tourism – on their own island. The air over nearby Antigua rocks with "Sunjets" and "Fiesta Jets". St Kitts only has brochures and plans; the airfield can only take Viscounts. It is unspoiled; the tourists do not come. The feeling among the young is that Papa Bradshaw has sold out to the sugar interests and wants no change.

And Bradshaw's victories were only of St Kitts. They meant little to the peasant farmers of Nevis, and nothing to the long-independent farmers and fishermen of Anguilla, seventy miles away. The Nevisians and Anguillans never voted for Bradshaw. Bradshaw didn't need their votes, but he was irritated. He said he would put pepper in the soup of the Nevisians and bones in their rice; he would turn Anguilla into a desert and make the Anguillans suck salt. That was eleven years ago.

"Gahd bless Papa Bradsha' for wa' he do." It is only the old and the devout among the plantation Negroes in St Kitts who say that now. They remember the *ola* or trash houses, the cruel contract system, the barefoot children and the disease. Bradshaw himself worked as a young man in the Basseterre sugar factory; he carries a damaged hand as a mark of that service. Like many folk leaders, he never moved far beyond his first inspiration. It is also true that, like many folk leaders, he is responsible for the hope and the restlessness by which he is now, at the age of fifty-one, rejected.

The weatherbeaten little town of Basseterre also has a stage-set simplicity. There is a church at the end of the main street. PAM hangs its home-made board in the veranda of a rickety little house. Directly opposite is a building as rickety, but larger; this is labelled "Masses House" and is the headquarters of the Bradshaw union. At times of tension this section of the main treet is known as the Gaza Strip.

Masses House has a printery which every day runs off 1,200 copies of a ragged miniature newspaper called *The Labour Spokesman*. Even with large headlines there isn't always enough news to fill the front page; sometimes a joke, headlined "Humour", has to be added. Sport is good for a page or two or three. A cricketer like Sobers can make the local sportswriter ambitious. "The shy boy of seventeen, not yet lost his Mother's features on his debut against England in the West Indies in 1954, has probably rose to the pinnacle of being the greatest cricketer both of our time and the medieval age. If W. G. Grace were to twitch in his grave at the comment he would only turn over on the other side to nod his approval."

A few doors away from Masses House is Government Head-quarters, a modernistic building of three storeys. Grey air-conditioners project from its façade; a pool in the patio is visible through the glass wall. The hotel is opposite, a converted old timber house. The manager is a gentle second-generation Lebanese whose nerves have been worn fine by the harassments of his large family, his staff, untrained or temperamental, the occasional assertive Negro group, and the political situation. "Have you seen our Premier, sir?" He supports Bradshaw but avoids controversy; he knows now he will never see Beirut.

A short side street leads to Pall Mall Square: the church, the timbered colonial-Georgian Public Library and Court, the St Kitts Club, the private houses with lower floors of masonry, upper floors shingled, white and fragile, and steep four-sided roofs. The garden is unkempt, the wire fences around the central Victorian fountain trampled down, the lamp-standards empty and rusting; but the trees and flowers and the backdrop of mountains are still spectacular. Pall Mall Square is where PAM holds its public meetings. It is also, as all St Kitts knows, the place where, among trees and flowers and buildings like these, "new" Negroes from Africa were put up for auction, after being rested and nourished in the importers' barracoons, which were there, on the beach, not far from today's oil-storage tanks.

The past crowds the tiny island like the sugar-cane itself. Deeper and deeper protest is always possible.

At about ten every morning the guards change outside Government Headquarters. The green-bereted officer shouts, boots stamp; and the two relieved soldiers, looking quickly up and down the street, get into the back of the idling Land-Rover and are driven to Defence Force Headquarters, an exposed wooden hut on high ground near ZIZ, the one-studio radio station.

Against the soft green hills beyond Basseterre, the bright blue sea and the cloud-topped peak of Nevis, a Negro lounges in a washed-out paratrooper's uniform, thin and bandy-legged, zipped-up and tight, like a soft toy.

It seems to be drama for the sake of drama. But there are bullet marks on the inside of the hut. These are shown as evidence of the armed raid that was made on Basseterre by persons unknown in June 1967, at the beginning of the Anguillan crisis. The police station was also attacked. Many shots were fired but no one was killed; the raiders disappeared. Bradshaw added to his legend by walking the next morning from Government Headquarters to Masses House in the uniform of a Colonel, with a rifle, bandolier, and binoculars.

The raid remains a mystery. Some people believe it was staged, but there are Anguillans who now say that they were responsible and that their aim was to protect the independence of their island by kidnapping Bradshaw and holding him as a hostage. The raid failed because it was badly organized – no one had thought about transport in Basseterre – and because Bradshaw had been tipped off by an Anguillan businessman.

Days after the raid leading members of PAM and WAM were arrested. They went on trial four months later. Defence lawyers were harassed; and Bradshaw's supporters demonstrated when all the accused men were acquitted. Ever since, the rule of law in St Kitts has appeared to be in danger. The definition of power has become simple.

I see them:
These bold men; these rare men –
Above all other men that toil –
That LIVE the truth; that suffer:
These policemen. We love them!

The poem is from *The Labour Spokesman*. There may no longer be a danger from Anguilla, but the police and the army have come to St Kitts to stay.

I first saw St Kitts eight years ago, at night, from a broken-down immigrant ship in Basseterre harbour. We didn't land. The emigrants had been rocking for some time in the bay in large open boats. The ship's lights played on sweated shirts and dresses, red eyes in upturned oily faces, cardboard boxes and suitcases painted with names and careful addresses in England.

In the morning, on the open sea, the nightmare was over. The jackets and the ties and the suitcases had gone. The emigrants, as I found out, moving among them, were politically educated. Copies of *The Labour Spokesman* were about. Many of the emigrants from Anguilla, which had been recently hit by a hurricane, were in constant touch with God.

The emigrants had a leader. He was a slender young mulatto, going to England to do law. He moved among the emigrants like a trusted agitator; he was protective. He was a man of some background and his political concern, in such circumstances, seemed unusual. He mistrusted my inquiries. He thought I was a British agent and told the emigrants not to talk to me. They became unfriendly; word spread that I had called one of them a nigger. I was rescued from the adventure by a young Baptist missionary.

I didn't get the name of the ship-board leader then. In St Kitts and the Caribbean he is now famous. He did more than study law. He returned to St Kitts to challenge Bradshaw. He founded PAM. He has been jailed, tried, and acquitted; he is only thirty-one. He is Dr William Herbert. A good deal of his magic in St Kitts, his power to challenge, comes from that title of Doctor – obtained for a legal thesis – which he was then travelling to London to get.

He came into the Basseterre hotel dining-room one morning. As soon as we were introduced he reminded me of our last meeting. The ship, he said, was Spanish and disorganized and he was young. He was as restless and swift and West Indian-handsome as I had remembered: his five months in jail have not marked him.

"I don't want to frighten you," he said, when he came to see me later that day. "But you should be careful. Writers can disappear. Two soldiers will be watching the hotel tonight."

We drove to a rusting seaside bar, deserted, a failed tourist amenity.

"Have you seen Bradshaw?"

I said that the feeling in Government Headquarters was that I might be a British agent. Mr Bradshaw wouldn't give an interview, but he had come over to the hotel one morning to greet me.

"He's an interesting man. He knows a lot about African art and magic and so on. It perhaps explains his hold, you know."

We went to look at Frigate Bay, part of the uninhabited area of scrub and salt-ponds which is attached like a tail to the oval mass of St Kitts. The government had recently announced a £29-million tourist development for Frigate Bay. Some in-transit cruise passengers had been taken to inspect the site a few days before; *The Labour Spokesman* had announced it as the start of the tourist season.

"Development!" Herbert said, waving at the desolation. "If you come here at night they shoot you, you know. It's a military area. They say we are trying to sabotage."

On the way back we detoured through some Basseterre slum streets. Herbert waved at women and children. "*How, how, man?*" Many waved back. He said it was his method, concentrating on the women and children; they drew the men in.

Herbert is the first and only Ph.D. in St Kitts. Beside him, Bradshaw is archaic, the leader of people lifted up from despair, the man of the people who in power achieves a personal style which all then feel they share. In St Kitts and the West Indies Bradshaw is now a legend, for the gold swizzle-stick he is reputed to bring out at parties to stir his champagne, the gold brush for his moustache, the formal English dress, even the silk hose and buckle shoes on some ceremonial occasions, the vintage yellow Rolls-Royce. He has a local reputation for his knowledge of antiques and African art and for his book-reading. He is believed to be a member of several book clubs. He reads much Winston Churchill; his favourite book, his PRO told me, is *The Good Earth*; his favourite comic strip, *Li'l Abner*.

It is an attractive legend. But I found him subdued, in dress and speech. I was sorry he didn't want to talk more to me; he said he had suffered much from writers. I understood. I looked at his moustache and thought of the gold brush. He is well-built, a young fifty-one, one of those men made ordinary by their photographs. We talked standing up. His speech was precise, very British, with little of St Kitts in his accent. He stood obliquely to me; he wore dark glasses. As we walked down the hotel steps to the Land-Rover with his party's slogan, "Labour Leads", he told me he was pessimistic about the future of small countries like St Kitts. He worked, but he was full of despair. He had supported the West Indian Federation, but that had failed. And it is true that Bradshaw began to lose his grip on St Kitts during his time as a Minister in the West Indian Federal Government, whose head-quarters was in Trinidad.

The Negro folk-leader is a peasant leader. St Kitts is like a black English parish, far from the source of beauty and fashion. The folk leader who emerges requires, by his exceptional gifts, to be absorbed into that higher society of which the parish is a shadow. For leaders like Bradshaw, though, there is no such society. They are linked forever to the primitives who were the source of their original power. They are doomed to smallness; they have to create their own style. Christophe, Emperor of Haiti, creator of a Negro aristocracy with laughable names, came from this very island of St Kitts, where he was a slave and a tailor; the inspiration for the Citadel in Haiti came from those fortifications at Brimstone Hill beside the littoral road.

The difference between Herbert and Bradshaw is the difference between Herbert's title of Doctor and Bradshaw's title of Papa. Each man's manner seems to contradict his title. Herbert has none of Bradshaw's applied style. His out-of-court dress is casual; his car is old; the house he is building outside Basseterre is the usual St Kitts miniature. His speech is more colloquial than Bradshaw's, his accent more local. His manners are at once middle-class and popular, one mode containing the other. He never strains; he moves with the assurance of his class and his looks. To all this he adds the Ph.D.

"Tell me," Bradshaw's black PRO asked with some bitterness, "who do you think is the more educated man? Herbert or Bradshaw?"

It would have been too sophisticated a question to put to the young and newly educated who went to Herbert's early lectures on economics, law, and political theory in Pall Mall Square.

"Studyation is better than education," Bradshaw said, comforting his ageing illiterates from the canefields. It became one of his *mots*.

But Herbert grew as the leader of literate protest. Everything became his cause. New electricity rates were announced: large users were to pay less per unit. Standard practice in other countries, but Herbert and PAM said the new rates were unfair to the poor of St Kitts. The poor agreed.

Bradshaw and one of his ministers became law students; Bradshaw was almost fifty. The faded notifications of their enrolment in a London Inn are still displayed in the portico of the Court in Pall Mall Square; both men were said to be eating dinners during their official trips to London. Then Anguilla seceded; PAM and WAM were as troublesome as their names; the world press was hostile. Herbert, jailed, tried, acquitted, became a Caribbean figure. Bradshaw was isolated. He appeared to be on the way out. But then he recruited a young St Kitts lawyer-lecturer as his Public Relations Officer.

This man has saved Bradshaw, and in a few months he has given a new twist to St Kitts politics. Bradshaw's tactics have changed. He is no longer the established leader on the defensive, attracting fresh agitation. He has become once again the leader of protest. It is in protest that he now competes with Herbert. The young PRO has provided the lectures and the intellectual backing. He is known to the irreverent as Bradshaw's Race Relations Officer. The cause is Black Power.

The avowed aim is the dismantling of that order which the geography of the island illustrates. The word the PRO sometimes uses is Revolution. The word has got to the white suburb of Fortlands and the Golf Club, where the little group of English expatriates is known as the Whisperers.

Someone put it like this: "What Bradshaw now wants to do is to make a fresh start, with the land and the people."

The politics of St Kitts today, opaque to the visitor looking for principles and areas of difference, become clearer as soon as it is realized that both parties are parties of protest, in the vacuum of independence; and that for both parties the cause of protest is that past, of slavery. What is at stake is the kingship, and this has recently been simplified. The difficult message of Black Power – identity, economic involvement, solidarity, as the PRO defines it – has become mangled in transmission. It can now be heard that Bradshaw, for all the English aspirations of his past, is a full-blooded Ashanti. Herbert is visibly mulatto.

Herbert's father was Labour Relations Officer for the sugar industry at the time of Bradshaw's famous thirteen-week strike. It was a difficult time for the Herbert family. They were threatened and abused by the strikers; and the St Kitts story is that Herbert, still a boy, met Bradshaw in the street one day and vowed to get even. Herbert says the meeting may have taken place, but he doesn't remember it.

I asked him now whether power in St Kitts was worth the time, the energy, the dangers.

"A man is in the sea," Herbert said. "He must swim."

There is still a Government House in St Kitts, a modest, wide-verandaed timber house on an airy hill. The butler wears white; a lithograph of a local scene, a gift of the Queen, hangs in the drawing-room; there is a signed photograph of the Duke of Edinburgh. The governor is a Negro Knight from another island, a much respected lawyer and academic. He is without a role; he is isolated from the local politics of kingship, this fight between the lawyers, in which the rule of law may go. He has spent much of his time in Government House working on a study of recent West Indian constitution-making. It is called *The Way to Power*.

The PRO on whom Bradshaw depends, the lawyer-lecturer to whom he has surrendered part of his power, is Lee Moore, a short, slight, bearded, country-born Negro of about thirty. Moore says that when he came back to St Kitts from London he rejected the view that what was needed in St Kitts was a Negro aristocracy. But the political usefulness of Black Power was only accidentally discovered, in the excitement that followed a lecture he gave on the subject.

Now, like Herbert, Lee Moore drives around the circular St Kitts road, mixing law business with campaigning, waving, mixing gravity with heartiness. On his car there is a sticker, cut out from a petrol advertisement: *Join the Power Set*.

I made a tour with him late one afternoon. Shortly after nightfall we had a puncture. He was unwilling to use the jack; he said he didn't know where to put it. He crouched and peered; he was confused. Some cars went by without stopping. I began to fear for his clothes and dignity. Then two cyclists passed. They shouted and came back to help. "We thought it was one of those brutes," one of them said. A van stopped. The jack wasn't used. The car was lifted while the wheel was changed.

Moore was in a state of some excitement when we drove off again, and it was a little time before I understood that it was an important triumph.

"It's how I always change a wheel. Did you hear what those boys on the cycles shouted? '*It's Lee Moore's car.*'"

Power, the willing services of the simple and the protecting: another man of the people in the making, another Negro on the move.

After a while he said reflectively, "If it was Herbert he would still be there, I can tell you."

Herbert, though, might have used the jack.

Anguilla: The Shipwrecked Six Thousand

The New York Review of Books, 24 April 1969

AMONG THE GREEN and hilly islands of the Caribbean Anguilla is like a mistake, a sport. It is seventeen miles long and two miles wide and so flat that when Anguillans give you directions they don't tell you to turn right or left; they say east or west. It is rocky and arid. There are no palm trees, no big trees. Mangrove is thick above the beaches, which look as they must have done when Columbus came. The forests that then existed have long been cut down; and the Anguillans, charcoal-burners and boat-builders, are the natural enemies of anything green that looks like growing big.

Sugar-cane used to grow in some places, but even in the days of slavery it was never an island of plantations. In 1825, nine years before the abolition of slavery in the British Empire, there were about three hundred white people and three hundred free coloureds, people of mixed race. Between them they kept about three thousand Negroes. The Negroes were a liability. On other Caribbean islands Negroes were let off on Saturdays to work on their own plots. In Anguilla they were turned loose for half the week to forage for themselves.

Today there are only about twelve thousand Anguillans. Half of them live or work overseas, in the nearby United States Virgin Islands, in Harlem, and in Slough in Buckinghamshire, known locally as Sloughbucks. But there are houses and plots for most of them to return to; the desolate island has long been parcelled out.

In mid-December last year, when I was there, the island was filling up for Christmas. The Viscount aircraft of LIAT, Leeward Islands Air Transport ("We fly where buccaneers sailed"), had stopped calling ever since Anguilla rebelled in 1967 and broke away from the newly independent three-island British Commonwealth state of St Kitts-Nevis-Anguilla. But the Anguillans (after chasing away an American and his DC-3) had set up three fiercely competitive little airlines of their own, Air Anguilla, Anguilla Airways, Valley Air Services, each with its own livery and its own five-passenger Piper Aztecs regularly doing the five-minute, five-dollar connecting hop from St Martin.

More than any other Caribbean community, the Anguillans have the sense of home. The land has been theirs immemorially; no humiliation attaches to it. There are no Great Houses, as in St Kitts; there are not even ruins.

For the Anguillans history begins with the myth of a shipwreck. This was how the white founders came, the ancestors of the now multi-coloured clans of Flemings, Hodges, Richardsons, Websters, Gumbs. About the arrival of the Negroes there is some confusion. Many know they were imported as slaves. But one young man was sure they were here before the shipwreck. Another felt they had come a year or two after. He didn't know how or why. "I forget that part." The past does not count. The Anguillans have lived for too long like a shipwrecked community.

They are not well educated. Instead, they have skills, like boat-building, and religion, which is a continual excitement. Few Anguillans act without divine guidance. The Anguillan exodus to Sloughbucks that began in 1960 had the sanction of God; and a similar certitude is behind the secession from St Kitts and the boldness of many recent Anguillan actions.

So close to God, the Anguillans are not fanatical. They have the Negro openness to new faiths. Eight years ago Mr Webster, the now deposed President, re-thought his position and, at the age of thirty-four, left the Anglicans for the Seventh Day Adventists. He would like to see more and varied missionary activity on the island. "If the Jehovah's Witnesses or any other denomination convert one or ten souls they are doing a good job and serving the community. Because our basic plan is to keep Anguillans as pious as possible. This keeps out partial and immoral thoughts."

8*

The island has its own prophet, Judge Gumbs, Brother George Gumbs (Prophet), as he signs his messages to the new local weekly. He is not without honour; he is consulted by high and low. When the spirit moves him he cycles around with a fife and drum, "a short black man with a cap" (an Anguillan description), preaching and sometimes warning. He is said to get a frenzied feeling about a particular place, a field, a stretch of road; a few days later the disaster occurs. In December, three or four days after Mr Webster said that Anguilla was going to leave the Commonwealth altogether, Judge Gumbs was out, preaching. I didn't see him, but I was told he had no news; he just asked the people to pray. No news from Judge Gumbs was good news.

Certain other reverences remain, to bind the community: certain families act or take decisions in times of crisis. The reverences follow the antique patterns, whose origins have been forgotten. Colour is accidental, and nothing angers the Anguillans more than the propaganda from St Kitts, seventy miles away, that their rebellion is the rebellion of a slave island, with the blacks loyally following the whites and browns. The reverences are of Anguilla, and the Anguillans describe themselves as Negroes. Mr Webster, who could be of any race between the Mediterranean and India, describes himself as a Negro. It is true: losing the historical sense, the Anguillans have also lost the racial sense. It isn't an easy thing to put across, especially to St Kitts, which is now playing with its own concept of Black Power.

Anguillans have never liked being administratively linked with St Kitts, and they have hated Robert Bradshaw, the St Kitts Premier, ever since, angered by their indifference, he said he would turn the island into a desert and make the Anguillans suck salt. They were frightened by the idea of an independent St Kitts-Nevis-Anguilla under Bradshaw's rule; and there was a riot in February, 1967, when, as part of the independence celebrations, St Kitts sent over some beauty queens to give a show in the Anguilla High School. The police used tear gas, but inefficiently. They gassed the queens and the loyal audience, not the enraged

Anguillans outside. Reinforcements from St Kitts's one hundred-man Police Force were flown in next day. Houses were searched; the Anguillan leaders took to the bush.

It was the signal for a general revolt. The Warden's house was set on fire; the Warden fled. From time to time during the next three months shots were fired at the police station at night. The hotel where the acting Warden was staying was set on fire; he too left. The next day the bank manager was attacked. Two days later several hundred Anguillans rushed the police station. The seventeen policemen offered no fight; they were put on a plane and sent back to St Kitts; and the Anguillans set up their own five-man police force.

Ten days later, fearing outside intervention (Jamaica nearly sent in troops), and guided now by that religious certitude, the Anguillans raided St Kitts and shot up the police station and Defence Force Headquarters. The raid, by twelve men, was openly planned; people went down to the wharf in the afternoon to wave as the fifty-foot cutter left for St Kitts. Five and a half hours later the cutter tied up, quite simply, at the main pier in St Kitts. Then the Anguillans discovered they hadn't thought about motor-cars. They had intended to kidnap Bradshaw; they had to be content with scaring him.

Some time later there was a report that thirty-five men from St Kitts had invaded Anguilla. The man who was the Provisional President flew over the reported landing area in an Aztec, dropping leaflets asking the invaders to surrender. But there were no invaders. The fighting was over. All that followed were words; secession was a fact. Anguilla had become the world's smallest republic.

Its status was ambiguous. It still considered itself within the Commonwealth. It looked to London for a constitutional settlement, for some sanction of its separation from St Kitts. London didn't know what to do. For more than two hundred years, in fact, no one had really wanted Anguilla or had known what to do with it. The place was a mistake.

*

It had its formalities. When you got off the Piper Aztec you went through Anguillan Immigration and Customs; they were both in one room of the two-roomed airport building. The Immigration man had a khaki uniform, an Anguilla badge, and an Anguilla rubber-stamp. You needed an Anguillan driving licence; it cost a dollar; you paid at the Police Station in the long low Administration Building. The five-man police force was enough; there was little crime. Women quarrelled and used four-letter words; the police visited and "warned"; that, in the main, was the routine. There was a jail, and there was one prisoner. He had been there for a year, a St Kitts man on a charge of murder. There was no magistrate to try him. Mr Webster was hoping to deport the man as soon as the secession issue was settled.

In the Post Office you bought Anguillan stamps, designed and produced by an English firm and sold by them to overseas collectors for a fifteen per cent commission. Incoming mails were regular; Anguilla had beaten the St Kitts postal ban by having two box numbers on the half French, half Dutch island of St Martin. In the Treasury, next door to the Post Office, there was a notice about the new two per cent income tax. Other taxes, on liquor and petrol, had been lowered, to increase consumption and revenue; and it had worked. People told me there were more cars in Anguilla than ever before.

The administration, spare and efficient, had been inherited with the Administration Building. An elected fifteen-man Council ruled. This structure of government was like sophistication in a community that had for long organized itself around its own reverences. The island ran itself; it worked. After half a day the visitor had to remind himself of size and quaintness. It was there, in the new flag, designed by some Americans: a circle of three orange dolphins on white, a lower stripe of turquoise. And in the fanciful anthem, composed by a local "group":

> ... *An island where the golden corn is waving*
> *in the breeze!*

An island full of sunshine and where Nature
e'er doth please.

The visitor heard that the beaches were watched every night, in case St Kitts invaded; that there were secret military exercises every fortnight; that the Anguillans had more than the four machine-guns, fifty-five rifles, fifteen shotguns, and two boxes of dynamite they had at the time of secession. There was talk of a repeat raid on St Kitts; there was even a hint of a fighter being called in. St Kitts was still claiming Anguilla and still advertising it in its tourist brochures ("Island of charm . . . for the holiday-seeker who wants to get away from it all"). But the Anguillans were secure. They knew that St Kitts had its own political dissensions, that many people in St Kitts were on their side, and that the 120-man St Kitts army had enough to do at home. The Anguillans didn't talk much about Bradshaw and St Kitts. They talked more of their own dissensions, their own politics.

Shipwrecked and isolated, the community had held together. With the quick semi-sophistication that had come with independence, the feeling that the island was quaint, famous, and tourist-precious, the old rules and reverences had begun to go. A few months before, on the quaint airstrip, the engine of a Piper Aztec had been smashed up at night with a hammer. Family rivalry was said to be the cause.

There is only one hotel with electricity in Anguilla, the Rendezvous. It is like a rough motel; and the lights go off at nine. It is owned by Jeremiah Gumbs, half-brother of Judge Gumbs, the prophet, and is run by Jeremiah's sister, who has spent many years in the United States and speaks with an American accent; the atmosphere of Negro America is strong.

I knew about Jeremiah Gumbs. He had been described to me as "the smart Anguillan", the only one who had made good in the United States. He was a considerable local benefactor; and he was Anguilla's link-man with the bigger world. He had given a number of interviews to American newspapers, had presented

Anguilla's case at the United Nations, and had led an Anguillan delegation to the OAS building (they found it closed).

He was there, assessing and formidable (I had been told in St Kitts never to laugh at Anguillans), while his sister showed me round.

"And here, young man, you can plug in your shaver. Which is more than you did this morning."

She was very large; she was called Lady B. I recognized her as a "character". Characters lie on my spirit like lead; and I resolved never to shave while I was at the Rendezvous.

At lunch Jeremiah, sucking fish, began to boom across the dining-room, at first as though to himself.

"They call it a rebellion." His accent too was American. "Most peaceful rebellion in the world. Rebellion? It's a rebellion against years of neglect, that's all. What's wrong with being small? Why shouldn't a small country have dignity? Why shouldn't a small country have pride? Why shouldn't – "

I tried to break into his harangue. "Gumbs. It's an old island name."

"One man," he said. "One man gave this island a library. One man set up the X-ray unit in the hospital. One man did all this. What did Bradshaw do? Police, plastic bombs, tear gas, things we never saw before. Now he says I am the big villain, the leader of rebels."

I had heard no such thing.

"One man. Joe Louis. Marian Anderson. You get no more than one in a generation. It's because I care. I remember when I was a child we had four successive droughts in this island of Anguilla. I know what poverty is. I remember days in New York in the Depression when I didn't have the subway fare and had to walk one hundred blocks to school. Days when I didn't even eat an apple."

It hadn't marked him. He was an enormous man. Fifty-five, sharp-nosed, with a moustache and thin greying hair, he was like somebody out of those Negro Westerns of thirty years ago, *Two-Gun Man from Harlem*, *Harlem on the Prairie*. It was the way he ate, the way he walked and talked; it was the rock and the dust outside. He was the man opening up a territory.

"You come to write something, huh?"

I said, with acute shame, that I had.

"You go ahead and write. They come all the time. They sit on the beach and write all day long." His voice began to sing in the American way: "Just like Nature intended."

I resolved never to set foot on his beach.

We met that afternoon on the dusty road, he in his high jeep, a territory-opener, I in the low exposed mini-jeep I had rented from him.

"You making out all right?"

I was choking with dust and had already been lost twice (those Anguillan compass directions), but didn't tell him: he had sold me a map.

"You write and tell them. You tell them about this bunch of rebellious savages."

For a short time after secession the Anguillans flew the flag of San Francisco, the gift of an editor who belonged to what is known in the island as the San Francisco Group. The Group took a whole-page advertisement in *The New York Times* in August 1967 for "The Anguilla White Paper", which they composed.

Anguillans, the White Paper said, were not backward simply because they didn't have telephones. "Do you know what one Anguillan does when he wants to telephone another Anguillan? He walks up the road and talks to him." But the absence of telephones was part of the case against St Kitts; and it isn't easy to get about the island without a jeep. There are people in West End (where the people are mainly blackish, with occasional blond sports) who have never been to East End (where many of the fair people are).

Anguillans didn't "even want one Hiltonesque hotel"; it would turn them into "a nation of bus boys, waiters and servants". They didn't want more than thirty "guests" at one time; it wouldn't be polite for a guest to go away without at least lunching with the President. They didn't want "tourists".

The White Paper – it offered honorary citizenship for $100 – made $25,000 for Anguilla. Some Anguillans felt they had been made ridiculous by the White Paper. But Mr Webster, who signed it as Chief Executive, told me he stood by it. Jeremiah Gumbs, though, was extending his hotel; other people had put up establishments of their own of varying standards (the tourist future could still be one of rough bars and souvenir-stalls and ice-cream stands, very private enterprise); and Mr Webster himself said that he would like to see Anguilla as a tourist resort.

It was part of the Anguillan confusion. Too many people had wanted to help, finding in Anguilla an easy cause, a little black comedy. The Anguillans, never seeing the joke, always listened and then grew frightened and self-willed.

One member of the San Francisco Group was Professor Leopold Kohr of the University of Puerto Rico, a sixty-year-old Austrian who went to live in America in 1938. Kohr has long promoted the theory of the happy small society; his book, *A Breakdown of Nations*, was published in London in 1957 (it is now out of print). In 1958 Kohr addressed the Welsh Nationalist Party that wants Wales to break away from England; he is now on a year's sabbatical at the University of Swansea. Kohr feels that small communities are "more viable economically than larger powers", and he thought Anguilla "the ideal testing ground". Immediately after secession the Anguillan leaders were beating up support in the nearby islands. They met Kohr and the San Francisco Group in Puerto Rico. "My team," Kohr says, "was accepted within twenty-four hours."

There appeared to be early proof of economic viability when it was rumoured that Aristotle Onassis had offered a million dollars a year for the right to use Anguilla as a flag base. The story is still current in the West Indies and Kohr still appears to believe in it. In St Kitts and Anguilla, however, it was dismissed as one of Jeremiah Gumbs's stories. Mr Webster, as Chief Executive, wrote twice to Onassis but got no reply. The commercial offers that did come from the United States were, in Kohr's words, from "interests of all shady shades".

A local man I met at the airport one Saturday – like market-day, then, with the cardboard boxes and baskets and parcels coming off the Aztecs, the women waiting for letters, messages, remittances from their men in the American Virgin Islands – a local man whispered to me about the Mafia and their agents among the local people. (From recent newspaper reports I feel he has been whispering to many other visitors.) I asked Mr Webster about this. He said, puzzlingly, that this whispering about the Mafia was official Anguillan policy, to keep the Mafia away. He also asked me not to pay too much attention to white "stooges". At this stage I began to feel I was sinking in antique, inbred Anguillan intrigue.

There were people, though, who, while not wishing to go back to St Kitts, had become less happy about the future than Mr Webster or Professor Kohr. They had seen no "development" in a year of ambiguous independence and they feared what would happen if Anguilla officially declared itself outside the Commonwealth. Anguilla, like Rhodesia, would be outlawed. It would attract outlaws.

The new weekly, *The Beacon* (typewritten and offset, the equipment a gift from a Boston firm), had run an editorial warning against a unilateral declaration of independence. It had created some doubt in the island; it made independence appear a little more difficult.

"If we sell away our rights to American businessmen now," the young electrician-editor said to me in a bar, "we will be the laughing-stock of the Caribbean and the world. Don't get me wrong," he added, speaking slowly while I took down his words. "If Britain don't do nothing, then I feel we should go on our own."

"I go put his balls through the wringer," a young man said angrily to Mr Webster at the airstrip, showing *The Beacon*. Such violence of language was once reserved for Bradshaw of St Kitts. Mr Webster, hiding his distress – it was Saturday, his sabbath – calmed the young man down.

The frightened, the bold, "stooges", "Mafia": this was the rough division at which the visitor arrived, feeling his way through intrigue that appeared to follow no race or colour line. Responsibility, acquired lusts and fears now balancing the old certitude, had brought dissensions, the breaking up of that sense of isolation and community which was the point of independence.

There was the Canadian with the idea for a radio station, for which for some reason he required stretches of beach. There was Jeremiah Gumbs's plan for a Bank of Anguilla (he actually started building), which frightened many people. There was Jeremiah Gumbs's plan for a "centre for physical medicine". "The trouble is, will I get my people to understand it? Or will they object to it like the American Medical Association?" I could never understand what he meant; I heard it said that he wanted to bring down an American who had a magic cure. I remembered Jeremiah's half-brother, Judge Gumbs.

The Anguillan faith in Jeremiah Gumbs as their guide to big American investment had been shaken by these projects and he had been dropped as an adviser to the Council. When I was in Anguilla I felt he was in disgrace, sulking at the Rendezvous. And his own attitude to Anguilla changed from meal to meal. Sometimes he was a patriot. "St Kitts will be sorry if they attacked us. When we have finished with them, the British Government will have to feed them on crackers and molasses, I guess." Sometimes he was despairing about Anguillans. "They don't know, they don't know." He could give this a gloss. "The trouble," he said during one gloomy meal, "is that colonialism has made the Anguillan a *shell*."

His changes of mood were linked with the arrival, examination, and dismissal of another American with an idea. This man was looking for a "fran-chise": a grant of land and, I believe, a twenty-five-year monopoly in the quarrying and block-making business. His examination by the Council and the Council's lawyer, who had flown in from Trinidad, lasted eight hours; and when he appeared at Jeremiah Gumbs's table at dinner, a young soft-bellied man in trousers of shocking Sherwood green, he looked bruised. I heard later that toward the end of his examination he was close to tears.

It was a subdued Jeremiah Gumbs who padded about the dining-room in his slippers, pouring water, offering bread, like a man still with a duty to his ranch-hands. Afterwards he led me through the wire-netting door to the open verandah. Sand-flies and mosquitoes pounced. He slapped and clapped his big hands, killing and calm.

"Who is this lawyer guy? Is he a constitutional lawyer, a company lawyer, a criminal lawyer? Does he know anything about economics? You tell Webster. He's got to have a development plan. Otherwise he's going to frighten off a lot of people. And they are not that many. They are not that many."

In the morning the sad American left, green check jacket matching his trousers.

Jeremiah Gumbs still suffered. "He was gonna invest plenty. He wasn't gonna make money for four years. *Then* you'll let someone *else* in? These people don't understand economics. If Webster could worry he'd be worried. He was gonna build that road, open up that whole area. Put value on people's property. Houses going up alongside the road. But these people don't understand. Look at me. *I* put this place up. *I* advertised Anguilla. Now other people have put down their little places. The tourist comes to the airport, the taxi-drivers rush him, take him this place, that place. *I* advertised." His voice began to sing. "It's not a way to live. I don't know. I feel there's another way to live."

I said I felt he had done enough for Anguilla.

He said he wouldn't rest until he had done a lot·more. "I love this country. I love the people. I know what poverty is like. I know what drought is like. I care. I remember when I was a boy. . . ."

On my bill there was a charge for an Anguillan flag. I told Lady B. I hadn't had one.

"You want one, young man?" She waved it at me when she

gave it, and did a gigantic little mimicry of a drum-majorette. "Anguilla, here I come."

I put it in my pocket, the flag of the territory that Jeremiah Gumbs didn't look like opening up.

Independence, as a smooth administration: that worked. Independence as the preserver of an old community: that made sense. Independence as "development" and quick tourist money: that, as the San Francisco Group romantically sensed, defeats itself. Anguilla was going to disappoint more of its supporters. Independence had only just come; and Anguilla already required pacification.

Pacification came, heavy-handed and absurd – but only to the outsider looking for comedy or a manageable cause. The Anguilla problem remains: the problem of a tiny colony set adrift, part of the jetsam of an empire, a near-primitive people suddenly returned to a free state, their renewed or continuing exploitation.

When I left Anguilla, Jeremiah Gumbs was giving instructions to the workmen (and a very slow, contemplative, sand-sifting workwoman) who were running up the barrack-like extension to the hotel. The other day, quite by chance, I saw him in a dark suit, his ring on the small finger of his large left hand, in the Delegates' Lounge of the United Nations. Four English journalists were taking down his grave words.

The British invasion was two days away. Jeremiah – an American citizen, his business in the United States the Gumbs Fuel and Oil Burner Service of Edison, New Jersey – was the petitioner that day for Anguilla, before the Committee on Colonialism. He spoke lucidly and without exaggeration; his tone was one of injury, familiar to me; but everything he said about the planned British invasion was true.

He was the official Anguillan spokesman again. He was back in favour in Anguilla. And it was not surprising to learn from newspaper reports that the American in green had returned to Anguilla. He had returned as a lawyer. He had no law degree, but he had "an extensive law library"; he was given a permit to

practise. He did more. He advised on the new Anguillan constitution. (The previous one, very short, had been drafted by a
Harvard professor, who had somehow ceased to be important in
Anguilla.) The *National Observer* gave some of the provisions of
the new constitution. Businesses, foreign or local, could not be
expropriated by the Anguillan government; foreign governments
could not bring tax suits against Anguilla-based businesses. A
judge of the Anguillan Supreme Court didn't have to be an
Anguillan or a lawyer; all he needed was a permit to practise law
in Anguilla, and he had to be over thirty-five. The *National
Observer* also gave some details of the franchise the American had
asked for in December, for his basic building-materials plant:
twenty-five years tax-free, the Anguillan government to get five
hundred dollars a year in return.

After the British invasion the American was put on a Cessna
and sent off the island.

"It may seem strange to people who have lost faith in the United
Nations," Jeremiah Gumbs said to reporters a week later, "but on
our little island the United Nations is still regarded, in spite of its
imperfections, as the great hope of small nations and people of
goodwill anywhere."

It was the *New York Times* Quotation of the Day. The *Times*
also presented, as news, some lines from the two-year-old
Anguillan anthem. Anguilla – as cause, as comedy – appeared set
for a re-run.

Power?

The New York Review of Books, 3 September 1970

THE TRINIDAD CARNIVAL is famous. For the two days before Ash Wednesday the million or so islanders – blacks, whites, the later immigrant groups of Portuguese, Indians, and Chinese – parade the hot streets in costumed "bands" and dance to steel orchestras. This year there was a twist. After the Carnival there were Black Power disturbances. After the masquerade and the music, anger and terror.

In a way, it makes sense. Carnival and Black Power are not as opposed as they appear. The tourists who go for the Carnival don't really know what they are watching. The islanders themselves, who have spent so long forgetting the past, have forgotten the darker origins of their Carnival. The bands, flags and costumes have little to do with Lent, and much to do with slavery.

The slave in Trinidad worked by day and lived at night. Then the world of the white plantations fell away; and in its place was a securer, secret world of fantasy, of Negro "kingdoms", "regiments", bands. The people who were slaves by day saw themselves then as kings, queens, dauphins, princesses. There were pretty uniforms, flags and painted wooden swords. Everyone who joined a regiment got a title. At night the Negroes played at being people, mimicking the rites of the upper world. The kings visited and entertained. At gatherings a "secretary" might sit scribbling away.

Once, in December, 1805, this fantasy of the night overflowed into the working day. There was serious talk then of cutting off the heads of some plantation owners, of drinking holy water afterwards and eating pork and dancing. The plot was found out; and swiftly, before Christmas, in the main Port of Spain square there were hangings, decapitations, brandings and whippings.

That was Trinidad's first and last slave "revolt". The Negro kingdoms of the night were broken up. But the fantasies remained. They had to, because without that touch of lunacy the Negro would have utterly despaired and might have killed himsel slowly by eating dirt; many in Trinidad did. The Carnival the tourist goes to see is a version of the lunacy that kept the slave alive. It is the original dream of black power, style and prettiness; and it always feeds on a private vision of the real world.

During the war an admiration for Russia – really an admiration for "stylish" things like Stalin's moustache and the outlandish names of Russian generals, Timoshenko, Rokossovsky – was expressed in a "Red Army" band. At the same time an admiration for Humphrey Bogart created a rival "Casablanca" band. Make-believe, but taken seriously and transformed; not far below, perhaps even unacknowledged, there has always been a vision of the black millennium, as much a vision of revenge as of a black world made whole again.

Something of the Carnival lunacy touches all these islands where people, first as slaves and then as neglected colonials, have seen themselves as futile, on the other side of the real world. In St Kitts, with a population of 36,000, Papa Bradshaw, the Premier, has tried to calm despair by resurrecting the memory of Christophe, Emperor of Haiti, builder of the Citadel, who was born a slave on the island. Until they were saved from themselves, the 6,000 people of Anguilla seriously thought they could just have a constitution written by someone from Florida and set up in business as an independent country.

In Jamaica the Ras Tafarians believe they are Abyssinians and that the Emperor Haile Selassie is God. This is one of the un-expected results of Italian propaganda during the Abyssinian war. The Italians said then that there was a secret black society called Niya Binghi ("Death to the Whites") and that it was several million strong. The propaganda delighted some Jamaicans, who formed little Niya Binghi play-groups of their own. Recently the Emperor visited Jamaica. The Ras Tafarians were expecting a black lion of a man; they saw someone like a Hindu, mild-featured, brown and small. The disappointment was great; but somehow the sect survives.

These islanders are disturbed. They already have black government and black power, but they want more. They want something more than politics. Like the dispossessed peasantry of medieval Europe, they await crusades and messiahs. Now they have Black Power. It isn't the Black Power of the United States. That is the protest of a disadvantaged minority which has at last begun to feel that some of the rich things of America are accessible, that only self-contempt and discrimination stand in the way. But in the islands the news gets distorted.

The media cannot make the disadvantages as real as the protest. Famous cities are seen to blaze; young men of the race come out of buildings with guns; the black-gloved hands of triumphant but bowed athletes are raised as in a religious gesture; the handsome spokesmen of protest make threats before the cameras which appear at last to have discovered black style. This is power. In the islands it is like a vision of the black millennium. It needs no political programme.

In the islands the intellectual equivocations of Black Power are part of its strength. After the sharp analysis of black degradation, the spokesmen for Black Power usually become mystical, vague, and threatening. In the United States this fits the cause of protest, and fits the white audience to whom this protest is directed. In the islands it fits the old, apocalyptic mood of the black masses. Anything more concrete, anything like a programme, might become simple local politics and be reduced to the black power that is already possessed.

Black Power as rage, drama and style, as revolutionary jargon, offers something to everybody: to the unemployed, the idealistic, the drop-out, the Communist, the politically frustrated, the anarchist, the angry student returning home from humiliations abroad, the racialist, the old-fashioned black preacher who has for years said at street corners that after Israel it was to be the turn of Africa. Black Power means Cuba and China; it also means clearing the Chinese and the Jews and the tourists out of Jamaica. It is identity and it is also miscegenation. It is drinking holy water, eating pork and dancing; it is going back to Abyssinia. There has been no movement like it in the Caribbean since the French Revolution.

So in Jamaica, some eighteen months ago, students joined with Ras Tafarians to march in the name of Black Power against the black government. Campus idealism, campus protest; but the past is like quicksand here. There was a middle-class rumour, which was like a rumour from the days of slavery, that a white tourist was to be killed, but only sacrificially, without malice.

At the same time, in St Kitts, after many years in authority, Papa Bradshaw was using Black Power, as words alone, to undermine the opposition. Round and round the tiny impoverished island, on the one circular road, went the conspiratorial printed message, cut out from a gasoline advertisement: *Join the Power Set*.

Far away, on the Central American mainland, in British Honduras, which is only half black, Black Power had just appeared and was already undermining the multi-racial nature of both government and opposition. The carrier of the infection was a twenty-one-year-old student who had been to the United States on, needless to say, an American government scholarship.

He had brought back news about the dignity of the peasant and a revolution based on land. I thought the message came from another kind of country and somebody else's revolution, and wasn't suited to the local blacks, who were mainly city people with simple city ambitions. (It was front-page news, while I was there, that a local man had successfully completed an American correspondence course in jail management.)

But it didn't matter. A message had come. "The whites are buying up the land." "What the black man needs is bread." "It became a phallic symbol to the black to be a log-cutter." It was the jargon of the movement, at once scientific-sounding and millenarian. It transcended the bread-and-butter protests of local politics; it smothered all argument. Day by day the movement grew.

Excitement! And perhaps this excitement is the only liberation that is possible. Black Power in these black islands is protest. But there is no enemy. The enemy is the past, of slavery and colonial neglect and a society uneducated from top to bottom; the enemy is the smallness of the islands and the absence of resources. Opportunism or borrowed jargon may define phantom enemies: racial minorities, "élites", "white niggers". But at the end the problems will be the same, of dignity and identity.

In the United States Black Power may have its victories. But they will be American victories. The small islands of the Caribbean will remain islands, impoverished and unskilled, ringed as now by a *cordon sanitaire*, their people not needed anywhere. They may get less innocent or less corrupt politicians; they will not get less helpless ones. The island blacks will continue to be dependent on the books, films and goods of others; in this important way they will continue to be the half-made societies of a dependent people, the Third World's third world. They will forever consume; they will never create. They are without material resources; they will never develop the higher skills. Identity depends in the end on achievement; and achievement here cannot but be small. Again and again the protest leader will appear and the millennium will seem about to come.

Fifty years ago, writing at a moment when Spain seemed about to disintegrate, Ortega y Gasset saw that fragmented peoples come together only in order "to do something tomorrow". In the islands this assurance about the future is missing. Millenarian excitement will not hold them together, even if they were all black; and some, like Trinidad and Guyana and British Honduras, are only half black. The pursuit of black identity and the community of black distress is a dead end, frenzy for the sake of frenzy, the self-scourging of people who cannot see what they will have to do tomorrow.

In *We Wish to be Looked Upon*, published last year by Teachers

College Press, Vera Rubin and Marisa Zavalloni report on surveys of high-school students in Trinidad they conducted in 1957 and 1961, at a time of pre-independence, messianic optimism. (Eric Williams had come to power, suddenly and overwhelmingly, in 1956.) The students were asked to write at length about their "expectations, plans and hopes for the future".

Black: I would like to be a great man not only in music but also in sociology and economics. In the USA I would like to marry a beautiful actress with plenty of money. I would also like to be famed abroad as one of the world's foremost millionaires.

Black: In politics I hope to come up against men like Khrushchev and other enemies of freedom. I hope I will be able to overcome them with my words, and put them to shame.

Black: I expect to be a man of international fame, a man who by virtue of his political genius has acquired so much respect from his people that he will be fully capable of living in peace with his people.

Black: I want to be a West Indian diplomat. I would like to have a magnetic power over men and a stronger magnetic power over women. I must be very intelligent and quick-witted: I must be fluent in at least seven languages. I must be very resourceful and I must say the correct thing at the correct moment. With these qualities and a wonderful foresight and with other necessary abilities which I can't foresee, I would be able to do wonders for the world by doing wonders for my nation.

East Indian: I will write a book called the *Romance of Music and Literature*. I will make this book as great as any Shakespeare play; then I will return to India to endeavour to become a genius in the film industry.

East Indian: I want to develop an adventurous spirit. I will tour the earth by air, by sea, and by land. I shall become a peacemaker among hostile people.

East Indian: When I usually awake from my daydream, I think myself to be another person, the great scientific engineer, but soon I recollect my sense, and then I am myself again.

Coloured (mulatto): Toward the latter part of my life I would like to enter myself in politics, and to do some little bit for the improvement and uplift of this young Federation of ours.

Coloured: I am obsessed with the idea of becoming a statesman, a classical statesman, and not a mere rabble-rouser who acts impulsively and makes much ado about nothing.

White: I am going to apprentice myself to a Chartered Accountant's firm and then to learn the trade. When I want to, leave the firm and go to any other big business concern and work my way up to the top.

White: I want to live a moderate life, earning a moderate pay, slowly but surely working my way in the law firm, but I don't want to be chief justice of the Federation or anything like that. . . . Look around. All the other boys must be writing about their ambitions to be famous. They all cannot be, for hope is an elusive thing.

White: By this time my father may be a shareholder in the company, I will take over the business. I will expand it and try to live up to the traditions that my father has built up.

Without the calm of the white responses, the society might appear remote, fantastic and backward. But the white student doesn't inhabit a world which is all that separate. Trinidad is small, served by two newspapers and two radio stations and the same unsegregated schools. The intercourse between the races is easier than inquiring sociologists usually find; there is a substantial black and East Indian middle class that dominates the professions. When this is understood, the imprecision of black and East Indian fantasy – diplomacy, politics, peacemaking – can be seen to be more than innocence. It is part of the carnival lunacy of a lively, well-informed society which feels itself part of the great world, but understands at the same time that it is cut off from this world by reasons of geography, history, race.

The sub-title of Rubin and Zavalloni's book is "A Study of the Aspirations of Youth in a Developing Society". But the euphemism is misleading. This society has to be more precisely defined. Brazil is developing, India is developing. Trinidad is neither undeveloped nor developing. It is fully part of the advanced consumer society of the West; it recognizes high material standards. But it is less than provincial: there is no metropolis to which the man from the village or small town can take his gifts. Trinidad is simply small; it is dependent; and the people born in it – black, East Indian, white – sense themselves condemned, not necessarily as individuals, but as a community, to an inferiority of skill and achievement. In colonial days racial deprivation could be said to be important, and this remains, obviously, an important drive. But now it is only part of the story.

In the islands, in fact, black identity is a sentimental trap, obscuring the issues. What is needed is access to a society, larger in every sense, where people will be allowed to grow. For some territories this larger society may be Latin American. Colonial rule in the Caribbean defied geography and created unnatural administrative units; this is part of the problem. Trinidad, for instance, was detached from Venezuela. This is a geographical absurdity; it might be looked at again.

A Latin American identity is also possible for Guyana and British Honduras. But local racial politics and servile prejudice stand in the way. The blacks of British Honduras, in their one lazy, mosquito-infested town, reject "Latinization" without knowing what they are rejecting. Until Black Power came along last year, the black flag of protest against Latinization was the Union Jack; and the days of slavery were recalled with pride as the days when blacks and their English owners, friends really, stood shoulder to shoulder against the awful Spaniards. The blacks, at the end of the day, see themselves as British, made in the image of thier former owners, with British institutions; Latin Americans are seen as chaotic, violent, without the rule of law.

There is an irony in this. Because in these former British territories the gravest issue, as yet unrecognized, is the nineteenth-century Latin American issue of government by consent. These Caribbean territories are not like those in Africa or Asia, with their own internal reverences, that have been returned to themselves after a period of colonial rule. They are manufactured societies, labour camps, creations of empire; and for long they were dependent on empire for law, language, institutions, culture, even officials. Nothing was generated locally; dependence became a habit. How, without empire, do such societies govern themselves? What is now the source of power? The ballot box, the mob, the regiment? When, as in Haiti, the slave-owners leave, and there are only slaves, what are the sanctions?

It is like the Latin American situation after the break up of the Spanish Empire. With or without Black Power, chaos threatens. But chaos will only be internal. The islands will always be subject to an external police. The United States helicopters will be there, to take away United States citizens, tourists; the British High Commissions will lay on airlifts for their citizens. These islands, black and poor, are dangerous only to themselves.

The Overcrowded Barracoon

Sunday Times Magazine, 16 July 1972

SIX CARPENTERS LEAVE the Indian Ocean island of Mauritius to go to Swaziland in Southern Africa to work for a year, and it is front-page news in *L'Express*, the leading Mauritius newspaper. Six mouths less to feed; six families saved, at least for a year. Twenty-five nurses, men as well as women, are chosen for hospitals in England. England will swallow them up; but for the moment they are famous in their island, with their names at the top of the front page of the *Mauritius Times*. Perhaps 10,000 applied for those twenty-five vacancies. That is what is believed; those are the odds.

"Your Majesty," a young Mauritian writes to the Principal Nursing Officer of a Scottish hospital, "will you please find me a seat?" The newspaper correspondent who reports the joke back, himself a Mauritian, one of the lucky ones who got away, says that flattery like this will get young Mauritians nowhere. The correspondent is not unsympathetic; he says he knows that the young people of Mauritius are obsessed with the idea of escape and are "all the time morally and physically fatigued"; but the only ones who will succeed are those with "a fair knowledge of up-to-date things and a (really) good character and a love for nursing".

But so many are qualified. Since the only Mauritians acceptable abroad are nurses, in Mauritius they all love nursing. They are a nation of nurses. And they hang around the ministers' doors in Port Louis, the capital, waiting for the call to serve. The ministers are all-powerful in Mauritius; nothing can be done except through a minister. But what can the ministers do? Once manna fell from heaven – this is how the Foreign Minister put it – and the Germans asked for five hundred nurses. But manna doesn't fall every day; the hope that the French would take five thousand units a year remains a hope.

There is a Minister of State for Emigration, a plump, chuckling mulatto, a former motor mechanic. But he can give no figures for emigration. He says he doesn't carry these figures in his head; and, besides, he is preoccupied with a local election. "All our energies are devoted to this by-election at Curepipe. We think that Mauritius must have a good political climate to solve our problems."

The Minister can give no figures because there are not many figures to give. So the young men hang around, sometimes for years, waiting for their careers to begin. They meet in little clubhouses of concrete or corrugated iron, decorated with posters from the British Information Services or cut-outs from foreign magazines, and talk and talk. Some of them begin to suffer from spells of dizziness and have to stay at home. Many of them get headaches, those awful Mauritian headaches that can drive an unemployed labourer mad, interrupt the career of a civil servant, and turn educated young men into mindless invalids.

It was on Mauritius that the dodo forgot how to fly, because it had no enemies: the island, 720 square miles, was once uninhabited. Now, with more than a thousand people to the square mile, the island is overpopulated.

The Dutch attempted to settle Mauritius in the seventeenth century. They cut down the ebony forests and introduced sugarcane. When the Dutch left – driven out, it is said, by rats – the French came. The French, mainly peasants from Brittany, stayed and continued to flourish after the British conquest in the early nineteenth century. They grew sugar-cane, depending for labour first on slaves from Madagascar and Africa, and then, when slavery was abolished, on indentured immigrants from India.

Throughout the nineteenth century labour was short, and immigration from India continued until 1917, so that today Indians make up two-thirds of the population. Even with this immigration the population held steady. In 1931 the population was more or less what it had been in 1901, just under 400,000. Then the disaster occurred. In 1949 malaria was finally eradicated. The population jumped. It is now about 820,000. Three Mauritians out of five are under twenty-one. No one knows how many unemployed or idle people there are – estimates vary from 50,000 to 80,000 – and the population grows by about 12,000 every year.

The economy, and the social structure, is still that of an agricultural colony, a tiny part of an empire: the island has been independent for only three years. The large estates, the big commission agents and the sugar factories are white (though there are many Indian landowners and there is an Indian aristocracy of sorts); rural labour is Indian; mulattoes are civil servants; Negroes are artisans, dockworkers and fishermen; Chinese are in trade.

Sugar remains the main crop and virtually the sole export. Sugar-cane covers nearly half the island, so that from the air this island of disaster looks empty and green, dotted with half-pyramids of stone that are like the relics of a vanished civilization. The stone comes from the sugar-cane fields: "de-stoning" – and the boulders are enormous – is a recurring task. Once the de-stoning was done by hand; now it is done by bulldozers. Sugar has always been an efficient industry, and in Mauritius the efficiency shows. Lushness has been abolished; order has been imposed on the tropical landscape. The visitor who keeps to the main highways sees an island as well-kept as a lawn, monotonous except for the jagged volcanic hills, miniature green Matterhorns.

An island roughly oval in shape, 720 square miles in the Indian Ocean, far from anywhere, colonized, like those West Indian islands on the other side of the world, only for sugar, part of the great human engineering of recent empires, the shifting about of leaderless groups of conquered peoples: to the travel writers, who have set to work on Mauritius, the island is "a lost paradise" which is "being developed into an idyllic spot". It is an island which the visitor leaves with "a feeling of peace". To the

9

Mauritian who cannot leave it is a prison: sugar-cane and sugar-cane, ending in the sea, and the diseased coconut trees, blighted by the rhinoceros beetle.

Twenty thousand tourists came to Mauritius last year. The lost paradise already has a casino, and the casino company, in tune with the holiday tastes of these low latitudes, has also put in fruit machines in the island's leading hotels. The tourists prefer the fruit machines. In the Park Hotel in Curepipe the fat women and their fatter girls start playing the machines after breakfast; in the late afternoon, when the television also blares, conversation in the lounge of this allegedly eighteenth-century building becomes impossible.

The casino is patronized mainly by local Chinese, sitting as blank-faced here before the bright tables in the dark-red hall as they do behind their shop counters in the villages, having apparently only changed from khaki shorts and singlets into suits. The Chinese are a race apart in Mauritius, and impenetrable; it is a cause for awe that people can be so reckless with money which, in the Mauritian myth, they have made by such tedious treachery. In the myth, the Chinese shopkeeper spends a part of every working day extracting one or two matches from every box in his stock, so that out of, say, twenty boxes of matches he makes twenty-one and so picks up an extra quarter-penny of pure profit.

The casino picks up more than quarter-pennies, and many Mauritians are pleased with the success and modernity of the place. I couldn't find out what there was in the casino venture for the Mauritius Treasury or the tourist trade. To enquire was only to probe a kind of native innocence. But everyone knew that the casino employed a number of people and that the white and mulatto girls who operated the tables – their satiny old-fashioned evening-dress uniforms labelled with their first names – had until a few months before been idle and unemployed. Now, very quickly, they had acquired this difficult modern skill: in this "adaptability" – a recurring Mauritian word – lay the hope for the future. In Mauritius it always comes to this: jobs, employment, a use of the hands, something to do.

The tourists come from the nearby French island of Réunion (technically a department of France), from Madagascar, England, India, and South Africa. Relations with South Africa are close. South Africa buys, at more than a fair price, every kilo of the somewhat flavourless tea that Mauritius produces; and to see what "Made in South Africa" looks like in Afrikaans, all you have to do is to turn over the ash-tray in your hotel room. Mauritius is no place for the anti-apartheid campaigner. Many French Mauritians have family or business links with South Africa; and during the period of French "over-reaction" before independence ("We always over-react here") – when the French rallied their loyal Negroes (anti-apartheid people really should stay away from Mauritius) and there were rumours of a French-South African commando takeover – during this period of over-reaction a number of French people moved to South Africa.

As visitors the South Africans are popular. And not all the South Africans who come are white. BLACKS IN SOUTH AFRICA SHOULD NOT COMPLAIN: this is the front-page headline in the *Mauritius Times* over a question-and-answer interview with a visiting South African Indian, Mr Ahmed Cajee Khan.

Q: Mr Khan, how do Indians fare in South Africa?
A: Very well economically integrated with the government. . . . Some of our people are multi-millionaires.
Q: How did this powerful position come about?
A: It's traditional among Indians. . . .
Q: Would you say that a lot of what we hear against South Africa is incorrect?
A: . . . In Mauritius I was surprised when somebody told me there were separate toilet facilities on board South African Airways. This is false. . . .
Q: But surely there are some inflexible situations?
A: All countries have their domestic problems.
Q: Mr Khan, there is a school of thought which believes that the political battle in South Africa is lost. Do you subscribe to this view?

A: Not for a minute. . . .

Q: Your happiness about this régime baffles me. Would I be right in saying that it's because you don't feel the pinch like the blacks?

A: No! Nobody feels the pinch. Everybody has a job . . . although we should make allowance for the eternal grumblers.

Earlier this year Black Power slogans in French and the local French patois appeared in many towns and villages: *C'est beau d'être noir, Noir ene jolie couleur, Noirs au pouvoir*. It was the idea of the Foreign Minister, Gaëtan Duval. Duval himself isn't black. He is a brown-skinned, straight-haired man of forty, as handsome as a pop star and with a pop star's taste in clothes. As part of his Black Power campaign he took to wearing black leather and making public appearances on a black horse called Black Beauty. For many years Duval was regarded as the leader of the island's blacks. But then two years ago, forgetting pre-independence disputes, he took his party into a coalition government; and since then, as the government's popularity has gone down, so has Duval's.

Black Power was Duval's way of fighting back. It was intended, so far as I could gather, to scare off political poachers. It certainly wasn't intended to frighten ordinary white people. Duval supports the idea of trade with South Africa, and he would like to see more South African tourists. He would like to see South Africans buying houses in special tourist developments. Statistics showed, he told me one day at lunch, that a hotel room provided employment only for two servants. A house provided employment for four.

The government recognizes a problem of unemployment. A White Paper says that 130,000 new jobs will have to be created by 1980. The government doesn't recognize a problem of overpopulation and discourages investigation of its effects. It disapproves of "crude" family planning programmes on TV.

Mauritius is a conservative, wife-beating society and the government doesn't want to offend anybody.

There are also good political reasons. At a seminar on unemployment, which began the day after I arrived, a spokesman for the Labour Party, the major party in the ruling coalition, said: "We have rejected the all too facile and simple explanation that unemployment is a consequence of overpopulation and the lack of capital and investment possibilities. . . . In fact it is clear that the holders of economic power, either for fear of inadequate protection of their interest or again out of a carefully elaborated political strategy, refused to be involved in the necessary development process. . . . The Mauritian situation, therefore, presents a picture where the holders of political power are separated by a wide, almost unbridgeable gap from those holding economic power."

So, by stressing unemployment and by playing down overpopulation, the government defends itself and seeks to remain the instrument of protest, as in colonial days. Protest against the rich, so often white, whose talents and money are yet needed; protest against the sugar-cane, the slave crop, hateful yet indispensable.

But the government is unpopular. If there were an election tomorrow the government would be overthrown, not by its old enemies, most of whom it has anyway absorbed, but by the young, those people who have grown up during the years of the population explosion.

The Prime Minister, an Indian in an island with an Indian majority, is seventy. The political party of the young, whose sudden popularity has rocked the government, was founded in 1968 by a French Mauritian student, then aged twenty-three and fresh from the events of Paris. The Prime Minister has a background of rural Indian poverty. Education and self-education, the long years in London in the 1920s, first as a student, then as a doctor, trade union work on his return to Mauritius, politics: it has been a long haul, against an almost "settler" opposition, and his achievement has been remarkable. Over the last twelve years he has created a rudimentary welfare state in Mauritius. There are extensive social services; there is a system of "relief work" for the

unemployed (4 rupees, 30 pence, four days a week); there is a
monthly allowance of 10 rupees, about 75 pence, for families
with three children below the age of fourteen.

This rudimentary welfare state has saved the society from
collapse; and the people who have benefited are the young. They
are better educated and better fed than their parents. An excellent
television service keeps them sharp and well informed. Their
expectations are higher; they are no longer an uncomplaining
part of the old serf society. The flaw is that this welfare state has
been created, perhaps at the expense of development, within a
static colonial economy where sugar is still king. The higher
skills are not required in Mauritius. Elsewhere, only those with
really good characters and a love of nursing need apply.

"They blame the government. Once they have the certificate
in hand they never think of anything else except securing a job
with government. There are organized groups in agriculture, but
the bulk would like to sit behind a desk and have papers to scratch
all day." "The government has made the people of Mauritius
beggars. The thing is we had an extended family system here we
could have made better use of. What has happened is that all this
government relief has weakened the family system." "Our people
have no sense of adventure." "People are becoming accident-
conscious. Malingering. My surgery is pestered with malingerers
hoping to get compensation from the government for their
'accidents'."

These are middle-class comments on the Mauritius welfare
state, and they are supported to some extent by a White Paper.
Too many people, the White Paper says, live at the "relief" level;
too many people do "unproductive" relief jobs (sometimes relief
workers are sent to clean the beaches); and as a result "the will to
work among those employed, who see it is possible to live with
less work or even without working, is being affected".

And it is easy for the visitor to be irritated. Those well-built,
well-dressed young men idling away the afternoons in the choked
village lanes: they are too well drilled, too ready to be an audience
and sit in rows in their clubhouses. The complaints come easily.

"If you want a job they put the Riot Unit against you. This happens three times in one month." "Every day you will see people knocking at the deputy's door asking for a job, because everyone believes, 'The deputy will give my son a job, daughter a job'." "To see a minister you have to pay people money. We only see the pictures of the ministers."

So they sit and complain, and threaten. "Change the government. Replace it by the socialist party. The government tolerates capitalism." The socialist party is the party of the young. What will it do? How will it replace capitalism? There is no clear idea. But the government must be punished. The government is the government, and can do anything it really wants. "The government has failed not because they are foolish or wicked but because they are selfish."

Is this really all to their life, this hanging about in the village lane, these games of dominoes, these endless political discussions in the clubhouses? Are there no other activities, no pleasures, no festivals? "No money, no pleasures, sir." Rum, at 55 Mauritian cents a nip, just under four pennies, is expensive, *bien, bien cher*; all they can afford is the local banana spirit, which sells at two and a half pennies a pint. The cinema is expensive, one rupee or seven and a half pennies in the third class, two rupees twenty-five in the first. "I haven't been to the cinema for ten years." "I haven't been for three years." "There is no pleasure for us even in Diwali [the Hindu festival of lights]. We can't buy presents for the children or give them new clothes."

But that fat, open-mouthed, jolly boy, who is on "relief", has just got married and is clearly the clown of the group. That handsome, stylishly dressed boy comes from a polygamous Muslim batch of seventeen. And that sullen man of thirty-five, with the pot-belly, has had six children in the six years he has been on relief.

But irritation is unfair. The sugar-cane, the cramped villages where the sugar workers and their families live, the little market towns: what the visitor sees is all that there is in Mauritius. There is little room for adventure, except at the top, for the French (who have always had large families), for the Chinese, for the well-to-do Indians. At the bottom, where life has been brutish, vision is more restricted, and there is only this communal sense of helplessness and self-disgust.

The relief worker, the father of six, knows he is doing a nonsense job; he doesn't attend; he goes only to sign and get his money. The weeding gangs on the sugar estate know that they are a substitute, and a less efficient and more expensive substitute, for herbicide. Everyone knows only that once the government was good and things appeared to be getting better; and that now, for reasons which both government and opposition say are political, things are getting worse.

The newspapers are so full of local politics they have no space for foreign news. So in the village clubhouses they talk politics; politics absorbs all their frenzy. Speech and elections are free; real power is unobtainable; and politics is the opium of the people.

A rainy Sunday afternoon, overcast yet full of glare, and sticky between the showers. In the gravelled back street of this new *cité*, an artisans' settlement of small concrete and corrugated-iron houses just outside the town of Curepipe, an election meeting warms up. It is only a municipal by-election, but in Mauritius an election is an election, and this one has been built up into a trial of strength between the party of Gaëtan Duval, the Foreign Minister, the Black Power man, and the party called the Mauritius Democratic Union, the UDM. Duval says the initials stand for Union des Mulâtres, the Union of Mulattoes. That is Duval's line of attack. There may be other issues; but the visitor, even after he has read all the newspapers, will not be able to detect them.

This is a UDM meeting. There is as yet no audience. Only a few Negro or mulatto boys, some in over-size jackets that belong to fathers or elder brothers; and little groups of unarmed policemen, many of them Indian, in peaked caps and slate-blue raincoats. A microphone on a lorry plays a *sega*, a Mauritian calypso in the local plantation patois.

Femme qui fume cigarettes
Mo' pas 'oulé.
Li a coule la mort tabac
Dans 'ous la gue'le.
(Woman who smoke cigarette I don't like.
She leaking stale tobacco in your mouth.)

More and more little boys come out. One thirteen-year-old boy in his brother's jacket (three brothers, seven sisters, father out of work, mother a cook) is against the UDM. Another boy of mixed race (four brothers, four sisters, no father, no mother) likes the UDM meetings, *parce qu'ils redressent le pays.* This is a version of the UDM slogan: elections here, like Christmas elsewhere, wouldn't be the same without the children. The road bristles with bony little legs; it is like a schoolyard at recess. ("When I go about now," Duval tells me later, "it's like Gulliver in Lilliput. Small children are trying to lift me up.") The UDM *sega* continues. A game of football starts in the sodden sunken field beside the road.

A motor-car rocks down a side road and pulls up next to the lorry. Stones fly. And all at once, to shouts and curses, enraged mulattoes and blacks are fighting around the car and the lorry. The football game breaks up; the children scatter, big jackets swinging above matchstick legs, and then stop to watch. The amplified *sega* continues. The gentle policemen intervene gently, leading away angry men in different directions, each man shouting over his shoulder.

The rain, the bush, the cheap houses, the poor clothes, the mixture of races, the umbrellaed groups who have come out to watch: the hysterical scene is yet so intimate: adults fighting in front of the children, the squalor of the overcrowded barracoon: the politics of the powerless.

The disturbance clears, the car drives off. The *sega* stops. The man on the lorry coughs into the microphone and the meeting begins.

"*M. Duval le zour li Black Power, le soir li blanc.* Mr Duval is Black Power in the daytime. In the night he white."

"Black Power?" the Negro girl in a pink blouse says. "For me it is a joke."

"*M. Duval na pas content créole petit chevé*. Mr Duval don't like black people crinkly head. '*Quand mo' alle côte z'aut' donne-moi manze macaroni et boire rhum blanc. Moi content manze un pé c'est qui bon.*' Hear him: 'When I go by other people don't give me no macaroni to eat and white rum to drink. I like eating a lil good food.'"

For the Negro girl the UDM is also a joke. "I don't care for politicians. I come here for *distraction*. There are many like me here. Seventy-five per cent of the girls and boys here don't work. The people are becoming poorer after independence. *Travaillent moins*."

She is twenty-one, small and thin, narrow shoulders quite square, her eyes hollow. She left school at the fifth standard in 1960. "I have done nothing since 1960. I have my typing certificate, but no work." But, like every other young person in Mauritius, she has a story of a job which once she nearly got. "There was a job advertised for a clerk in a filling station. I and another Muslim girl went. The Muslim girl was selected. Why? I cannot say. I called before the Muslim girl." She is calm now, will condemn no one; but she was angry at the time. "I returned home and said to my mother, 'But look what's happened. I didn't get the job.' I had been registered for five years, the Muslim girl for five months. I think the man at the filling station was a Muslim man, but I don't know. I don't know." The memory is fresh; but this happened three years ago, when she was eighteen. Anger is useless; she will not be angry, she will criticise no one.

Her father is a painter; her mother doesn't work. She has four sisters and three brothers. "I am the eldest. I was hoping to be a teacher. I've been to see Gaëtan Duval many times, but he's just promised and promised." When her father is in work he earns between twenty and thirty rupees a week, between £1.50 and £2.25. The rent of their house in the *cité* is twenty-five and a half rupees a month; electricity costs another nine rupees. "We eat rice, curry, salt fish. Sometimes we eat rice, oil and fried onions. Salt fish is dear now, a little piece for five cents [about a third of a penny]. It is very difficult for seven children. I can stay without food, but the young ones cannot."

Amusements? The cinema? "For five years I haven't been to the cinema. *On n'connaît pas. Connaît pas. Je suis découragée.*" She stays at home and reads poems; she has a schoolbook, *A Book of Longer Poems.* "In Mauritius there are no boy friends." She means that there can be no casual encounters; she cannot go out unchaperoned to mixed gatherings. To go out with a boy, the boy will have to write to her parents for permission; but there can be no boys because her family are too poor to invite anyone to their house. "I have a rich friend from school days. Her father is a policeman. She invites me to parties, but I can't go. Because my mother will not let me go alone. One day perhaps I may get married. By chance."

For another girl a little way up the road the prospects are brighter. She has a job as a teacher in a junior school. She is of mixed race—part of what, in Mauritius, is oddly called the General Population—and she is quite striking, with attractive, well-formed lips and almost straight hair, her looks marred only by a slight pimpliness. Her green pullover is tight over her little breasts; she wears a plaid skirt and a short fawn raincoat, a proper lined raincoat (lined because Mauritius is just outside the temperate zone and has a winter). The spirited girl supports all this stylishness on her salary of fifty rupees a month, just under four pounds. Of course she goes to parties; of course some boy has "written in" for her, and has been rejected.

The sun breaks through. The election speeches continue. Whole households stand outside the small houses, all up the road; and it is a little like a fair. This group is eating peanuts (locally grown: a new and profitable crop, planted between the sugarcane rows on the big estates, part of the attempt to "diversify"). There are ten people in this group, shelling peanuts, laughing at the speech, scattering peanut-hulls on the wet verge. Ten who live in the little house behind the little hedge. The tall man is out of work. Behind the hedge, at the end of the garden path, is the father, whom at first I couldn't believe in—couldn't believe what I had seen. A man sitting on the threshold, brought out for the afternoon's election entertainment, a man without arms, and with legs cut off just below the hips. Tetanus.

The symptoms of depression: dizziness, a heaviness in the head, an inability to concentrate.

The mulatto civil servant who is no longer young and no longer sure of his racial status becomes nervous about his job and his future and the future of his children. He wants to get away, to leave. But the talents that support him in Mauritius cannot support him in Australia or Canada; he has little capital; he can escape, with security, only if he gets his government pension. He can resign with the pension only if he is medically unfit. Depression, then, quite genuinely incapacitates him. In time he appears before a medical board; he is "boarded out", out of the civil service, out of Mauritius.

The unemployed young Indian labourer or labourer's son, seeing his twenties waste away, turns to studies, making un-lettered attempts at the Cambridge School Certificate—always big news in the press, the arrival of the papers from England, the arrival of the results—preparing himself for a job that doesn't exist. "I am twenty-nine. I am not married. I passed my School Certificate in 1965. I got a third grade. I applied for several posts. I never got it. Still now I am applying. I passed my School Certificate in 1968, when I was twenty-six. I got another third grade. I now work as a relief supervisor. It is not a promising job. According to my certificate it is not sufficient. I applied for Teachers' Training College six times. I like that very much." He is all right. But some break up. They yield to their headaches, give up the impossible goal of the Cambridge School Certificate and become horribly idle, at home or in the hospital.

The travel-writer, reporting on the happy-go-lucky island customs, will tell you that a bottle of rum will gain you admittance to a *sega* party. Local doctors will tell you that alcoholism is a serious and growing problem. Rum, at 8 rupees a bottle, 60 pence, is expensive, almost a tourist luxury; the standard drink is the local banana spirit, which sells at nine pennies a bottle. A few years ago one out of ten patients sent to the mental hospital was an alcoholic; now it is one out of seven. These figures are unverifiable; the government, perhaps correctly, disapproves of such investigations.

It is no secret, however, that many cases of mental disorder are caused by malnutrition and severe anaemia. Just as it is obvious that this very thin young woman in the family planning clinic is starved and quite withdrawn. No amount of family planning will solve her problems now. This morning she had tea; yesterday, for dinner, she had a kind of soup: boiled rice soaked in tea. With lacklustre eyes in a skeletal and already moronic face, she sits listless on the wooden bench. She wears a green sari; there is a small handkerchief in her bony hand, a trace of powder on her face. Mauritius is not India; there is no longer that knowledge of fate, *karma*, in which distress is absorbed. Everyone is responsible for himself, everyone is genteel.

Three years ago a woman of thirty-five decided to allow one of her children to starve to death, to save the others. She did so; then she fell into a depression.

For the past ten years and more economists have been visiting Mauritius and writing alarming reports, making "projections" of population and unemployment. Disaster has always appeared to lie in the future; it is assumed that at the moment people are somehow carrying on. A Mauritian journalist told me that the common people had their own little ways and could live on 25 cents a day, two pennies. It isn't true. But how can the journalist, or anyone else who has to live in Mauritius, be blamed for not seeing that the disaster has occurred?

The Mauritius economy, a government white paper says, "is not technically backward". The sugar estates are as efficient as can be; they engage in continuous research and are far more efficient than the small farmers. Any plan for breaking up the estates into smaller units runs the risk of damaging efficiency, and it is uncertain whether it will actually create more jobs.

Such a fragmentation may be socially satisfying. The party of the young, the Mouvement Militant Mauricien (MMM), says in its New Left-ish manifesto: "*On ne fait bien sûr pas d'omelette sans casser d'oeufs.*" That New Left omelette again; but the MMM's analysis is not all that different from the government's. They both recognize the efficiency of the economy, and its brutality. They both speak of the need to diversify agriculture and selectively to industrialize. They would both like to separate the sugar factories from the sugar estates, to separate, that is, management and money from the land. And they both seem to recognize that, at the end of the day, they will be left with what they started with: an agricultural colony, created by empire in an empty island and always meant to be part of something larger, now given a thing called independence and set adrift, an abandoned imperial barracoon, incapable of economic or cultural autonomy.

Both the MMM and the government speak, as they must speak, of a Mauritian nation. As though immigrant nations are created by words and exhortation and not by the possibilities of the land. No one has yet devised, or attempted to devise, a political philosophy for these independent island-barracoons; and it may be that their problems defy solution. The French, with their strange imperial-linguistic dreams, have made the nearby island of Réunion a department of France. Of what country can Mauritius be a department?

The MMM talks of "a global solution". Faced with the problems of Mauritius, even the New Left founders, and compromises. Tourism is degrading, the MMM manifesto says; and for two well-documented pages it catalogues the disasters that have befallen some Caribbean islands. But, the manifesto concludes, the situation in Mauritius is so desperate that tourism must be developed, though of course "*un tourisme visant non la classe très riche des pays étrangers, mais la classe moyenne de ces pays*". The MMM would like to see 300,000 tourists a year, fifteen times the present number; this is also the stated target of the government.

In the circumstances, the concrete plans that are put forward often have a Robinson Crusoe, boy-scout quality. Set the unemployed to plant trees on river banks, create a National Youth Service (to do what? to be financed by what?): these were ideas put forward by the Labour Party at the seminar on unemployment.

Mr Duval, the Black Power man, has his own *Projet Cochon*, Operation Pig. He distributes piglets to potential minders and hopes in this way to create a pig-rearing industry. A good idea, I was told, with export possibilities; and there have been some successes. But it happens that pork is the Negro's favourite food; and the Chinese of course dote on it. In an island of hungry Negroes and epicurean Chinese a piglet-distributing scheme runs certain risks. I could get no figures; but it seems that enough of the distributed piglets have been eaten for *Projet Cochon* to be known now to some people as the *cochon projet*.

The tenement stands on the site of a great house in Port Louis, the capital. The high concrete wall of the great house survives; within, the front of the yard is rubbled, with faded cigarette packets, dusty cellophane wrappers and dead leaves between the stones and crushed old masonry. In one corner, right against the wall, some boys and young men, seated on boxes, are playing cards, in the middle of this hot morning. Beyond the rubble, and below two old trees, the tenement sheds of corrugated iron and wood, much repaired and added-to, run down in two parallel lines, past the communal tap and many ancillary little sheds, to the communal lavatories. The ground is rocky here; the earth, where it shows, damp and black.

A red-tiled floor in the first room on the right, quite dark below the naked corrugated-iron roof. A bed, two tables, some boxes, a clothes-line. A *Playboy* pin-up above the bed, a little bundle on the bed: a tiny red-brown baby, ten days old. The mother went out this morning to get some milk from the Child Welfare Centre, but was sent back because she hadn't taken the correct papers. Yet the "papers", frail with handling, are there, on the table, in a little plastic envelope. She will go again tomorrow. Her fourth child: now six sleep in that room.

Her husband, an electrician, has been out of work for ten months. Once he worked in the Fire Brigade; and his Fire Brigade belt hangs on the line, the only unnecessary object in that room. He is out on the wharf this morning, hoping to get 50 cents, three and a half pennies. Yesterday there wasn't even 50 cents; and this morning she borrowed 25 cents from a neighbour. She sent a girl to buy some food, but 25 cents couldn't buy enough for a meal. So the girl bought a loaf and some chutney for 11 cents – that loaf there – and brought back the change, 14 cents, there, on the table, next to the tin of Nivea Creme, the broken comb, the worn powder puff, the half-full bottle of Cologne Impériale (a gift to the baby from the hospital nurse), the rubber dummy, and a pencil. Possessions.

She used to do family planning. But she quarrelled with her husband once and he threw away the pills, and she didn't go back to the clinic. Her husband gets angry when there is nothing to eat. He beats her then and she goes away. But then she thinks: what can the poor man do? So she stays outside for a little, cries for a bit and then goes back. She thinks now she'll put the children in a nursery and see if she can't get a job. According to her customs – she is a Tamil – she shouldn't go out for forty days after the birth of her child. But she has already broken that rule, and she needs money. So now she will go out. She will go from house to house, asking whether there are clothes to mend or dishes to wash. She'll probably make about 3 or 4 rupees a week, between 20 and 30 pennies.

The next room is larger, brighter, lighter: pale ochre walls, lino on the floor. No kitchen area at the front: the kitchen is in an adjoining room: this is an apartment. An Indian girl, a Bihari, pale and fine-featured, lives here, with a Negro girl, a friend perhaps, who has now cast herself in the role of maid. They are both very young, about eighteen, and both very small. The black girl looks shrunken and undersized. A transparent pinkish blouse shows her brassiere and the simplicity of her bony body. No sexual intent there; there is a curious guilelessness about the black girl. She is the maid; she lives through her young mistress. The Bihari girl is perfectly proportioned, even plump-thighed as she sits on the edge of the bed, occasionally nervously rocking her knees together in the Indian way. The mistress is obviously as anaemic as the maid, and perhaps even more unwell; she has the sunken, too-bright eyes of the hysteric.

A large photograph of a sailor hangs on the wall. The Bihari girl says he is Swedish.

"Is why she take *two* rooms," the black girl says in English. "She cook in other room. She stay here all day."

The Bihari girl says in patois, "My mother is at home in Petite Rivière. She lives alone since my father disappeared. My father went mad." It is said just like that. "Five years ago my father stopped working. He used to work as a cane-cutter. Then he began to get headaches and went to hospital. And then he disappeared. I was fourteen. My mother did a little cleaning and washing to get some money. In December of that year I came here to Port Louis. I told my mother I was coming to Port Louis. But it was my own idea. I go to see my mother sometimes; she doesn't come here. I have two brothers in school. One does a little work in a *magasin*. Here now I just sit and read and talk."

"She no tell you," the black girl says. "But she no work. All month this man" – the man on the wall – "give this girl money. Fifty, sixty rupees, I don't know. She have baby for this sailor. The baby die. Two years now."

There are other photographs of men stuck in the door of the glass cabinet. All the men are Europeans.

"*No Mauritius!*" the Bihari girl says in English, seeming to shriek as she switches language. "No have job here for man."

On the oilcloth-covered table, a Post Office savings book.

"*Fini,*" she says. "*Fini.* All fi-neshed."

She began to save in 1967. Twenty rupees after a year; 15 rupees after eighteen months. Then the regular monthly deposits – 10, 20, 25, even 30 rupees – until the later months of her pregnancy and the miscarriage. For six months the account bleeds, and for a year after that it seems dead. In February 1971 a miraculous transfusion: 600 rupees, £45, from an English boy, commemorated by that coloured snap in the glass cabinet: a family snap, clearly from England. Only 40 rupees remain now. She has paid off her debts. She has bought a transistor, and she has bought medicines. She feels tired. She has bought Sanatogen, for her nerves, and *Sirop des Chiens*, for her blood. All there on the table, with the savings book. Above the door, a Sacred Heart, to protect this Hindu girl and her maid.

They are free now, and independent. But the pimps and gangs of Port Louis await, and the new Chinese-run brothels at Pointe aux Sables. It was at one of those places, some days later, that I saw the two girls: the maid, very demure, keeping an eye on her mistress.

A lawyer says, "I've seen many people going into prostitution just to give a chance in life to their eldest brother or youngest brother. The girls who go aboard the ships are from the best schools in the colony."

The gangs started four or five years ago. They grew out of job-seeking and job-sharing street brotherhoods; they became pimping groups; they became gangs for hire. A recent gangster's job: throwing acid on the face of a manager who sacked a worker. The fee: 65 rupees, £5.

In this country court consider this gang, had up for damaging property: three black boys, brothers, and a badly mutilated young redskinned mulatto. Consider the procession of shabby youths with bright faces had up for the pettiest of petty larceny. The scene is almost domestic. Much of Mauritian official architecture is on a domestic, plantation-house scale, and the little wooden court-house is as small as a drawing-room. The magistrate sits against the back wall; there is a window on either side of his chair; and there are fruit trees just outside the windows.

The law is the law, and in Mauritius a job is a job. But the police officer is depressed by his duties. He says, "This district is one of the poorest in the island. After the crop season they have nothing to do. They fish a little and they collect acacia seeds, for which they get 12 cents [one new penny] a pound. So life is hard. It takes a lot of acacia seeds to make one pound."

A Muslim lawyer says, "We were more serene in 1962. We hope this is a passing phase. But that is what everyone says: 'It cannot last, it cannot go on.' And now this new party, the MMM, adds to the desperation. People withdrawing their capital. Prices going up. Taxes going up. Probably once a month we say, 'It is only a passing phase.'"

A mulatto doctor says, "The boy who in a richer society might have gone into another, mixed social group, in the end here, through depression and frustration, collapses into his old society and resigns himself to it. It is what is saving Mauritius, this climate of acceptance of fate, of things as they are, which the Indians irradiate to the others. We are ruled by two myths. The government; and the sugar estates, the malignant white god. The white man has become a myth. If the white man didn't exist, in Mauritius we would have to invent someone like him."

A huge swastika is painted on the main road that runs through the little Indian town of Triolet. The swastika is the Indo-Aryan good-luck sign and part of the decoration of a Hindu house, but here it is used politically, the emblem of a new party called the Jan Sangh, which seeks to remind Indians of their racial loyalties. Both swastika and Mr Duval's Black Power are responses to the inter-racial, New Left MMM. Fantasy responding to fantasy: it was in Triolet that the MMM won its first election victory, but in this clubhouse, just a few weeks after the election, nothing seems to remain of MMM doctrine.

There are the standard stories of Mauritian weariness, of School Certificate people who cannot get jobs and "just stay at home pursuing their studies. They are sick with life, tired with life." About thirty or forty have gone to England to do nursing. "But most of us don't get it. That depends on the minister. Sometimes he doesn't allow us to go. They give favours to their families." There is the story of the boy – that young man just passing in the

road outside – who "drank away" the little land that was his patri-
mony and is now like everybody else. "Now he is in crisis."

And there is a version of the Mauritian legend of the missed
job. This is the story of a boy who two years ago lost a government job through the trickery of a clerk: a job as a messenger,
worth $5\frac{1}{2}$ rupees a day, 40 pence. Everyone in the clubhouse
knows this story and has his own version; and the failed messenger, when he appears, a handsome, energetic young man, is
clearly a glamour figure. His neighbour got the job. "I am not
angry with him. I leave the matter in the hands of God." In the
meantime he wears a mauve MMM shirt, to express his defiance
of the government.

Someone says, "People here help one another in cases of accident. But it's different when it comes to jobs. Then families are
jealous. And the bad blood comes out when they're drinking."

They have such a developed sense of injustice. Have they no
sense of danger? They have such confidence in their rights, their
votes, the power of their opinions. They regard their independence as settled and permanent; they do not see its fragility. An
internal coup, an armed takeover from outside: neither hard to
imagine in this area: have they no thoughts of that?

The young men in the clubhouse say, "The government will
look after that."

But as the afternoon fades and the traffic lessens and many
radios are turned on to the Indian music programme, as the talk
becomes slower and less aggressive, it becomes clear that these
young men are beyond the sense of danger. They see themselves,
profoundly, as victims; the enemy won a long time ago.

"Today in Mauritius there is the rhinoceros beetle which can
damage a coconut tree. These beetles were introduced deliberately
for the medicines to be sold. Our forefathers never knew these
beetles. So they made money two ways. They destroyed our
coconuts and they sold the medicines. We can't suppose that the
Ministry of Agriculture did this. We can suppose that some
strangers did that."

"They uprooted our orange trees, in order to get us to buy

oranges from South Africa. We suppose it. They came and told us that our orange trees had a certain fungus."

"Day after day now we hear of our people being struck down by illnesses which we did not possess."

"Malaria."

It was the eradication of malaria that led to the population explosion.

"No. Malaria was common here."

"Cholera. For example, cholera was not common here. There are other illnesses now. I cannot say their names. But people do suffer from them. We suppose that certain things happen in Mauritius."

"Sysillis."

He is corrected. "Syphillis. That's on the increase, especially at Port Louis. The government is taking steps to legalize prostitution. They give the girls licences nowadays."

It is the Japanese, whose trawlers use the harbour, who have introduced a system of licensing.

"On the one side the government is fighting prostitution. On the other side it is encouraging it."

"They are right to do so, become prostitutes. They are suffering from poverty. They should do it. As I myself know – "

"I will kill my daughter if she does that."

"But prostitution is good for them, if it gives them money. Many students have become prostitutes, especially at Port Louis."

"They are building a new hotel here. The government will give permits for girls to work there as prostitutes."

The talk is gentle, slow, without anger. Outside, on the road, the swastika, emblem of threat and power, and the walls scrawled and counter-scrawled with political slogans and the initials of parties.

But some are lucky. Some get away. Like this very small twenty-year-old boy, encountered not far from the Government Buildings in Port Louis, still delicately holding his "papers", the duplicated foolscap sheet with the precious ministerial signature and ministry stamp. He is off to England; a hospital has accepted him. He is very small and pared-down, his frailty the result of an illness when he was six. He got his School Certificate in 1968, when he was seventeen, and for the last three years he has been doing nothing, just waiting for this. He is solemn and slightly defiant, as though afraid to express pleasure and ready to defend his success. He is clearly of good character. But does he have a real love for nursing? He says that he's wanted to do nothing else, ever since he was a boy; he even joined the St John's Ambulance Brigade.

His father works in a sugar factory and earns 150 rupees a month, just over £11. He has four sisters and two brothers. Their usual breakfast is bread and butter and bananas. During his years of idleness he would help with the housework in the mornings; then he would go to the British Council library to read, returning home for a lunch of rice and vegetable curry. Sometimes he fell ill and couldn't eat. Sometimes he was just too miserable to eat. He went out walking then with his friends and they had "nice baths by the river". His headaches could come at any moment, especially when he was alone; and as he found it hard to sleep he would stay out on the road talking to his friends until midnight. He visited his friends a lot. They would tell one another that in a year's time they would be "safe", they would get a job; in this way they "inspired one another with confidence".

Certain problems remain: the raising of the £50 surety and the 1,640-rupee fare to London, the two sums equivalent to his father's wages for fifteen months. But the bank will help, and he will be able to repay from the eight or nine pounds a week he will be getting from the English hospital. He is absolutely unconcerned about racial problems in England; it will not matter to him what people say to him or about him; and he doesn't care if he never sees Mauritius again. He and his friends have given up local politics. Politics can't help anyone in Mauritius now. The government can't help anyone now. "The MMM is also the same. It is better to depend on yourself."

In a bigger, richer country Gaëtan Duval, the Foreign Minister, might have been an actor or a pop-star. He has the disquieting attractiveness (though, at forty, his looks have begun to go, and he is concerned about his softening waistline); he has the hair, the clothes; and he has the actor's needs. His enemies say politics provides him with a "periodic mob-bath"; he says, as an actor might say, that he is in politics for "the love". "You get people to love you and you feel love for them." And he was especially pleased, when I met him, with his "Black is Beautiful" campaign. "In these few weeks I have created a psychological revolution in the mind of the black man in this country."

But he was also advocating trade with South Africa. How was that linked with Black Power?

"They're *not*! That is the point." And he roared with laughter, rocking back in his chair, his lace-trimmed black shirt open all down his milky-brown chest. He called, "*Madame Bell! Madame Bell!*" And when the middle-aged white receptionist-secretary came in from the outer office, he asked her for the text of the speech that had been made in his praise a fortnight before in Paris, when he had been presented with the Gold Star of Tourism by the Société des Gens de Lettres de France.

The speech was brought in, a foolscap sheet, and – though there was really no need: in the morning the text was to be in the newspapers – Duval began to read it out. "*Monsieur le Ministre, laissez-moi d'abord saluer le Ministre des Affaires Etrangères, l'Homme d'Etat, l'Ecrivain, le Penseur, l'Homme d'Action. Vous êtes le symbole de tout ce que nous aimons en l'Ile Maurice. . . .* That's the sort of thing that makes our Franco-Mauritians mad. That a black man should be a symbol of French culture. And I am the sort of man who rubs it in."

Until recently, Duval said, the French believed that there were only 10,000 French-speaking people in Mauritius – the French Mauritians. Now they knew that one-third of the island, and that meant a lot of black people, spoke French. "The French are pouring money on me. They gave me four million rupees. Another million this week. And now we've sent fifty-three workers to France. I'm fighting this election on my *foreign* policy." But the

South Africans were *slow*. "They're slower than the old Boers."
He had asked them for a three-year supply of subsidized pig-food
for his pig scheme, but so far they hadn't done anything.

Someone came into the office.

"Meet François," Duval said. "Factotum, friend." We were
all going to lunch in Curepipe. As we were leaving the courtyard,
Duval called out to someone, "Good news. Germany is taking
thirty-six more. Lufthansa, in Frankfurt." Thirty-six workers.

"In addition to the hundred?"

"Yes. I will announce it at the meeting today." And as we
drove along the scenic highway (its flowering roadside shrubs
and roundabout gardens maintained by relief workers) he said,
"I told the Germans when I was there that if they had anything
to give me they had better give it to me before the election.
Otherwise they would have to give it to somebody else. . . . It
doesn't matter at all whether we lose this municipal seat or not,
because we have such a majority. But I create this atmosphere of
tension. I can't live otherwise. I can do these things because
everyone thinks I am a little mad and do not act altogether
rationally. . . . What do you think of these?" He passed me, from
a full box, his new publicity photographs, taken especially for
the election: sitting in his black leather suit on Black Beauty,
sitting astride a motorcycle, and standing with crossed legs
against the front of his sports car. "They are for the women. I
appeared on French television in an Indian outfit and I am still
getting letters. The English don't like me, even when they try.
The French are different. Do you know what they said about me
in the French papers? A handsome black god."

When we were in the restaurant in Curepipe I told him – after
a glass or two of wine – that I found it hard to think of him as a
politician. He said he could leave politics; he was a farmer. I said
I'd heard that some of the piglets he had distributed had been
eaten. He was instantly serious and offended; but then, almost at
once, he said that perhaps some had been eaten, but that wasn't
what he had heard.

François, factotum, friend, spoke in patois.

At the end Duval said, "I've just been hearing a sad story. The father of all the little pigs died. Black Power."

A waiter came and said, "*M. Duval, téléphone pour 'ous.*"

"*Qui sanne là-ça?*"

"*Consul africain.*"

"The South Africans," Duval said.

When he came back he said, "The consul has just had a telephone call from South Africa. They've offered a gift of fifty sows and two boars and free food for them for one year. I told him to tell Pretoria to send me a telegram." No doubt for the meeting.

I said, "I thought you asked for pig-food for three years."

"That was subsidized. This is free. They're scared."

There was a French consulate wedding party in a private room of the restaurant. A young Frenchwoman came out, became ecstatic at the sight of Duval and, ignoring the rest of us, embraced him and began to talk. Then a blue-suited man came out and said, "*Gaëtan, ils te demandent de venir les bénir.*"

"*Je n'ai pas mon collier de maire.*"

But he got up and went. He came back many minutes later. His eyes were champagne-bright and he was smiling. "I've just heard something very funny. This girl who's got married, you see, is half Belgian and half Polish. Typically French. She was there with her brother. I said to them, 'If you are Polish, why aren't you more beautiful?' And the brother said, '*Parce que nous sommes habillés.*'"

Later, in the crowded town hall, Duval had some of his supporters sing one of his campaign songs for me.

> *Black Beau-tee! Black Beau-tee!*
> *Black is beautiful!*
> *Beautiful, beautiful*
> *Is black.*

"This is going to be the uniform," Duval said, showing some bits of material. "Black and red. Black belts with red trousers. Black shirts. Wet look."

The following day, when I went to the Foreign Ministry to

check my notes of our lunch, Duval introduced a little Negro boy
in the outer office as the composer of his campaign *sega*. The boy
beat time on Madame Bell's table and sang:

> *Mo' dire 'ous: la frapper.*
> *Laisse-mo' trappe-li.*
> *Laisse-mo' batte-li.*
> *Mo' alle condamné,*
> *Jamais mo' va laisser mulâtre*
> *Faire mari de mon endroit.*

(I tell you, hit them. Lemme catch them,
lemme lash them. I rather go to jail than let
a mulatto man boss me around.)

"The level of political thought here is *fantastically* low," Paul
Bérenger, the twenty-six-year-old French Mauritian founder of
the MMM, said. He had been shot at a few days before from the
town hall in Curepipe where Duval's men had sung the Black
Beauty song for me. And now – in Port Louis, in this new
air-conditioned basement restaurant, almost empty after lunch –
Bérenger was with his bodyguard, a black giant called Muttur,
running slightly to fat, but still famous locally as a boxer.
Bérenger was in his own way as stylish as Duval, and in Mauritius
as exotic. Small, slender, soft-spoken, with tinted rimless glasses,
a thin handlebar moustache, and a black leather jacket hanging
over his shoulders, he was like a European, of Europe. There was
no trace of Mauritius in his speech or accent; and he looked what
he was, a man from the Paris barricades of '68. "A good year, if
I may say so."

He said, "Of course the government talks only of *unemployment*. That word tends to make it only an issue of economics, to
take the human and political aspects out of it. . . . Before
1968 in Mauritius people didn't have to think or offer serious
economic or political programmes. They simply had to play the
racial card. In the past the people at the top sought to take the
pressure out of the situation by having the different races fight and
kill each other, and they would start the same thing again if they

could. . . . The history of this country is the history of several different struggles succeeding one another and then fighting each other. That's the drama of this place. The first struggle was the struggle of the slaves. The head of a rebellious slave, a Malagasy chief, was kept in our museum here in Port Louis for many years. Then you have the rise of the coloureds [mulattoes]. In 1911 there were riots here in Port Louis between coloureds and whites. Then the Indians. The coloureds, following the white example, became anti-Indian. Then the creoles [blacks] also fell for that. And the main agent of that change was Duval. That is the importance, the malefic importance, of Duval: bringing over the blacks on to the side of the whites. Duval is a myth. He is a creation. He is King Creole. Created by the newspapers. It's a myth that's dead. But he doesn't want to die."

Bérenger snapped his fingers. The black bodyguard brought out a paper-bag of what looked like sweets. Bérenger took one; the bodyguard took one. Bérenger said, "Hack's Cough Drops."

Bérenger comes from an old French Mauritian family. His father was a civil servant. Not a planter, not a landed man; and there are people in Mauritius who say that this is at the heart of Bérenger's own rebellion. In 1963, at the age of eighteen, before going to university (North Wales), he worked for a while as a sailor. "The MMM was started during a holiday in Mauritius in 1968. Though that makes it sound more casual than it was. The government made us a present. We planned to demonstrate peacefully against Princess Alexandra's visit. The government threw eighteen of us into jail. Why Alexandra? Well, Alex's husband is Ogilvy, Ogilvy is Lonrho, and Lonrho is extremely powerful here – hotels, sugar factories, import–export. Plus the waste involved in the reception. I've been in jail four times since then. . . . The situation is bad. People feel it can blow up at any moment. I doubt whether we'll go past this year without the government crumbling or an uprising or general elections."

I told him I had found no trace of MMM doctrine in Triolet. The socialism his party had expounded seemed to have been absorbed into the paranoid myth of the enemy.

He didn't answer directly. He said, "There is always *something* behind the myth." And then, tentatively, like a man thinking aloud, he began to talk around the subject of myth-making. "Things can go fantastic distances in the minds of people here. I suppose the size of the island has something to do with it. . . . There is a definite melodramatic tendency. In Port Louis, for example, I was said to have an *electric* baton. I don't know what they meant by that. In Curepipe it was a baton with a chain. And my black leather jacket is supposed to be bullet-proof. And I suppose that if as I walk past the municipality office in Curepipe I am shot at; and if there is a minister, supposedly the protector of the black, who wears black leather and sits on a black horse; then you are in a situation that can give rise to any kind of myth.

"You live with certain things; you don't put them together. There's one of our ministers – it's only now, as I am talking here, I see how extensive this myth-faculty is – this minister, on election day he wore his paratroop uniform. Ramgoolam [the Prime Minister] used to be a myth. The *chacha* or uncle of the Hindus. Very active and powerful, but somehow floating above it all. There is a biography of Ramgoolam by one of our local writers. It's a biography without a date. It's fantastic mythology and poetry and things. . . . I believe the real depression comes when you go through our education system. There's the linguistic aspect. The language we all use is despised." (The MMM is romantic about the local patois, which it sees as an important part of a "national" culture.) "The Franco-Mauritians too have their myths. When I came back the story among them was that *I* had brought de Gaulle down. You can find it still. 'If Paul brought de Gaulle down, what chance does poor old Ramgoolam have?' They all deal in fantasies. And it's rooted in the colonial situation."

He made the two hours pass quickly. As he left with his body-guard he smiled and said, "I've got to go now and get some 'tough guys' for the forum this afternoon."

But the tough guys were not needed. No one tried to break up the MMM meeting that afternoon, which was in the town of Rose Hill. The hall was packed with several hundred students.

A racially mixed audience, a mixed platform, ideas being treated like news: it was the brightest gathering I had seen in Mauritius. And by its very existence it was – but perhaps only in the eye of the visitor – a tribute to the liberal administration that was being rejected.

"It is an imitation," Sir Seewoosagur Ramgoolam, the Prime Minister says. "They are trying to imitate Mao, Fidel Castro. Fantasy? They are not dealing in fantasy; they think their ideas will take root here. There *is* poverty. But we are trying to contain that by social services. We spend about thirty million rupees on assistance. People criticize us for that, for giving things like family allowances. My reply is: 'Children are born. I cannot allow them to grow up stunted. If they are well fed, well educated, they are not a burden on society. Otherwise they will become backward, mentally.' "

A different vocabulary, different concerns: a different life. The Prime Minister is nearly as old as the century; and that poetic biography Bérenger spoke about is an attempt to do justice to a subject which – though the scale is small, the setting restricted – is worthy of legend: the rise to power of a man born into a depressed and leaderless community, in an agricultural colony, in the darkest age of colonialism. Few colonial leaders have shown such courage and tenacity as Ramgoolam; few, having achieved power, have been so anxious to heal old enmities and rule humanely. But already the new state, as incomplete as it ever was, is threatened, and from more than one direction.

Bérenger says, "This hanging around ministers' offices, people looking for jobs, this is encouraged by the ministers. Each minister is trying to succeed Ramgoolam and each is trying to play his card."

The Prime Minister says, "Now we have the Public Service Commission. This waiting outside the doors of ministers is a mistake. It is a relic of colonial days."

The old enemy. And also the new: "Colonialism is a destructive institution. It creates parasites and hangers-on. And they are still with us – people of all races who profited from the stay in this country of a foreign power. I don't know whether they've completely reconciled themselves to the changes. I think this new movement, the MMM, is a devious approach by these same people to revive themselves. I think they want to have their own back on me especially and my party."

The Prime Minister has one bad eye, damaged by a cow's horn when he was a child. The drawing-room of his new house in Port Louis, built on the site of his old house, is full of the mementoes of his long political life: signed portraits, photographs of airport meetings, ponderous official gifts in a variety of national styles. Here, among his souvenirs, he constantly entertains. He likes informal dinner parties, conversation, chat. He would like to retire, to become his legend, to be "above it all".

But tranquillity recedes. The barracoon is overcrowded; the escape routes are closed. The people are disaffected and have no sense of danger.

ABOUT THE AUTHOR

V.S. Naipaul was born in Trinidad, to which his grandfather had come from India, but he has lived most of his life in London. His fifteen books—eight of them novels—have been accorded several of today's most distinguished literary prizes, among them England's Booker Prize.